Orrin E. Klapp is Professor of Sociology at San Diego State College, Vice President of the Pacific Sociological Association, and Associate Editor of the Pacific Sociological Review. In addition to numerous published articles in various scholarly journals and reviews, he is the author of *Ritual and Cult, a Sociological Interpretation* (Washington, 1956).

HEROES, VILLAINS, AND FOOLS

A SPECTRUM BOOK

Prentice-Hall, Inc.

Englewood Cliffs, N.J.

ORRIN E. KLAPP

HEROES, Villains, and FOOLS

THE CHANGING AMERICAN CHARACTER

Current printing (last digit):

11 10 9 8 7 6 5 4 3 2

Library of Congress Catalog Card No.: 62-12909

Printed in the United States of America
12800-C

To Evelyn, Merrie, and Curtis

PREFACE

The main purpose of this book is to survey the major social types of American society which serve prominently as its models. By models, I mean images that guide people positively by imitation or negatively by avoidance. Major role-models are here called heroes, villains, and fools. From such a survey, we get a look at a role-network of types, an important part of the structure of our society, that is not, I think, to be obtained in any other way.

The second undertaking is to interpret the various types for what they may tell or suggest about us as a people. While I do not think social types are a crystal ball, they are important symbols made by people; and the only way to attack a symbol is through its meaning in various contexts. Meanings have to be supplied by somebody, and I tell what I see in them in the light of what other people have seen in them.

Some leading ideas of this book may be stated here. One is that Americans have considerable freedom of role-choice and self-typing, and that this creates some role-conflicts. Another is that many of our types show considerable alienation and anomie, especially flaws in contemporary models that I have called "deterioration of the hero." Even in some which on the surface seem to indicate that everything is "all right" there may be trouble beneath. One of the ideas presented in this book is that a hero can have compensatory functions, to console people, as it were, for a recognized lack of what the hero represents (a distortion of the proper function of a hero, which is to stimulate people to do better). The "good Joe," I think, is a compensatory type which reflects a condition of anomie and alienation (disguised as pseudo-integration) precisely opposite in many ways to that lamented by foes of the "organization man."

My approach to heroes, villains, and fools is primarily through language. This is not a study of persons, but of abstract types named and embedded in language. My assumption is that if a thing is important to many people, they will find a name for it and talk about it (unless some pressure keeps it taboo—a situation which does not apply to most social types). Popular language, then, provides a basis for sampling, classification, and study of types, though many are drawn from other sources— literature, news, art, biography, even mythology. I think language not only shows what is consensual and common but also reveals generalized features of persons and situations, therefore sparing us many distracting particulars; more important, it is systematic and it reveals a social structure. Because of this focus, *Heroes, Villains, and Fools* does not deal adequately with real persons. Though scores of celebrities are mentioned and some biographical material is used, this book makes no claim to represent or analyze the personalities named as they really are. Let it be said for all real people used as examples of social types: if Mr. X happens to fall into a category with, say, John Wilkes Booth, it means only that some people did think of him in this way—a fact of how some people think, not a fact about Mr. X. It may well be that more think of him as a genius or a saint. A type-rating is not the whole range of opinion about a man, let alone the truth. In short, this is a study, not of personalities, but of abstract roles or types registered in popular language.

I regret exceedingly that practical limitations have made it impossible for me to mention all of the persons whose ideas and researches have helped me in writing this book. Yet I do feel that some acknowledgment will help the reader understand its background and orientation. It is an investigation that belongs somewhere in the series stemming from the work of Robert E. Park and his colleagues, including Ernest W. Burgess, Clifford Shaw, Nels Anderson, Harvey Zorbaugh, Louis Wirth, and others equally known; nor would I forget Samuel M. Strong, whose study of the types of the Negro urban community was a definitive and pioneering one. Especially important to me are Park's concept of consensus (reformulating Durkheim's collective representations) as the basis of social structure, and George H. Mead's theory of the self. I am grateful to those teachers at the University of Chicago who opened these lines of thought to me. I am most personally thankful to Herbert Blumer, who encouraged me to study popular heroes. In this initial study I also received considerable help from Louis Wirth and Everett C. Hughes. I mention these teachers without implying that they are in any way responsible for the present project, which was done long after I was out of their reach. I am indebted to Anselm L. Strauss for having criticized the entire manuscript; Bernard C. Kirby of San Diego State College, and Otto N. Larson of the University of Washington, who read the chapters on the deterioration of the hero; and Frank and Ruth Young and Kingsley Widmer of San Diego State College who have kindly criticized a good part of this book. Finally, Herbert Blumer's painstaking criticism has been invaluable to me in getting the manuscript into its present form.

O. E. K.

TABLE OF CONTENTS

I MPORTANCE OF SOCIAL TYPING

The Typing Process

Abraham Lincoln is said to have grown his beard as a result of a letter from a twelve-year-old girl who wrote that if he would "cultivate whiskers" she would not only like him better but would try to persuade her two Democratic brothers to vote for him. Four months later, in February 1861, Lincoln stopped his train at the town of Miss Bedell, the writer of the letter, called for her to come to him from the crowd, kissed her, and said, as he touched his beard, "You see I let these whiskers grow for you, Grace." [1]

Whether or not all politicians so cooperate with the typing process, all

[1] *Yankee*, February 1959, p. 39.

must deal with it. They must try to make it work for them, at least avoid having it work against them. Even in daily life we can see its importance— the crucial effect of facial hair (present, absent, or of the wrong style), men whose children did not know them when they returned from a voyage, marital tensions from shaving or adding a moustache. One man, after removing a well-established moustache, was asked by so many people whether he was "sick" that he lost courage and grew it back. Another found himself in the following predicament: he looked too young without hair on his lip, but was forced to abandon a moustache after he found that it made him look like a slicker, or, as someone put it, like a cat that had gotten into the cream. He finally decided that he would rather look young than sinister. Yet another, who happened to be a college professor, found that a rather bushy moustache aided his role, made him look like an English intellectual in-tweeds-with-pipe, or as another saw him, like an "honest German toymaker." He, too, when he shaved his moustache, was persuaded to grow it back.

Traditional societies may dictate the style of hair as part of a cultural type, as with the patriarchal beard. If one wants a respected status, he may have to grow the hair that goes with it. In our society we do not have, as one might at first suppose, freedom *from* typing but a *choice* of type. Free role-choice is characteristic of a democracy, and is reflected by such things as faddism in costume—indicating that people are trying to type themselves in certain ways, presumably consonant with the status they wish to occupy. If, in after-hours or private life, a person cultivates a type inconsistent with his formal status, we may guess that he wishes to build a new self.

TYPING ONESELF AND OTHERS

When they are moving and not well-known, people have much initiative in role-assumption, as in the well-publicized case of Fred Demara the *poseur* who passed himself as a research physicist and Navy surgeon. Our relations with strangers depend almost entirely on superficial cues provided by dress, hair-do, facial expression, tone of voice, vocabulary, and props such as cigarette holders. A person may also type himself by friends, style of life, or conspicuous public roles. In any case he has great freedom to create his type by manipulating cues, so long as people do not know him well enough to "have his number" and put him into an inescapable category. Once so categorized, he can change his social identity only by moving on.

Fashion, I hold, is basically a matter of self-typing, an effort to mold oneself according to certain social types which currently have prestige; fashions, however come in and go out, and one is forced to make nice decisions. Paradoxically, you can't stay yourself unless you change yourself skilfully with the fashion. While it may seem that fashion is simply blind imitation by thousands, it is for each person a highly selective process of picking one's type and avoiding other types which are now square, vulgar, or passé. Rather than stress the imitative side of fashion, I would stress this creative side. In a world where the types themselves are numerous and changing, the effort to maintain an attractive self-type may amount to zeal, even desperation.

Some go to extremes in their type and become the faddists—hep-cats, beatniks—or the sectarians of our modern society. A principal difference between a faddist and a sectarian, I think, is that the faddist seeks "individuality" whereas the sectarian admits he wants to acquire a type by closely identifying with a group. Both reject the prevailing model of their society in favor of something different. The faddist is probably the more deceived because he thinks he is being himself whereas the cultist embraces the group-type, finds in it his salvation.

All kinds of deviant behavior, I believe, are processes of self-typing—the deviant is not just being antisocial, aggressive, etc. We may well adopt the premise that everyone in modern society is vitally interested in creating a type for himself, the deviant no less than the Philistine. Self-typing gives psychological content to the quest for status. Indeed, the desire to be a type of person may be, consciously or unconsciously, what makes us desire a particular status (more than money, that is, and the other externals). The deviate may have a status-problem (let us say he is a homosexual) because he is typing himself in a manner that causes people to deny him a satisfactory status; if he were willing or able to conform to a normal type, he would have no difficulty keeping his status. Or, if he found a world that would allow him to be the type he wanted to be, he would have no status-problem because the other statuses denied him would not matter.

I might summarize this by saying that "finding oneself" is, in my opinion, to a large extent building a type for oneself—whether it is a type donated by some group or created by individual effort. (It is always a question how much a type can be built without collaboration.) A person who is not sure of his type is not sure of who he is, of what roles are appropriate for him. A person has "found himself" when he has established a type in his own mind which is satisfying to him (it is possible to dislike one's type) and which gives people the assurance that they know him well. If we accept this premise of finding oneself, we cannot attempt

to make predictions about people, analyze their problems, still less understand society as a whole, without knowing a lot more about the types
with which individuals identify and which comprise a kind of structure
for the entire society. Personality-typing is less a matter of measuring
"traits" than of finding out how people type themselves, and to what degree their actual qualities and behavior agree with their self-styled type.
Part of this process involves considering a person's role as a strategy of
presenting himself to others.[2]

The effort to type oneself, of course, also includes the effort to type
others. We are continually creating, as it were, the other fellow. A
common kind of conversation in almost any company is characterizing
people by what they have been doing or what is being said about them.

Social relationships hinge upon fitting the other into a category that
makes it possible to deal with him successfully. We normally try to put
a person into a pigeonhole of the same scheme from which our own self
was derived—I don't mean attribute our self-image to him but make both
images belong to the same system. The other fellow is trying to bring us
into his scheme (which may be the same or different from our own). Thus,
when Americans come together, they type each other variously as good
Joes, smart operators, heels, easy marks, and so on. They may disagree in
using the same system (Mr. X thinks Z is a such-and-such, but Y thinks
Z is a so-and-so). But when persons have different type systems (Mexican-
American, Frenchman-American, and so on) the result is likely to be
more frustrating, unless they happen to be familiar with each other's
systems and to have worked out certain equivalents for themselves. (We
know little enough about the American social typology at present, let
alone how much it is equivalent to the Mexican, German, Russian, and
so on.) When persons have inadequate relationships because of different
type systems you have what is properly called stereotyping. But social
typing within the same system is useful and fairly accurate; it is needed
in a mobile society where status is insecure, identities are uncertain,[3] and
people do not know one another well; it does what a personnel file might
do: provides us with a convenient *précis* of the one with whom we wish to
deal.

It is impossible, except conceptually, to separate this typing of others
from the typing of oneself, because by the theories of Charles H. Cooley
and George H. Mead and modern reference-group theory, the other *as we
type him* is a key to our construct of our self. We find ourselves by the

[2] Erving Goffman, *The Presentation of Self in Everyday Life* (University of Edin-
burgh Social Science Research Centre, Monograph No. 2, 1958).

[3] See Anselm L. Strauss, *Mirrors and Masks* (Glencoe, Illinois: The Free Press, 1959).

responses of others (Harry Stack Sullivan calls it consensual validation); but it is not simply the response of the other that makes our self but the way we see ourselves in his eyes as we have typed him. Without knowing what kind of fellow the other is, we cannot know what significance to attach to his approval or disapproval, how to rate ourselves by him. We cannot, then, without knowing him, know who we are.

People in public life feel typing as a powerful force. It is a key to their failures and successes. Unfavorable typing can "dog" a celebrity throughout his career. In my opinion, it was unfavorable typing more than anything else that caused the defeat of Thomas E. Dewey as a Presidential candidate in 1948. Richard Nixon, also, was impeded in his candidacy for President in 1960 by unfavorable typing. Both of these men have lived lives as correct as one has a right to expect a politician's to be and considerably more exemplary than those of many American favorites.

Favorable or unfavorable, an almost inevitable result of the typing process is that a public personage has at least two selves. People build up an image that satisfies them. Celebrities typically feel that they have a public self that is different from what they feel themselves to be. Of course, anyone may have this experience; but it is aggravated by the intense and continuous force of popular typing as well as studio build-ups and public relations techniques which foster and create images. Movie stars complain of restrictions on their private lives by the demands of the public image. We notice, for example, that Kim Novak cries and shows frustration from "the system" which manipulates her life; she is rigorously supervised, told whom to date and whom not to date; her name was changed from Marilyn to Kim (to avoid similarity to the public image of Marilyn Monroe); she is one of the most recent versions of the screen goddess—a human being who has been converted into a piece of valuable property. Again, Marlene Dietrich, at fifty-five, projects an image of glamor, with the help of make-up, massage, and dresses costing $12,000— the image of a "world weary woman"—but in real life a friend describes her as "an old German shoe."

The mystery of why some celebrities are severely criticized and others receive no blame for (are even helped by) the same kind of conduct is, in my opinion, largely a matter of getting out of touch with one's public self. As is well known, misbehavior does no great harm to some entertainers (the dope-scandals of Gene Krupa and Robert Mitchum, the alcoholism of John Barrymore). Others may be taken to task for minor faults. A television singer, Eddie Fisher, lost his sponsorship after six seasons on NBC because of a falling off of rating, due in good part to a love triangle of comparatively innocent proportions as triangles go—

breaking an idyllic marriage with Debbie Reynolds to marry glamorous "Liz" Taylor. Countless stars have gotten by with worse; it is even expected of some of them, but Eddie, somehow, got characterized as a "sneak" in the minds of many Americans. It seems plain that were it not for the type established by his "idyllic" first marriage and fatherhood (belonging to that species of marriage illustrated in the popular mind by Doug Fairbanks and Mary Pickford) and the ballyhoo of this theme by television and magazines, fans would not have been so outraged by a typical American readjustment. The key to the mystery, I say, is staying in contact with the nature of the established type (through feedback in the form of fan mail, and so on), and acting consistently with it in public. The same standards are *not* applied to all—even in the same field or profession. Consequently, when a person's career depends upon a public image, a type-analysis is called for. He must know his type to know what criticisms he is vulnerable to, and also what other types might be alternatives (conversions) within the social type system, that could change his character for better or worse.

W. Lloyd Warner shows how popular definitions of a Yankee City politician, Biggy Muldoon, changed from hero to villain to clown, with little relation to the real man.[4] Such vagaries within the typing process shows the need for understanding it and seeing more clearly its repertory —the typology we are all exposed to. Many candidates for popularity have smashed on the rocks of social typing, while others have inexplicably succeeded. I believe this depends less on what people are than how they are dramatically cast.

Deliberate type-casting is possible on the stage. Not only does a director choose a person who best fits a part and coach him for it, but the drama itself imposes a role by the dynamics of plot-development. Plainly this kind of knowledge can be extended to public affairs—to the management of the roles of celebrities, politicians and so on. Political type-casting was formerly left to "history" or "circumstance"; but today leaders are asking, in a histrionic sense, "What is my role?" and looking upon public affairs as a kind of stage, for example, getting help from make-up men and dramatic coaches on such things as "stage presence." Success or failure, in this new art of political type-casting and role playing, depends on a knowledge that could be made more explicit by a survey such as we are attempting here. The American social typology might be looked upon as a repertory of roles for those who wish to act, a set of dangers and pitfalls

[4] *The Living and the Dead, a Study of the Symbolic Life of Americans* (New Haven: Yale University Press, 1959), p. 16.

for those who act carelessly, just as it is a set of tools for those who wish to manipulate the social scene or public opinion regarding it.

COLLECTIVE ASPECT OF THE TYPING PROCESS

But the typing process is more than just pigeonholing people, as a psychologist might see it, that is, an individual process, whether self-building or perceiving others. It is a vast collective undertaking to be studied with the social system as the focus. In this sociological aspect, we are concerned with a stock of images and symbols, as part of a culture, and the way this stock changes and works in the system.

There are two major phases of typing as a collective undertaking. One can be called dramatic-personal, namely, how people are cast in public roles as defined by audiences, and the consequences of this casting upon them and the audience. Historic events are in good part a matter of dramatic typing, for much of what we remember of people like Mary Queen of Scots, Sir Walter Raleigh, George Washington, consists of parts they have played in certain dramas that struck the popular imagination. Probably in this way, more than any other, history enters society, as distinguished from the information to be found in reference books.

The other phase of the typing process might be called collaborative-structural. This is the longer-run work in which definitions of particular persons are part of a stock of type images which society maintains. In this view, social types comprise a system, more or less stable though ever-changing as the typing process acts on particular individuals, audiences, and human relations. We see an invisible network of rules, an informal structure, registered in symbolic residues of language—the way people think and talk about others (gossip, story telling, legend building, and so on). Within the second phase, we are concerned with at least three questions:

1) how types are formed,
2) how the types build a social structure, and
3) how types function within the system and *as* a system, for example, for control of human behavior, character-shaping.

Through the second phase, we see that people work together to maintain a system although they may not be aware of its extent and they are almost surely unaware of its functions.

This structure provides a milieu that is distinctly American. It gives a flavor to our life, our values, our problems, and our world. If properly interpreted, it is a key to our national character. Other societies have their own type milieux, each of which should be investigated. Typing can reflect trends such as the emergence of "sick" humor or the rise of the "good Joe." The study of social types like the climber, crasher, smart operator, and great lover tells us something about such matters as oligarchy, democracy, conformity, individualism, leisure, social climbing, secularization, anomie, and alienation. For the social type, as I shall try to show, is capable of reflecting a society in at least two ways: as a model which people try to approximate; and as a kind of photograph, though abstract, of what people have been doing.

Social Types as Concepts

Let us consider social types in general before surveying those which serve as major role-models for American society.

TYPES IN SLANG

A tribute to slang, that treasurehouse of popular wit, is perhaps first in order. The names Americans call one another have a pungency, if not a poetry, that puts slang, according to H. L. Mencken, among the gorgeous creations of the human mind. His tribute to "rubberneck" might be extended to scores of American types:

> It may be homely but it is nevertheless superb, and whoever invented it, if he could be discovered, would be worthy not only of a Harvard LL.D., but also the thanks of both Rotary and congress, half a bushel of medals, and thirty days as the husband of Miss America.[5]

Picturesqueness—literally the quality of being able to give a picture—is notable in slang; it is almost like a sightseeing tour to scan such a list. The power of slang is also felt in those epithets that strike a personality or a reputation with the stinging power of a whip. But most important here is realism, slang has the ability to name the situations and kinds of people we meet in everyday life and are important to us. Any collection of slang is a rich source of types. Indeed, I believe the making of slang has much to do with the making of types and roles, the slang vocabulary contains most of the important type-names of American society, and it works for the popular mind as a set of tags or strings attached to the informal social structure.[6]

[5] *The American Language, Supplement II* (New York: Alfred A. Knopf, Inc., 1948), p. 647.
[6] Edward Sapir, *Culture, Language and Personality*, (Berkeley and Los Angeles: University of California Press, 1957), pp. 68-69.

On these assumptions I have used slang as the basis for sampling American social types. By combing various lists, I compiled a list of words describing kinds of persons or roles, which I presented to groups; I asked them to supply descriptions and add any other types they could think of. The collection came to over eight hundred before growth slowed and repetition predominated. While not exhaustive, I believe my list is representative of the major categories of generally familiar[7] types.

WHAT IS A SOCIAL TYPE?

However vivid, a social type is plainly an abstraction. Even proper names like Simon Legree refer to a *kind* of person. The name is the symbol of a class present in our minds as a concept. Social types are not, however, logical categories. Unlike scientific and logical categories, they are based on practical experience, common sense judgment of situations as lived rather than as observed. They result from insight rather than reasoning. They have the truth of the proverb rather than that of the proposition or hypothesis. Though simplified, they are by no means necessarily distorted pictures. Our satisfaction when a person has been typed as a climber, tightwad, or good-time-Charlie, is not just because it is a good joke on him but because we see that it is true.[8]

Types can be created through any medium which can evoke in the popular mind a durable, vivid image. Many types have been created by witty naming. "Egghead" was apparently coined by John deKoven Alsop to refer to followers of Adlai Stevenson,[9] later extended to intellectuals

[7] Aside from generally familiar types, each professional subculture also seems to have its own social types, for example in boxing: puncher or mauler, cream puff, miller, butcher, tanker, mechanical fighter, punchy, old man (S. K. Weinberg and Henry Arond, "Occupational Culture of the Boxer," *American Journal of Sociology*, Vol. 57 (1952), pp. 460-69); cabdrivers have a working classification of cab-users: jerks (slobs, yokels), sports, blowhards, businessmen, lady-shoppers, stiffs, live ones (Fred Davis, "The Cabdriver and His Fare," *Ibid.*, Vol. 63 (1959), pp. 158-65.

[8] A well known American comedian, Jackie Gleason, analyzes his ability to mimic social types:

"I Like your Bartender," I said.

"That's because you've known guys like him," Gleason told me. "Most of the characters I break myself up into are people we run into somewhere, only I magnify their oddities. Reggie is two playboys I've known rolled together. The fact that people recognize such characters is what gives them appeal. We call such bits nudge numbers. When they're on the screen people nudge each other and say, 'Get him, will ya? Uncle Harry did that last week when he was having that argument with Aunt Jo. Remember?' Mr. Loud Mouth, he's insecure, he picks on little guys."

Pete Martin, "I Call on Jackie Gleason,"
Saturday Evening Post, July 6, 1957. p. 56.

[9] Cleveland Amory, "First of the Month," *Saturday Review of Literature*, XLI (January 4, 1958), p. 5.

generally (its possible relation with the Nazi Eierkopf[10] must also be con-sidered). Some were made by comic cartoonists (Sad Sack, Dennis the Menace), others by fiction writers (sheik, Simon Legree, Sherlock, Fauntle-roy, Babbitt). Dickens, Shakespeare, Molière, Balzac, Thackeray, Sinclair Lewis, Arthur Conan Doyle, and Zane Grey were great type-makers, how-ever different their abilities otherwise. Actors have "created" some types by immortalizing a scene or character—tying it down in the public mind by a conspicuous performance (Valentino as sheik, Raymond Massey as Lincoln, Charles Laughton as Captain Bligh and Henry VIII, Lionel Barrymore as Scrooge, Edward G. Robinson and George Raft as gangsters in "Little Caesar"); they became synonymous with their particular role so that one can not think of it without thinking of them. It is about the same to say that the type made them or they made it. Casting directors and others who help make such dramas can also claim to be creating types. Psychologists produce social types when their technical terms (introvert, masochist, sadist, inferiority complex) pass into popular language to designate something rather different from what the author intended.

Yet, when all is said, the vast majority of social types are anonymous and one does not know how they were formed. Even when an author can be named, the people often take over his type and change it. Sinclair Lewis' Babbitt "clicks" with the people's judgment that there are persons like Babbitt in real life, and we can see them better for having the type. The new type may fill a perceptual gap or merely supersede a less satis-factory one (heel for cad, chick for flapper). But, however well the artist does his job, he loses control over what he has made. Shylock no longer means a Renaissance Jewish money-lender with curious notions about collecting debts, but almost anyone who is stingy and a little hard-hearted. Social psychologists, in studying what happens to rumors, tales, and judg-ments when they are shared, have collected evidence which shows that they are changed according to the interests, needs, and capacities of the groups through which they pass.[11] Relevant, also, is the literature on legend building.[12] I believe that the functional needs of a group deter-

[10] Crane Brinton, *Shaping of the Modern Mind* (Prentice-Hall, Inc., Mentor Books reprint, 1953), p. 17.

[11] For example, F. C. Bartlett, *Remembering* (Cambridge University Press, 1932); G. W. Allport and L. Postman, *Psychology of Rumor* (New York: Holt, Rinehart, and Win-ston, Inc. 1947); Muzafer Sherif, *The Psychology of Social Norms* (New York: Harper & Brothers, 1936); Warren A. Peterson and Noel P. Gist, "Rumor and Public Opinion," *American Journal of Sociology*, 57 (September, 1951), 159-167.

[12] See, for instance, Roy P. Basler, *The Lincoln Legend* (Boston: Houghton Mifflin Company, 1935); H. Delehaye, *Legends of the Saints*, trans. V. M. Crawford (London: Longmans, Green, & Co., Ltd., 1907); Arnold van Gennep, *La Formation des legendes* (Paris: E. Flamarion, 1910); S. G. Fisher, *Legendary and Myth-making Processes in*

mines its stock of social types—their form and how they are applied. Although individuals may invent social types, society is the co-author—one, indeed, often eager to erase the original artist's name.

Viewed in such terms—as part of popular language and thought—the social type is plainly a group product and group property, related to the *Elementargedanken* of Bastian, the crowd ideas of LeBon, and the collective representations of Durkheim. I think of it as a collective norm of role behavior formed and used by the group: an idealized concept of how people are expected to be or to act. The type may describe the way people should be, should not be, or simply are predicted to be. And, though it is found in various media, often as the creation of artists, it is really made by the people who use it.

STRANDS IN THE TYPING PROCESS

When "is" a person a social type? A man arrested in San Diego for a violent crime appeared in court wearing a full beard, blue jeans, and an Ivy League cap. Police described him as an "original" beatnik, a frequenter of beach-area coffee houses. A reporter asked him, "Are you a beatnik?" He replied, "No, man. I don't even know what a beatnik is." Now, how does one decide when a person "is" a type if he does not think of himself that way? Is it just consensus about him? If so, then many slanders and myths would have to be accepted as evidence along with fair reputations. Yet it seems to me that you cannot wait until a man accepts a type for himself before typing him, nor can you accept his claim to a type (for example, prophet) that others do not see in him. The best criterion—for all its vagaries—is the judgment of people who "know," who can see things which the individual may be unaware of. While the opinion of the individual must be respected, we cannot let him be the paramount judge of what he is. I would say that the man arrested was a beatnik if many knowledgeable people in his social world called him one. A person belongs to a social type when his appearance and behavior

Histories of the American Revolution (Philadelphia: S. G. Fisher, 1912); A. L. Guerard, *Reflections on the Napoleonic Legend* (New York: Charles Scribner's Sons, 1924); George Willison, *Saints and Strangers* (New York: Reynal and Company, Inc., 1945); H. G. Creel, *Confucius: The Man and the Myth* (New York: The John Day Company, Inc., 1949); John T. Flynn, *The Roosevelt Myth* (New York: The Devin-Adair Co., 1948); Hamilton Basso, "The Roosevelt Legend," *Life*, November 3, 1947, pp. 126 ff; Keith Sward, *The Legend of Henry Ford* (New York: Rinehart & Company, Inc., 1948); W. E. Woodward, *George Washington, The Image and the Man* (New York: Penguin Books, Inc., 1946); Richard J. Walsh and Milton S. Salisbury, *The Making of Buffalo Bill* (Indianapolis: The Bobbs-Merrill Company, Inc., 1928); Bernard Mayo, *Myths and Men* (Athens, Ga.: University of Georgia Press, 1960).

approximate it so closely that he is widely recognized as an example of it —whether or not he is willing to declare himself as such.

Celebrities are visibly subject to typing, feel its pressures strongly, and develop public images distinct from themselves as real people. It is safe to say that one cannot become famous or notorious without being typed. Individual opinions crystallize into consensual images. Opinions about any famous man can be sorted into thematic categories and labels which sum him up, for example:

> A little man in a big pair of shoes . . . folksy, homespun, common . . . plucky, outspoken, with the courage of his convictions . . . a little too cocky . . . (Harry Truman during his Presidency)

> Super-patriot, red-baiter, fanatic, gloryhog . . . misuse of power to abuse people . . . a real patriot and defender of the Constitution . . . has done what others lacked the guts to . . . an opportunist with some admirable qualities of energy who has stumbled upon a popular issue which he exploits . . . (Senator Joseph McCarthy)

> Brain, genius, character, highbrow, egghead, crackpot . . . (Einstein)

> Energetic, intelligent, good looking, strong character, good family, aggressive, dynamic, outspoken, too young, too smart, truthful, not afraid to express himself, family man, determined, a good Catholic, likeable, millionaire, headline-hunter, smart-alec, honest, up-and-coming, knowledgeable about politics, from good background, all-American, firm, well educated, straightforward, a leader not a follower, independently wealthy, a go-getter, excellent statesman . . . (Senator John Kennedy.)[13]

While by no means consistent, definite themes are evident, including explicit types such as go-getter, red-baiter. I have no doubt that some celebrities would be recognizable from characterizations alone. People have no difficulty matching up celebrities with lists of types. This kind of opinion about famous people is the raw material of typing, some of which "catches on," gets repeated, and is molded until it dominates the image and becomes the man's public character. There is a striving to hit the nail on the head; a nickname may sum the celebrity up (The Voice, The Babe, The Sheik, The Million Dollar Legs, Old Firesides, The Crying Crooner, The Blonde Bombshell, Schnozzle, Harry the Haberdasher, The Manassa Mauler, The Kingfish). Such things convert a public figure into a socially comprehensible image. He enters society and becomes a social fact in Durkheim's sense.

There seem to be two strands in the typing process. One is the degree to which persons penetrate popular consciousness (measured by fame and crystallization of consensus). Some have superior ability to stamp them-

[13] The last characterization is drawn freely from a sampling of opinion, by George Gallup, the American Institute of Public Opinion, August 16, 1959.

selves upon the minds of others by personal "color" or drama of roles (Will Rogers, Tallulah Bankhead, Huey Long, Babe Ruth). They enter and persist in popular thought as *personalities* rather than just abstract types. Rudolph Valentino was remembered, long after contemporary actors were forgotten, as he appeared on the screen—Vaselined hair, burning looks, sideburns, Arab costume, tango-dancing, and all. Gradually he became more abstract as "The Sheik," "The Great Lover." There is a kind of battle between individuality and typing. The less penetrating power, the quicker does a celebrity become a mere abstraction and merge into the anonymous stock of types. Of course, without a minimum of penetrating power he would not even pass the symbolic threshold of fame.

The other strand of the typing process is what people do to a personality, rather than the impact of a personality on the people. I refer to the creative work of imputation, which can produce a legend even about living persons. The growth of reputations—whether of great men like Lincoln or characters like Al Capone[14]—is helped by seemingly gratuitous themes and anecdotes. It seems clear that people fashion a hero— or a villain or a fool—into a figure more to their liking, or fears. Whatever his original character, he becomes functional: he becomes what is needed in a situation—a martyr like John Brown, a "Robin Hood" like Capone, a "savior" of the people like Hitler. For such creative work, however, people do not usually invent fresh images but draw from the stock of concepts. So it often results that there is something very similar about "saviors" of various eras; or outlaws like Billy the Kid, Jesse James, Pancho Villa, John Dillinger, and Al Capone. Almost identical stories have served for many. Even coined names for celebrities, such as "bubblehead" (Henry Wallace), "Lone Eagle" (Lindbergh), may not be as unique as they seem but merely versions of generic types. If a figure is fashioned into an ancient type by imputation (Napoleon into Caesar, for example[15]) it seems reasonable that he meets archetypal needs of social organization; he is doing a job that has been done a thousand times before.

The typing of ordinary persons is not so abstract or developed as that of celebrities. When a person is typed by acquaintances ("You know George," or "He's a skinflint") there is less gratuitous elaboration because people know him better and have neither the freedom nor need to build a legend. There is less penetration (fame): his image may be confined to a limited circle. The image is likely to be more concrete—less typical—

---

[14] See Fred Pasley, *Al Capone, the Biography of a Self-Made Man* (Garden City, New York: Garden City Publishing Company, 1930); Basler, *op. cit.* and other works on legend formation previously cited.

[15] Friedrich Gundolf, *The Mantle of Caesar,* trans. by J. W. Hartmann (New York: Macy-Masius, The Vanguard Press, 1928).

because not abstracted through the interaction of thousands. It is a more complete personality because people know several "sides" of the person. He might better be called a personal idea[16] than a mass symbol. Fewer people are using him and he is less perfected as a daydream image. Yet the difference between the typing of ordinary persons and that of celebrities is of degree rather than kind—the degree of abstraction, elaboration, and truth.

Celebrities, by their greater impact and color, by their ability to "project" themselves—doubtless also by the greater need for that particular type—burst through the circle of acquaintances and enter popular consciousness. As they do so, they are transformed by imputation and abstraction more and more into what people want of a *public* figure. Every durable image is presumably functional; but ordinary typing has different functions from that of celebrities: ordinary types mediate personal relations, whereas the mass symbol is a vehicle for the imaginings of thousands; also, the mass symbol is part of a drama or story rather than a personal relationship. Being a dramatic character, he is likely to have perfected dramatic form as hero, villain, or fool. An audience uses a type for anonymous, private, vicarious experience, and for a quick (stereotypic) kind of consensus; while in real life types are validated in interaction. Because of this difference of function as well as of development, the "good Joe" in ordinary life is not the same as the "good Joe" of mass communication. But they are cousins from the same stock.

In short, the strands of penetration and imputation are shorter in the typing of ordinary persons than celebrities.

STEREOTYPES VERSUS SOCIAL TYPES

It is time to deal with stereotypes. Some will say that wherever mass judgment results in an image of a celebrity, it is only stereotyping and there is no need to discuss it as something different called social typing. Much depends, of course, on definitions. If you define stereotyping as rigid, inaccurate popular concepts applied indiscriminately to individuals without due regard for their actual characteristics, then I deny that what we have been talking about is properly called stereotyping and hold that a distinction is needed.

For one thing, mass judgment of celebrities, especially with the help of television, is often accurate and revealing. Anyone who has met an audience knows how penetrating its scrutiny can be. Much depends on

[16] Charles H. Cooley, *Human Nature and the Social Order* (New York: Charles Scribner's Sons, 1922), pp. 118-119.

who judges. Shrewd appraisers of human nature "hit the nail on the head" with social types. Even where popular judgment builds a double image of a celebrity—that is, a public image different from that of some who "know him better"—it may be that something true of him in one situation is selected and enlarged into the whole reputation. Any extensive list of social types shows that they reflect dimensions of social life for which there are few equivalent—let alone more accurate—technical terms. What sociological or psychological concept could adequately replace crasher, hepcat, hot-rodder, tightwad, good-time-Charlie, ladies' man? Viewing the many slang words for which there are no substitutes, it seems to me we have little choice but to stay with the insight of the people, as it is crystallized in social types, to understand what is going on in society.

My criticism of the stereotype concept focuses mostly on this point: it overstresses the perceptual and cognitive deficiencies of some popular ideas and at the same time neglects their truth and social function, perhaps by lumping them under some head such as prejudice. The orientation of the stereotype theory (Lippmann's treatment for example) is predominantly individualistic and rationalistic—a kind of Lockean we-are-all-going-to-think-clearly-together view of ideal democracy. The assumption is that there is a realistic kind of knowledge, available to the common man as well as to philosophers, that with the help of education is going to replace crude popular ideas. On the contrary, I see no way of getting along without social types. The connotation of "stereotype" is too disparaging to be applied to them *in toto*. There is no reason to think of them as more inaccurate than other concepts commonly employed by people, such as cow, chair. They are as accurate[17] as we have a right to expect concepts used in everyday life to be. They can become rigid, banal, inaccurate; but this can happen to any idea—scientific, philosophical, technical, artistic, theological—and is no peculiarity of social types. Should one wish to extend the meaning of "stereotype" to accurate and revealing judgments by popular concepts, then there would be no objection to considering stereotyping and social typing as synonymous.

[17] Some studies have found that stereotyped judgments of persons are more accurate than judgments by persons trained to abandon stereotypes and respond to individual differences. See W. J. Crow, "The Superiority of Stereotyped Judgments in Person Perception," paper read at Western Psychological Association meetings; 1959; and N. L. Gage, "Judging Interests from Expressive Behavior," *Psychol. Monogr.* 1952, 66, No. 18 (Whole No. 350). The fruitful application of accurate social typing to social casework, even "the development of a classification system that has diagnostic validity," is visualized by Max Siporin, "The Concept of Social Types in Casework Theory and Practice," *Social Casework*, XLI (May 1960), 234-242.

On the other hand, it may be more useful to stress the differences. I would prefer to say that social types promote insight into relations within a system, whereas stereotypes hold people at a distance and portray outside groups in an inaccurate way. Stereotypes emphasize error while social types represent real roles being played; stereotypes refer to things outside one's social world, whereas social types refer to things with which one is familiar; stereotypes tend to be conceived as functionless or dysfunctional (or, if functional, serving prejudice and conflict mainly), whereas social types serve the structure of society at many points. People often talk as if they would like to be rid of stereotypes but it is hard to conceive of society without social types.

FUNCTIONS OF SOCIAL TYPES

By using social types we pass a judgment on ourselves. Words like jerk, eagerbeaver, good Joe, playboy, express approval or disapproval of what some Americans have been doing. Three main categories seem to be praise, condemnation, and ridicule (heroic, villainous, and foolish). This suggests that the basic interest of a group in forming concepts is not just to know but to control—put things in place within an order. Because control is so important, group concepts normally carry built-in sanctions to bring individuals into conformity. A person can resist these sanctions, but he cannot escape them, for they are there in the language and social structure.

I asked people to sort[18] social types according to how they felt "people generally" regarded them, or "how you would understand them if used by somebody else." In other words, the individual's estimate of *consensus* was sought. Combined ratings gave, as it were, a consensus about consensus. Some, such as good Joe, champ, and wheel, came out predominately as heroes; others as fools or villains. Some were ambivalent, for example, the rogue or smart operator (the rogue has a character as cut-up that counterbalances somewhat his status as villain). "Neutral" types, which got few strong positive or negative ratings (e.g., draftee, hashslinger, hiker, pollster, southpaw), were dropped from further consideration, though it may be added that comparatively few were neutral. This book, then, is concerned with types predominantly or ambivalently rated as heroes, villains, or fools.

Why were such categories used? Perhaps here is the place to explain my belief that the hero, villain, and fool represent three basic dimensions of

[18] The method is described in "American Villain-Types," *American Sociological Review,* 1956, 21:337-340.

social control in any society. Heroes are praised, followed, set up as models, and given a central part in dramas. Villains and fools are negative models, respectively, of evil to be feared and hated, and absurdity to be ridiculed. Heroes, villains, and fools represent three directions of devition: (1) better than, (2) dangerous to, and (3) falling short of, norms applied to group members or status occupants. These basic kinds of models are used by all societies to maintain the social system, especially to control persons and put on significant dramas and rituals. Typing, then, holds up models for the way people should be and act. Ethically, the hero might be thought of as the bull's-eye of a target, the ideal achievement of right conduct. He gives impetus to rise above the ordinary. Negative types represent deviations and failures important enough to be memorialized by society. An individual feels success to the extent that he lives up to heroes, at least stays comfortably above the folly and wrongdoing represented by the other extremes. The middle ground is "safe"; but once a person leaves the ordinary role he has three main alternatives: to slay the dragon, stab Siegfried in the back, or fall off his horse, armor and all, onto the surprised dragon. It is impossible to speak of ethics, in my opinion, without getting into the realm of these socially produced images of the hero, villain, and fool. Man lives stretched in painful tension between these extremes, symbolized by Don Quixote. He is a whole only in terms of the triad of ideal possibilities which add to his discomfort quite as much as they goad him into being, into becoming, himself.

Just as these types affect the individual, so they help society maintain its structure and orient its members. For example, a trouble-maker gives vivid representation[19] of the way people ought not to act in a status. The more important role models for the social system are institutionalized in symbolic media that reach the average member reliably: in a preliterate society, the oral tradition, myth, and ritual (Maui, Cuchulain, Odysseus); in our modern society, various media, usually labeled neither as myths, ritual, nor models (Westerns, professional wrestling, comics, soap opera,

---

[19] Because I am in this chapter using words like social type, model, and norm almost interchangeably, let me explain that I do not consider them synonymous. A type is an abstract concept, whereas a model is always concrete enough to illustrate—to spell out—the meaning of a concept, whether as a picture, figure, dramatic role, tale, or a real person. It is possible to speak of a character like Babbitt as the model of a social type to the extent that he enables people to visualize clearly what a "Babbitt" is and so can use this knowledge in guiding their lives. If people use a type concept not only as a way of understanding reality but as an image of what ought or ought not to be, then it is a norm; and then an example which spelled this out would be a model of a norm. In short, all social types are abstract concepts, but only those which are positively or negatively valued are norms; and models are concrete things that make a norm or type tangible or visible.

romances, "true stories," "Dragnet" and "Gangbuster" types of drama, recurring themes in human interest news, success stories—whether in Rotary luncheon speeches, fiction, or biographies—typed styles of comedians, actors who portray certain kinds of character consistently, political oratory, pageants and processions depicting well known figures or scenes).

When models are working well, they compose a more or less consistent system, and there is a visible correlation between them and the members of a society. A group normally supports its models and recruits, trains, and controls members in accordance with them. The stronger the control system, then, the more closely the average person should come to the heroic norm of his status and the more widely should he shun the negative ones. Highly cohesive groups—sects, monastic orders, some military organizations—achieve their type so successfully that almost any member could be taken as a model. Georg Simmel writes of depersonalization which subdues individuality until only the type is visible. Even in less cohesive groups, a certain "look" sets them apart from others (some criminals say they can spot a cop in plain clothes the moment he enters the room; and some police say the same about criminals). Where the control system is weak and models are inconsistent, it may be impossible to guess models from looking at members. Society may be ambivalent toward even major heroes and there may be latent conflict, alienation, potentialities for deviant roles, liking for heroes which support an opposite ideal. We shall consider American society as an inconsistent and mutually cancelling model system.

Let us review some of the major services of social types under the following heads: (1) role discrimination, (2) defining and institutionalizing emergent roles, (3) professionalization, (4) providing individuals with self-images, (5) control by status modification, and (6) general contribution to consensus.

First, *role discrimination*. Social types provide knowledge which is especially useful in a complex, mobile, and anonymous society like ours, where sharpness and versatility in role playing are called for. We must be able to put on and take off roles. The number of choices and discriminations is great. We must know how to play roles that do not belong to us, empathize with strangers, display enthusiasm for people or jobs we don't like, and detect "front." If a person is familiar with American types, we expect him to be better able to fit into various situations, "find his way around," deal with people—perhaps also do special jobs requiring role knowledge, such as cast plays, write stories, or work in propaganda and public relations. The service of social types to role playing and discrimination has been badly obscured by the stereotype concept. Properly used, social types, rather than "lumping" people together and causing misunderstandings and conflicts, make for better organization and understanding and finer discrimination of roles than the formal structure defines. That is, no formal status explains how to deal with the *kinds of people* one is likely to meet in that status, nor much about deviations and undercover activities within the status. Happily for the newcomer, there is a kind of knowledge that "fills in" between knowing a person's formal status only and knowing him intimately. For example, bankers may be hard-headed but Mr. X is a "good Joe." This information, quickly transmitted, serves to orient a person, say a loan-seeker, more effectively in the social structure. The social type[20] is his substitute for really knowing the person he deals with—often not a bad substitute at that.

Since formal structure labels only a limited number of roles, it is left to social typing to specify much of the informal structure and special situations that develop, for example, variations in people within a status (character, trouble-maker, eagerbeaver, boondoggler, has-been, yes-man, applepolisher, upstart.) *Sub rosa* and illicit organizations are also well indicated by social types such as the call girl, pimp, pusher, cops' stool-pigeon, payoff man. They enable members to make vital distinctions between outsiders and insiders, degrees of professional attainment, or specialties within the same professional area. Call girls, for example, speak of themselves as being in the racket, in the life, a regular girl, one of the girls. They distinguish among chippies (amateurs or inferior professionals), party girls, hustlers (call girls who operate on an appointment basis), and whores (who are further divided into house girls and street walkers).[21] One can judge the degree to which a person knows a social world by his knowledge of the types that belong to it. A participant in the jazz world must know the difference between Dixie, swing, bop, hot, and cool, otherwise he is hopelessly square (an outsider rather than a

---

[20] A distinction between social type and social role is also in order. First, roles vary greatly in degree of consensus, ranging from those on which there is little consensus, perhaps because unique and personal, to those on which there is virtual unanimity throughout the society such as a doctor's obligation to administer emergency treatment. Social types are roles which, though informal, have become rather well conceptualized and on which there is a comparatively high degree of consensus. Second, while many roles are widely allocated and do not "belong" to any particular kind of person, some get conceptually linked with a particular kind of person. At this point we may speak of the role-consensus as having developed into a social type, that is, a "tightwad" is not only a consensual concept of a stingy role, but a kind of person who characteristically acts that way. This stress on the kind-of-person-who-acts-that-way helps also to clarify the distinction of social types from formal roles, which tend to be more abstract and impersonal.

[21] Harold Greenwald, *The Call Girl* (New York: Ballantine Books, Inc., 1958), pp. 23-26.

cat.) In smaller jazz circles distinctions are even more refined. People who deal with strangers, such as detectives, bellhops, waiters, use social types to size them up. Important power relationships are made plainer by types such as upper crust, top dog, big shot, wheel, front man, yes-man, stooge, that might remain invisible without the language of social types.[22] Also, hidden conditions of exploitation and parasitism become clearer by words like chiseler, operator, boondoggler, five percenter, fat cat, expense-account aristocrat. Thus social types supply important information about people as individuals and also make more visible a kind of connective tissue in society—an informal network of roles and linkages that, however subtle, is highly important for anyone who wishes to enter those worlds.

Social types also *define emergent roles*—new ways that people are acting—and link them consensually to the social structure. A changing society is marked by emerging and disappearing types. Comparatively new ones in America would be egghead, cat,[23] five percenter, hotrodder, and beatnik. Obsolete types (Lord Fauntleroy, Lady Bountiful, vamp, carpetbagger, mugwump) remain like linguistic fossils. For Negroes in the northern United States, Uncle Tom is a fairly obsolescent type. Typing casts a net over a new role and brings it within the social structure. Naming brings it into group consciousness and enables people to organize their opinion toward it and put it into a status system. This is what I mean by consensual definition of new roles. Take "hotrodding." Such a name helped people to become aware of what juveniles were up to, ultimately to institutionalize it in car clubs, drag racing, and drag strips, some of which, at least, are an accepted and controlled part of the community. Thus social typing helps a group institutionalize roles and articulate them with the social structure.[24] News-writers, historians, and novelists, have an important part in making types and consensus explicit.

The end of the institutionalizing process may be for a type to become an office with formal rights and responsibilities, for example, the fool.

[22] See Floyd Hunter, *Community Power Structure* (Chapel Hill: University of North Carolina Press, 1953), p. 42.

[23] See Harold Finestone, "Cats, Kicks and Color," *Social Problems*, 5 (1957), 3-13.

[24] Another aspect is control of new movements by names like crank, crackpot, egghead, which discount them and make it difficult for them to get serious attention. The person who named that literary movement in England represented by John Wain, John Osborne, Kingsley Amis, and John Braine the "Angry Young Men," did much to weaken the validity of their disturbing protest. More marked has been the effect of "red" on the socialist movement in America. Here we see the other side of the status-giving power of typing, its ability to push things out of an important place in the social structure (into Villain and Fool roles).

People might appoint someone to be a clown or life of the party, or look around consciously for a yes-man or fall guy. I visualize the entire process from informal type to institutionalized office somewhat in this way: first a person plays a new role important for a group. Maybe they cannot name it at first but can only say, "He's an institution around here," or "You know Charlie." But in attempting to talk about the role, some wit may hit the mark with a name; or people may use the name of the person who first played the role conspicuously in pointing out new players, saying, "He's a Charlie." (Some social type names in our slang were originally proper, for example, Babbitt, Uncle Bim, Judas, Fagin, Shylock, Fauntleroy, sloppy Jane, good-time-Charlie.) After a type gets named, people may come to realize they need it, even make it into an office. They may say, "We elect you as our official Charlie." The foregoing is a picture of how an unnamed role becomes an institutional office—to use Max Weber's terminology, personal charisma becomes routinized by the typing process. In this transition, typing plays a mediating part between the unique personal role and the formal organizational office. But the main function of social types is to supplement, not to supplant, formal structure. Their main ground is the informal area between the purely personal role and the rational social structure. They emerge as a kind of "common sense" consensus, not as rational as that of ideal bureaucracy.

Typing also helps *professionalization*. When an office comes into existence, suitable people with training and pride in their work, must be recruited to fill it. A type can become a model for work performance and a basis for selecting members of a profession. Thus, Everett Hughes notes that a white male Protestant of old American stock is the preferred kind of person to fill the status of physician in our society. Many types have become recognized as suited to certain professions, for example, a glad-hander suits a city greeter's job; a "life of the party," a professional party-giver; a tough guy, a cafe-bouncer or a loud and domineering army sergeant. Confidence teams need a fast talker; a social worker or minister is expected to be a do-gooder; chambers of commerce seem to draw booster and goodfellow types; William Whyte suggests that good Joes are often selected by personality tests to meet the corporation's image. Typing often helps a profession to be better understood by the public and its own members, recruit people better fitted to its work, and have models building morale and pride in the profession, for example, distinctions between rookie and regular, the old-timer and apprentice, "pro" and amateur. Indeed, since a profession is a group, almost all the functions of social types apply to it.

A major function of types is *providing the individual with self-images* and corresponding motivation. I believe that social types provide the main motivational force for the individual to relate himself to the system—accounting for his mobility, seeking and finding a place, orientation toward one goal or career rather than another—even deviation. It may seem a paradox to speak of types as a reason for both conformity and deviation, but this is resolved when one considers the variety of groups in the United States and the possible disturbances in human relations that could cause a person to reject one type in favor of another. It seems plain that most young people are concerned with building types and finding identities. Once a person has chosen a type as a major part of his personality structure—say, as a result of hero-worship—it affects his choices and vulnerability to influences[26] and gives direction to his "gravitation" [27] from group to group. For example, a person may think of himself as a tough guy and seek company where he can prove it, or a smart operator and look for someone on whom to "operate," or a good Joe and let friends impose on him. Little details of behavior, such as insisting on one-hundred-proof liquor or always dining on white tablecloths, can "give away" a man's self-type. Much of what we call "front," "affectation," and mental conflict is a struggle to achieve or maintain a self-type out of line with one's ordinary status. If a man has trouble with his job, he may have to lead a double life in after-hours to build himself up again. The self-type is a major clue to a man's character: he will reject suggestions and memberships inconsistent with it and prefer those which build it up; phrases such as he "cramps my style," "makes me sick," or "brings out my better side," indicate that the individual is seeking associates who will let him be the kind of self he wants to be. Negative types provide identity too; that is, the desire *not* to be a fool, coward, softie, has-been, easy-mark, can influence a career and the way one acts.

From the outside, a person finds a more or less deliberate[28] effort by society to mold him in accordance with certain types that may not be the same as he has chosen. This includes not only simple pressure but *status-*

[26] Walter C. Reckless, Simon Dinitz, and Barbara Kay, "The Self Component in Potential Delinquency and Potential Non-Delinquency," *American Sociological Review,* 22 (1957), 566-570.

[27] The term is used by Albert K. Cohen to describe the movement of people with status problems toward congenial groups. *Delinquent Boys* (Glencoe, Ill.: The Free Press, 1955).

[28] An example of deliberate typing is use of the term "litterbug," even in roadside signs warning the motorist of legal penalties connected with this behavior.

modification. It is plain that calling a person a "party-pooper" tells him, "Don't leave early," and subjects him to pressure not to leave and derision if he does; "eager-beaver" says "Don't work so hard," or "What are you trying to do, make things hard for the rest of us?" Beyond such simple pressures, there is status-modification: person who fails to conform may find himself demoted informally without losing his formal status. Let us say that because of certain behavior, the boss has come to be regarded by employees as an old grouch, a fuddy-duddy, or a ladies' man. He might, on the other hand, be regarded as a regular guy, live-wire, wheel, brain, so that his employees have much loyalty and respect for him. Either way, his formal status has been modified by social typing, so that it is boss-plus-X or boss-minus-Y. Unfavorable typing may be a punishment and rob him of influence, just as favorable typing can promote him beyond his office. Probably every formal status, high or low, is modified by types which pressure incumbents to conform to the status. No American is free from having social types modify his status, nor can he avoid pressures resulting from modification. This applies with greater force to leaders and others in the public eye; because of their prominence and because higher standards are set up for them, people watch closely to see if they will slip; "bobbles" will be deprecated, for example, in a President (Truman) that would have been overlooked in an ordinary man. Even powerful leaders are hedged by types that limit what they can do (big-head, tyrant, bully, incompetent, brass hat, authoritarian). Negative typing can act as an informal impeachment for those who ride too high or have grown "too big for their britches."

Last, there is the *general contribution of social types to consensus*, whether to interpersonal relations or to society as a whole. I mean the ability of minds to meet and act together (often called morale, we-feeling, sometimes crowd-mindedness, prejudice). This aspect has been rather overdone and distorted by the stereotype concept, as though the main contribution of popular types to consensus was clichés and superficial judgments. Yet it seems that the ability of Americans to get together and work well together is based upon recognition of each other as belonging to certain types (such as good Joe), and having a common type system by which to classify people with whom they deal. Loyalty to a nation or to a team is built by identification with hero types and hatred for villains. A group forms its self-image from social types. The general contribution of types here is to various kinds of role consensus[29]—what we are doing, what

[29] See the exploratory study of role consensus by Neal Gross and W. S. Mason and A. W. McEachern, *Explorations in Role Analysis* (New York: John Wiley & Sons, Inc., 1958).

our nation is doing, what the other fellow is doing, how we do different things or the same things together. Without a quick, informal role consensus helped by social types, I doubt that Americans could get much done together.

Let us now look more closely at the various kinds of American models, under the headings of heroes, villains, and fools.

PART I

POPULAR AMERICAN SOCIAL TYPES

CHAPTER 1

Heroes

Heroes state major themes of an ethos, the kinds of things people approve. The heroes here presented are types judged "heroic or admirable" by most raters, though some are markedly ambivalent.[1]

Each represents certain themes of value and achievement.

Category	Theme
1) Winners	Getting what you want, beating everybody, being a champ.
2) Splendid performers	Shining before an audience, making a "hit."
3) Heroes of social acceptability	Being liked, attractive, good, or otherwise personally acceptable to

[1] Types without strong approbation or disapprobation, such as hiker, southpaw, hashslinger, whitecollar, are not considered as heroes, villains, or fools.

	groups and epitomizing the pleasures of belonging.
4) Independent spirits	Standing alone, making one's way by oneself.
5) Group servants	Helping people, cooperation, and self-sacrifice—group service and solidarity.

Each of these five categories seems to correspond to a different Weltanschauung. Looking at winners, one gets the impression that they live in a world in which life is a battle of champs, even dog-eat-dog competition, in which the strong man is king. Splendid performers, on the other hand, seem to live in a world of showmanship, where everything is for the grand impression and little matters except whether or not you make a hit in front of an audience. The show-off rather than the able man (unless also a show-off) is king. The third category, heroes of social acceptability, suggests a world of conformity where everyone is concerned to be liked and accepted—whether or not he shines, whether or not he is strong and able. Independent spirits have yet a different emphasis: the important thing is to stand alone, as on a frontier or where there is a loose social structure in which people are more interested in being themselves and freely moving than belonging—or, on the other hand, a confining structure from which they wish to escape. The last class, group servants, epitomize team spirit and solidarity—a world in which everyone is loyal to the cause and working with and for his neighbor. These worlds, of course, do not fit into a closely coherent, let alone a simple, picture. Modern society is a complex pluralism, and its system—or lack of system—contains contradictory hero-types. (Can one be both a do-gooder and a smart operator, for example?) I shall describe the types against their respective backgrounds.

Winners

The first category includes heroes who beat everybody, get what they want, and come out on top. Speaking generally, they are competitive, self-assertive, invidious, and oligarchic, favoring the king-of-the-hill principle in some form. Winners include strong men, top dogs, underdogs, brains, smart operators, even great lovers.

The *strong man* of modern times is plainly related to the conquering hero of primitive legend (Achilles, Sigurd, Beowulf, Rama) who is invincible and can't be stopped or even hurt because of his extraordinary, even magical power.[2] American slang shows admiration for indomitable persons:

> champ, ace, winner, superman, iron man, Tarzan, Samson, big operator, big leaguer, big timer, big spender, titan strong-and-silent man, man's man, lumberjack, bronc-buster, buckaroo (also some ambivalent figures like two-gun-man, Billy the Kid, and tough guy, who are predominantly villains though they have appreciable heroic ratings).

Asked to name a strong man, Americans are likely to mention Atlas, Hercules, Samson and Tarzan; after that a range such as Jack Dempsey, Napoleon, Popeye, Superman, Paul Bunyan, Joe Louis, Teddy Roosevelt, General MacArthur, Floyd Patterson, Johnny Weismuller, John L. Lewis; also some negatively valued characters, such as Hitler, Stalin, Khrushchev, Perón, Batista, Franco, Goliath, James Hoffa, Premier Tito, and Fidel Castro. These indicate that the strong man, while predominantly a hero, is also a villain when he abuses power in certain ways (to be discussed later). Americans are not, however, squeamish about accepting some pretty rough customers as heroes, whether Western two-gun men,[3] ruthless empire-builders of politics or finance,[4] even the Big Bankroll of a crime syndicate.[5]

A seeming reaction against the tough guy has been noted in favor of a gentlemanly kind of hero, exemplified by Gregory Peck, Henry Fonda, and James Stewart, aware that the problems of life can "not all be solved by a breezy manner, a gun, or a punch in the nose." [6] Some cowboys of film and TV, too, are ceasing to be strong-and-silent men. Yet there is little reason to believe that the strong man is ceasing to be a popular type. The mass media are full of the crudest exemplars. Politics is also a scene of swashbuckling.

Very like the strong man is the *top dog* (indeed, it may seem that stress is simply on point of arrival rather than what brought him there).

[2] See my study of such legendary types, "The Folk Hero," *Journal of American Folklore* (Jan.-March 1949), pp. 17-25.

[3] Mody C. Boatright, "The Western Bad Man as Hero," in Mody C. Boatright, et al., eds., *Mesquite and Willow* (Dallas, Texas: Southern Methodist University Press, 1957), pp. 96-104.

[4] See Gustavus Myers, *History of the Great American Fortunes* (New York: Modern Library, Inc.); and some of Veblen's remarks about captains of finance.

[5] Leo Katcher, *The Big Bankroll* (Harper & Brothers, 1959), a story of the life of a gangster Arnold Rothstein; Fred Pasley, *Al Capone, the Biography of a Self-Made Man* (La Salle, Ill.: Open Court Publishing Co., 1931).

[6] Leo Gurko, *Heroes, Highbrows and the Popular Mind* (Indianapolis. The Bobbs-Merrill Company, 1953), p. 193.

Americans may call such a person a wheel, big shot, boss, head guy, king-pin, Mr. Big, V.I.P., tycoon; or, somewhat derisively, brass hat. Often mentioned as top dogs are: Eisenhower, Churchill, Franklin Delano Roosevelt, Nasser, Castro, Khrushchev, Hoffa, Rockefeller, Dave Beck, Du Pont, Carnegie, Walter Reuther, Governor Faubus (nominations are, of course, affected by current news). A dictator or oppressor may seem a top dog in villainous aspect; but this is by no means the predominant way in which the big shot is viewed in America; as many have observed, our business structure is markedly authoritarian under its surface of good Joeism.

Every top dog, of course, must have an *underdog,* whether as loyal subordinate, victim of bullying or domination—or, as it may be, rival destined to upset him. I refer here only to the kind of underdog who could properly be called heroic because he commands admiration and is ex-pected to win, by pluck or luck, over the big guy. He might be thought of as a plucky little guy, a dark horse, a little David or a poor boy (who is going to become a self-made man). Well known stories, such as Cinderella and The Ugly Duckling, depict this theme in literature.[1] Unexpectedness is an essential part of his victory against overwhelming odds—epitomized by the famous flight of Lindbergh. Americans mention Harry Truman, Fidel Castro,[8] and Richard Nixon as underdogs who overcame odds.

The strong man is in a curious position of conflict with the underdog. If he fights him, he may seem a persecutor; if he doesn't, he may look like a coward. His safest course, other than avoiding the little guy altogether, is to defend him from another big guy. An example of the embarrassment a strong man can get into by fighting an underdog was the historic boxing match of Jack Dempsey with Georges Carpentier, the overmatched but sentimentally regarded champion of France. It was one of Dempsey's most unpopular fights. But in describing this tactical advantage of the underdog I do not wish to give the impression that his path is easy; even in America, negative types such as upstart, whippersnapper, fall guy, Sad Sack, butt, and low man, may be assigned to him.

Pausing to comment on these winner types, we may say that the strong man, top dog, and underdog reflect a world rather like a tournament in structure: sharply hierarchical, competitive, consisting of a series of en-counters in which rivals are matched—the results are invidious, if not ruinous, for many. He who holds his position as king of the hill becomes top dog. The fall of a top dog—especially a disliked one—to an underdog

[7] See David Malcomson, *Ten Heroes* (New York: Duell, Sloan, & Pearce, Inc., 1940).
[8] Prior to his vilification in the American press.

is a source of delight to audiences that like a good fight and are pre-occupied with winning or watching others win. In such a world, where the facts of life are distinctly not equalitarian (whatever the ethical ideals), the supreme goal is winning one's way (fairly) to the highest place.

Oddly, for all the stress on top dogs, *climber* is not a term by which Americans designate successful ones. The one who climbs is not *called* a climber if he is admired. This type has a derisive flavor, with some resentment too. It may denote a striver who cannot make the grade, or has been clumsy in his maneuvers; or be used by those on higher levels to disparage crashers, upstarts and pretenders; or by rivals to express envy and the hope that another will not succeed. Why do Americans resent the climber but admire the top dog? I would say that they like achievement but despise anyone who concentrates on small tactics—finagling, climbing itself—as a substitute for the abilities a hero should have.

Another type seems opposite to the strong man if we accept the familiar antithesis of brains versus brawn: that giant of intellect, *the brain*. Americans also call him genius, mastermind, Einstein, pundit (sometimes professor, brain-truster, intellectual, intelligentsia, expert, specialist). Even such lesser lights as quiz kid, panel-game expert, and commentator come in for their share of glory. Asked to name a brain, Americans overwhelmingly choose Einstein, though Werner Von Braun, Robert Oppenheimer, Leonardo da Vinci, Socrates, Webster, or Aristotle are often mentioned. My data show that intellect is highly esteemed by Americans. This is borne out by polls of the National Opinion Research Center at the University of Chicago, which show that college professors rank high in prestige among other professions, at least on a par with bankers and Congressmen, though below physicians. Anyone who watches television can see that there is considerable respect for pundits, mathematical wizards, mind-readers, and people who can answer the sixty-four-thousand-dollar question.

This may seem hard to square with distrust of pure scholarship and the reputed anti-intellectualism of Americans. Seymour M. Lipset says American intellectuals don't really have low status but just *feel* that way, possibly from comparing their status with that of European professors or from taking salary as the sole index of status. The key to the question, I think, is the *kind* of intellect that Americans admire. Contempt for dreamers, eggheads, and crackpots is well known. Philosophy is neglected in colleges. But let the idea-man produce cures, bombs, and gadgets—or enter the stock-market to become a successful analyst, a debate to win by smashing argument, or television contests to give the precise date that Shakespeare wrote his twelfth sonnet—and suddenly he is respected. What is common to these? It seems to me they are all tangible, public demonstrations of power. Not so much ideas per se but their results are appreciated. If so, the brain is consensually closer to the strong man than at first supposed—he might even be called a conquering hero of intellect. According to this, Einstein did not become the popular symbol of genius because the people appreciated his ideas but because they could feel and understand the impact of his ideas; he became a kind of demiurge generating a force that changed the world.

Also like the strong man, the brain supports hierarchy. He separates the thinker from the non-thinker; we see the master-mind directing what others do but cannot understand, as the top dog of a planning elite. If active thinking were the prerogative and pleasure of everyone, we would expect champions of intellect; but they would probably not be superstitiously revered as brains and wizards, nor, would they be despised if the results of their ideas were not immediately practical.

A third winner type is the *smart operator*. He is neither a brain nor a strong man, but he is similar in one essential: even though he does not claim knowledge or overcome everyone by smashing arguments or fists, somehow, when the game is over, the smart operator has the chips.

He may be called a smoothie, promoter, fast worker, diplomat—or when disapproved (with undertones of admiration): fast talker, sharpie, fox, con-man. Asked to name a smart operator, Americans may mention: Louis Wolfson, Phil Silvers (Sergeant Bilko), Maverick (TV), Richard III, Richard Nixon, Perry Mason, Frank Costello, Lucky Luciano, Dave Beck, Mike Todd, Walter Reuther, Joe McCarthy, Mayor Curley, Khrushchev, Ford, Hamilton, Lyndon Johnson, to name but a few. A fairly flattering picture of the smart operator is found in Cameron Hawley's *Cash McCall,* the hero is a bafflingly shrewd gentleman who buys up weak companies and turns them over for a profit; no one knows how many deals he is involved in or where he will turn up next; he is the mystery man behind the front man. As depicted in the novel, he is ethical in the old-fashioned "rugged" sense: he does not swindle innocents but outsmarts not quite so smart operators. (Other literary pictures include Becky Sharp, Julien Sorel, Cassius, and—as an outright villain—Uriah Heep.) Asked what a smart operator does, Americans say he puts things over on people, gets what he wants by slick deals, comes out on top, can talk you out of your eye-teeth, knows how to make a fast buck without being a crook, a smooth apple, you never catch him with his guard down.

It is easier to understand the popularity of the smart operator if we recognize him as a modern version of the clever hero of folklore, extolled in most cultures.[9] His basic role is to overcome more powerful opponents (some of whom happen to be exponents of law and order) by a trick. Anyone can understand such a universal figure; yet doubtless special things in America, such as laissez-faire business competition, favor such types. Also the good Joe and good-Christian ideals encourage sharpies to be smoothies and smile more without showing their teeth.

The victims (rivals) of a smart operator are seen as chumps, fall guys, or pompous clowns who have a fall coming. If his victims were viewed sympathetically, the smart operator would simply be a crook. What saves him, often, is that they are equally crooked and more powerful, so that bringing them down seems like a kind of justice.

Yet, the smart operator reflects a Machiavellian world of exploitation or dog-eat-dog competition in which those who don't have force use trickery. You can get to the top by being a fox. It may look as if a conventional surface masks a great deal of nastiness, but the smart operator is really playing *by* the rules of a game that necessitate, if they do not justify, his acting the way he does. One of the conditions of this game is that moral definitions are unclear, and, without a universally recognized umpire, it is impossible to be entirely right or wrong. In such a world it is to be expected that he who manages to avoid being exploited or, better yet, exploits the exploiter, will have some of the qualities of a hero. On the other side, there is less sympathy for victims because it is assumed that people should be on their guard and have only themselves to blame if they are taken. In short, the smart operator as hero "makes sense" where exploitation and unclear moral definitions are the rule. In such a world, one may find oneself despising the honest fellow as an "idiot" [10] and punishing the con-man for not being smart enough.

Last in our parade of winners is the *great lover,* who bears little resemblance, at first glance, to the smart operator or the strong man, but has features of both. Although sentimentally a Prince Charming, he also succeeds so well in the game of love that he is a kind of champion. America, says Roussy de Sales, is the only country where "love is a national problem," so one expects outstanding performers in this field to be celebrities of some consequence.

The great lover's success goes begond matrimony to amorous conquest— a string of hearts—even making thousands swoon. The hero is the one who makes the most people swoon the deepest. For these reasons Prince

---

[9] See my study of this type, "The Clever Hero," *Journal of American Folklore,* 67 (Jan.-Mar. 1954), 21-34.

[10] See Dostoevski's novel with this title.

Charming with his monogamous ideal is far from an adequate symbol.

By all odds, Rudolph Valentino (The Sheik) remains the major American example. After him come Don Juan, Casanova, Romeo, and a variety of movie stars and playboys such as Clark Gable, General Rafael Trujillo, Cary Grant, Eddie Fisher, Errol Flynn, John Barrymore, Charles Boyer, and "Ruby" Rubirosa. Any male who has or claims unusual prowess in affairs of the heart may be referred to, seriously or jokingly, as Casanova, Don Juan, Romeo, Adonis, or lady-killer.

There is little point in trying to specify what traits are common to great lovers. The essential thing is that he triumph consistently. For this reason I put the great lover among the winners with the strong man and the smart operator.

On the feminine side we have *love queens,* such as Rita Hayworth, Marilyn Monroe, Elizabeth Taylor, Marlene Dietrich, Jean Harlow, Clara Bow, Greta Garbo, and Mae West, who are rather like great lovers, though in a more fetching and less conquering way. Women have traditionally been too passive to have great lover properly apply to them. They might, however, have titles such as love goddess, Venus, Cleopatra, charmer, it-girl, oomph-girl, glamor girl, pin-up girl, and beauty queen. Let us note, however, that the *vamp* (seen in early film roles of Theda Bara and Pola Negri, or Marlene Dietrich's destruction of the professor in *The Blue Angel*) is no longer typical of American love ideals. She is a *femme fatale* —a sorceress who ensnares and ruins men. Were the vamp active today, she would probably fall into the category of golddigger, cheat, coquette, siren, heart-breaker (see villains). The American love queen is an attractive girl but lacks fatal charm. ("Can you imagine anyone killing himself over love for Marilyn Monroe or Lollobrigida?" asks Alberto Moravia.)

The great lover has a negative side as a *wolf;* the wolf is crafty, crass and ruthless; does not play according to the rules but short-circuits the higher emotions—cheats to win—and therefore is a villain. The romantic ideal calls for success of an idealistic sort, not just territorial acquisition, as it were. People who admire the great lover see that the wolf really spoils the game and condemn him accordingly.

Another negative view of the great lover is as a fool—a ladies' man, sissy—perhaps a lady-killer who boasts and imagines he is a Don Juan. These fool types do not contradict the great lover ideal any more than the wolf does. Rather, they are penalized departures from it, and to make fun of false great lovers is to reaffirm the true one.

Such types are part of an important aspect of our culture: a game which most Americans expect to enter at one time or another, and which is a spectator sport for almost any age. Most sit on the sidelines watching

heroes succeed better than they do, but this is the distinction between
the big league and the sand lot. As with other sports, the game as ideally
conceived is not always the same as that actually played. On the romantic
level the great lover role leads to the happy ending of perfect marriage
(it impairs the ideal to leave a trail of broken hearts without definite
progress toward the altar). On another level there is a battle-of-the-sexes,
an exploitative game,[11] in which people try to "take" someone for money,
sex, status advancement, or simply the pleasure of conquest. Playboys
become glamorous from the number of women they have been involved
with. It is hard to say that such a great lover role actually reinforces
"true love" as a cultural theme. One could reasonably argue that it
favors the opposite.

Splendid Performers

Mass communication has brought to the fore another variety of heroes,
whose specialty is a shining impression—some remarkable thing they do
before a crowd, camera, or microphone. It is hard to specify just what
this thing they do is except that it makes a hit (sometimes it is called
"clicking," or "wowing" an audience) by almost any means, from parachute jumping to crying into a microphone. An unending succession of
tricks ("gimmicks") for making a hit tells us that the limit is far from
reached. Rather than specifying what they do, we admire splendid performers for shining in front of an audience.

Of course, if the performer "wows" the audience by a knock-out punch,
he belongs among the "winners" previously discussed. But shining does
not require winning, indeed, many splendid performers are neither
dominant nor strong. Conversely, the big shot who runs the show and is
a real "winner" may not be out in front making a hit with the public.
The splendid performer may be a front man who has little power aside
from his popularity and effectiveness as a spokesman for policies made
by somebody else. To summarize, the splendid performer aims primarily
at impression rather than at beating or controlling others (though they
may be conjoined); he is directed towards audiences; he is colorful and
tries to set himself off (whereas the man of power or ability may be
inconspicuous); his goal is to steal the show, not run it; basically he is
a showman.

That our society admires splendid performance is indicated by the

[11] Willard Waller has carefully analyzed competitive and exploitative aspects of
courtship in America. See Willard Waller, *The Family*, revised by Reuben Hill (New
York: Dryden Press, 1938), pp. 101, 136-7, 142-3, 163-4, 168.

enthusiastic followers of headliners and stars, sacks full of fan mail, and the impact of splendid performers on people's lives (children marching on streets twirling batons, adults practicing the fast draw, taking vocal lessons or public speaking). The wish seems to be to get out in front and do something—anything that will make a hit. "Theatrical" has risen from a mild reproach to a title of glamor. Once when Margaret Truman dined at a swanky hotel, she was given table number eleven; the next time she got table one. Asked the reason for this promotion, the hotel explained that last time she had been only a President's daughter, since then she had become a radio and television actress.

I shall divide splendid performers into those who are in show business and those who show off as an incident to sport or play. Those who shine among professional *showmen* are often referred to by names like:

> star, maestro, impresario, showgirl, entertainer, crooner, torch-singer, disk-jockey, master-of-ceremonies, soloist, virtuoso, artist, premiere danseuse, prima donna, comedian, fashion-model, stunt artist, and daredevil—all of which get predominantly heroic ratings.

Some are featured soloists, some, though members of a team or cast, get the spotlight and most of the news stories. Typically they are veterans who have come up the hard way and mastered some art, stunt, style, or gimmick that reliably clicks with audiences.

Splendid performers also include those not strictly in show business who play so hard at a sport or recreation that they find their way into the limelight consistently and become drawing cards, even headliners. Let us call them *heroes of play*. This includes athletes, amateur or professional (Babe Ruth, Joe Louis, Bob Mathias, Jim Thorpe, Ted Williams, Babe Zaharias, Jackie Robinson, Sugar Ray Robinson, Archie Moore, Goose Tatum, Maureen Connolly, Mickey Mantle, Roy Campanella, Jessie Owens, Red Grange, Sam Sneed, Rocky Marciano), and outstanding sportsmen like Sir Walter Lipton, Aly Khan, or King Gustave of Sweden, whose play has attracted wide attention for one reason or another; even Bernarr McFadden's parachute-jumping at the age of eighty has been widely publicized. Others who get into the limelight by play are indicated by names like: water-skier, skindiver, polo-player, drum majorette, pompon girl, baton-twirler, mountain-climber, hell diver, parachute-jumper,[12] and life of the party (all of which have predominantly heroic ratings). Many American sports and hobbies have been so changed—even overshadowed—by grandstanding that it is hard to tell where fun in the game

---

[12] A growing fad in America. It was estimated that in 1959 there were about 3000 sport jumpers in the United States, double the number of the preceding year. *Life,* August 10, 1959, p. 101.

stops and playing to the crowd begins. You rarely see a water skier except as close as possible to a crowded bathing beach. The rage of sports cars in America is at least in part an expression of a desire to put on a show by sitting in the cockpit of a racy car wearing a snappy little hat. Another example is the conversion of the workaday cowboy into the rodeo dude. The rodeo has become a spectator sport in which people who have never been within miles of a cattle range dress up and parade in expensive, silver-inlaid outfits. Also among splendid performances should be put highly publicized amours and escapades of movie stars, sports,[13] and playboys, whose recreation is popular entertainment. It may even be motivated by a desire for publicity.

All of this is likely to improve the status of the *playboy*,[14] still predominantly a derided type. People have considered a person who plays too hard, too dangerously, or too expensively, or who shows off, or goes to extremes,[15] a kind of fool. Yet things are changing; more and more we see in America a world where everybody is playing or watching others play. Wider participation in conspicuous leisure seems bound to take the puritan curse, as it might be called, off play, and at the same time projects more splendid performers into the limelight. As people have more time to be baton-twirlers, bathing beauties, flycasters, and surfboard riders, their concern will be more centered on stars of such activities—indeed, heroes of work may have to take a back seat as playboys take over.

Mass communication should increase the prominence of showmen and spectator sports. Television's moving eye provides innumerable arenas for new play heroes to appear in. It seems inevitable that as more publicity is given to people playing and performing, the public will get wrapped up in watching—or trying to become—splendid performers; young people will direct their ambitions more toward shows—indeed, it seems as though we are all becoming stage-struck. I envisage a future world of grandstanders, where people who do a good but inconspicuous job suffer in comparison, and where entertainers are a major elite who crash into the "best" society. Also, people at the top of the power structure will feel they need to be showmen to compete with all these celebrities. The strong man will have to become a splendid performer.

[13] A type recognized by cab-drivers, who can be relied upon to give a good tip and put on a good display of living-it-up. Davis, *op. cit.*

[14] The striking rise of *Playboy*, a new man's magazine, to a circulation outstripping that of *Esquire* is some indication, perhaps, of a change in the status of playboy from fool to a hero type. See Martin Ryan, "Portrait of *Playboy*," *Studies in Public Communication* (Communication Research Board, University of Chicago), Number 1, Summer 1957, pp. 11-21.

[15] Jitterbug, jazz-fiend, dance-fiend, bridge-shark, hifii-addict, hot-rodder and drag racer have predominantly foolish ratings.

Heroes of Social Acceptability

"So if you want people to like you,
Rule 2 is: Smile."
                    DALE CARNEGIE

"I never met a man I didn't like."
                    WILL ROGERS

Will Rogers was a rough-cut wit who had the courage to "be himself" and criticize the big man, but equally important to his success was his capacity to make himself liked—a friendliness that has rarely been surpassed. He rolled Dale Carnegie and George Bernard Shaw into one. This paradoxical mixture, more than the development of either side, made him a unique figure in America.

The bland side of his character might have made him just a good Joe. He epitomized the deep desire and persistent effort to be liked, one of the strongest traits in the American character. A number of heroes, ranging from dazzling pin-ups to fervent gladhanders, men of good will to fashionable smoothies, embody perfected likeableness of one kind or another. I call them heroes of social acceptability. Often one is called a favorite, favorite son, social lion, or man of the people.

When we try to delineate the hero of social acceptability, we encounter the same difficulty we did with splendid performers: the same person may have several parts, say strong man, great lover, smart operator, splendid performer, and hero of social acceptability. Rogers himself, besides being the "best-liked man in America," was a splendid performer in his movies and in his Ziegfeld Follies roles. To sharpen the distinction, let me say that the hero of social acceptability need not stand out by shining; in fact, he is more likely to fit or blend in. Conversely, to be a brilliant performer does not require a person to be personally acceptable—indeed, the word *prima donna* (she shines but is bad-tempered or conceited) implies this.

There are various styles of personal acceptability. F. D. R. was almost the opposite of Will Rogers—rather a highbrow. Dapper Jimmy Walker was the toast of New York City though almost a dude. Al Smith made it as a plain man with the five-cent cigar, Sophie Tucker by shouting jazz songs, Perry Como by singing and talking in such a relaxed way that it was hard to believe his success cost him any effort. But all were very likeable. I have tried to sort heroes of social acceptability under four main heads: (1) pin-ups, models of bodily perfection; (2) social lions and charmers with remarkable magnetism; (3) goodfellows whose main appeal is friendliness;

and (4) conformers (subdivided into moralists and smoothies) who adhere
in such an exemplary way to group standards that, paradoxically, they
stand out by fitting in. It would not be easy to sort real people neatly into
such classes; but the types, I believe, can be conceptually distinguished.

The *pin-up* is found on thousands of magazine covers, bedroom walls
and locker doors as a secular ikon, the titles include doll, cover girl, beauty
queen, model, Adonis, Mr. Universe, Miss America. Such a model of
bodily perfection need be neither a great lover nor a social lion. Photo-
genic perfection is enough. It may be surprising to say that a pin-up need
not be unusual even in looks (many people have complained of the
monotony of American cheesecake and Hollywood beauty). Fashion,
cosmetology, and hair styling actually increase the resemblance of pin-up
types.

I would distinguish the *charmer* as one who actively magnetizes people,
casts a spell of a kind, whether by wit, conversation, manner, or eloquence.
He can be called a social lion, spellbinder, or personality kid. Neither
Samuel Johnson nor Will Rogers was a pin-up, but they surely fascinated
people. As charmers, Americans name persons like: Zsa Zsa Gabor, Charles
Boyer, Cary Grant, Leonard Bernstein, Cleopatra, Adlai Stevenson,
Salome, Mark Antony, Clark Gable, Maurice Chevalier, Perry Como,
Liberace, Harry Belafonte, Rubirosa, and Franklin Delano Roosevelt. The
ability to captivate people might be possessed by an evangelist, diplomat,
politician, super-salesman, great lover, or child actor.

Third among highly acceptable types is the *goodfellow,* also known as
regular guy, regular fellow, good scout, good sport, good egg, good Joe,
McCoy, everyone's friend (sometimes implied by terms like extravert,
democrat, G.I. Joe, social lion, socialite, booster, life of the party; and
derisively, gladhander, good-time-Charlie). He may not be mysteriously
magnetic, and often is not pretty enough to put on a bureau mirror; but
for friendliness he is hard to beat. Along with friendliness may go a kind
of rough-and-ready willingness to take a joke and people as they come.
(You can see it in a group of campers: no one stands on ceremony,
everyone is a good sport, all drink from the same cup.) At a formal affair,
the goodfellow is more friendly than required. He need not, however, be
a "common" man. Both Jimmie Walker and Franklin Delano Roosevelt
might be called Fancy Dans. Roosevelt had an aristocratic manner and
dared to use a cigarette-holder; yet a study shows that the chief thing
people liked about him was his warm personality, second that he did
things for people, third his ability to handle situations.[16] The boss who

---

[16] The study concluded that Americans like a "tremendously powerful man who *still*
is personally very human and who still champions the little man's cause." Fillmore H.

wants to be a regular fellow need not be a backslapper and gladhander. The essential thing is a good-heartedness that is naturally, continually, and effectively demonstrated, preferably in a democratic manner though the grand man may also show it. Such good-heartedness is displayed by those who are often mentioned by Americans as goodfellows: Arthur Godfrey ("and his friends"), Perry Como, Bing Crosby, Lucille Ball in the television show "I Love Lucy" (women can be goodfellows too), Will Rogers, Tennessee Ernie, "Ike" Eisenhower, Pat Boone, Abe Lincoln, Falstaff, Santa Claus, Eddie Cantor, Bob Hope, and Harry Truman. One movie star, William Holden, refers wryly to his "Smilin' Jack" parts. In comics, an outstanding example of the goodfellow is Joe Palooka, a good-natured fighter who visits kids in hospitals, takes care of doctor bills, and helps people do the right thing. It is not his fighting (he is, in fact, more a second-rater than a champ), but his good heart, personality, and his kind deeds that have won him a warm place in the hearts of millions; a poll of teen-agers showed that he ranked third behind Ted Williams and Gene Autry among those they admired most.[17]

Trying to appraise this type, I think one would have to say that amiable though he is, he is not strong as heroes go—plainly, no Siegfried. The relative weakness of the goodfellow may imply something about our national character. What weaknesses might be expected in a zealous goodfellow? Perhaps he would be too friendly for his own good—hobnob with the wrong people, be too "easy," earn titles like yes-man, sentimentalist, bleeding heart, easy touch, pushover. He might try so hard to help people that he became a meddler, busybody, quixotic do-gooder. He might seem so excessively friendly that people called him a hypocrite, a gladhander; he might be accused of mediocrity. When he is placed beside a classical strong man like Achilles or Beowulf, one suspects that Joe has a heart of gold but he lacks the strong arm of the primitive superman; he is willing to get himself into trouble for others but may not have the strength to get himself out of it.

On the other side, he represents an ideal of happiness and adjustment very important in American life—the good man surrounded by friends and secure in the confidence that he will have friends and can make them wherever he goes (not a Willy Loman riding on a smile and a shoeshine but a genuine person for whom the world cannot collapse). This is the

Stanford, "The Follower's Role in Leadership Phenomena," in Guy E. Swanson, et al., eds., *Readings in Social Psychology* (New York: Holt, Rinehart, and Winston, Inc., 1952), pp. 332, 335.
[17] Lawrence Averill, "Impact of a Changing Culture Upon Pubescent Ideals," *School and Society,* 72 (July 22, 1950), 1-3.

side of the good Joe that Americans take pride in. They might add that
he is a comfortable person to have around, no troublemaker or rebel,
doesn't needle people, never sets himself too far above others, measures
success in acceptance rather than achievement, no prodigal but a plodder,
not a fireball but a friend.

Last among heroes of social acceptability I would place *conforming
heroes*, super-conformers who stand for the letter of the law, the rule
perfectly applied: the sticklers, Puritans, saints, paragons—Lord Chesterfield the model gentleman, Cicero the ideal Roman, Washington the
perfect patriot—for whom the good Joe may be a little too easygoing.
Even in a society where almost everyone is corrupt, usually someone is
regarded as incorruptible. The conforming hero stands out because most
of us are poor conformers;[18] most Americans are fashionable, but how
many are fashion-plates?—most are loyal, but how many are 100% Americans, Yankee Doodle Dandies? Yet, however far he goes, a super-conformer
cannot stand out as do individualistic types like the strong man and
splendid performer.

Two classes of conforming heroes can readily be distinguished. *Moralists*
adhere closely to an ethical standard implied by names like:

saint, angel, puritan; also in a sense, patriot, superpatriot, 100% American,
martyr, Job, Galahad, idealist, missionary, reformer, boy scout, booster,
do-gooder, also unflattering names such as prude, prig, and diehard.

As "outstandingly correct or moral persons," Americans may mention
Pope Pius XII, Billy Graham, Norman Vincent Peale, Queen Elizabeth,
Fulton J. Sheen, Eleanor Roosevelt. They also think of Emily Post and
Amy Vanderbilt as models of correctness in etiquette and protocol. It is
easy enough to distinguish good or correct models from the likable goodfellow. True, one should be good to be liked, but one does not have to
win any gold stars (roisterers like Falstaff and Gargantua would pass
muster as good Joes). On the other hand, moralists are a little too austere,
even unfriendly, to be good sports.

This difference may be pinpointed by saying that the one thing a conforming hero may not do is "give" on the principle of which he is model.
Since this principle in a moralist is not friendliness, he will sacrifice friendliness to it and so seem rigid to a good Joe. In David Riesman's familiar
terminology, he is inner-directed.

This gives a basis for distinguishing the *smoothie* as an other-directed
superconformist who suavely fits current group requirements—is "hep" to

---

[18] Floyd Allport's well-known concept of the J-curve is applicable here. "The
J-Curve Hypothesis of Conforming Behavior," *Journal of Social Psychology*, 1934,
5:141-183.

the latest thing, "in the know." His main goal is to stay "with it" (whatever "it" is), and he is so smooth on the surface that people can find no fault in him—he plays roles adroitly, dresses smartly, and is a model for climbers who envy his ability to get into the "right" groups. Such a hero might be referred to by titles like man-about-town, fashion-plate, fashion leader, best dressed woman, hep-cat, slick chick, glamor girl, socialite, perfect gentleman, diplomat. Americans see something of the smoothie in: Adolph Menjou, Cary Grant, Maurice Chevalier, Rafael Trujillo, Jr., Errol Flynn, Bob Cummings, Bret Maverick, Tony Curtis, Fred Astaire, Mickey Cohen, Richard Nixon, Charles Boyer, Perry Como, Rudolph Valentino, Bing Crosby, Frank Sinatra, Eddie Fisher, Rubirosa, and Dinah Shore. Somewhat surprising mention is a cowboy (Maverick) and a gangster (Cohen), though one must admit that in modern times neither of these activities preclude being smooth. It may be hard to distinguish a fashion-plate from an authority on protocol such as Emily Post, yet one could maintain that the former is other-directed in trying to keep up with changing standards while the latter belongs more with inner-directed moralists in trying to define a standard and hold to it consistently. A smoothie knows the latest styles, beliefs, and points of view; but his commitment is neither moral nor permanent. He stands for relativity and perfect adaptability to the situation rather than the "right." He abhors absolutes, which are, sooner or later, a source of trouble. He is diplomatic in manipulating people so as to compromise their absolute stands; his whole skill is devoted to keeping "in," not standing out or differing. He shuns squares, creeps, oddballs, characters, eccentrics, troublemakers. He is conservative but not a diehard. Though he will not "rock the boat," neither will he stay with a sinking ship. However "good" he is, it is hard to imagine him caught in the predicament of a Joan of Arc.

I have described five major models of social acceptability—the pin-up, the charmer, the goodfellow, the moralist, and the smoothie. They seem to represent the persistent effort of Americans to belong and to be liked. Groups need such types and they are sought after and readily admitted. Once in, they do not usually rub people the wrong way (though a moralist can be a diehard or a stickler). Nor do they arouse envy by invidious striving and achievement as do splendid performers and strong men, for their tendency is to blend rather than to stand out; they are usually surrounded by a crowd whose imitation is their sincerest flattery.

Lack of invidiousness in heroes of social acceptability should not lead us to neglect their ability to climb. Though not seeming to wish to, they find themselves in the best company, well fixed, well placed, living it up, marrying above their class. Indeed, the demand for highly acceptable people may be so great that money and votes are available to them in large quantities. While the moralist in politics may be (like Cincinnatus) reluctant to accept office, the smoothie will decline two times in the hope of being asked the third. I can imagine a government by smoothies and good Joes, and a "high society" crowded with pin-up cuties and movie stars. When highly acceptable people climb, they become models for others who choose the socially acceptable route rather than the more aggressive ones of winner, splendid performer, or independent spirit (to whom we shall soon turn).

Through such models we glimpse a world with a surface different from the harsh competition of winners and splendid performers. Its theme is belonging and conformity. Were it totally achieved, life would be like the Happy Knolls Country Club. Even if this world were far from achieved, I should think such types could function as a vicarious compensation for not being liked and not belonging—symbols of a wistful hankering for solidarity.

Independent Spirits

It is hardly fair to stress goodfellows and conforming heroes without mentioning a thin but strong thread of individualism in the same fabric— models who act and stand alone. Names like individualist, trail-blazer, enterpriser, lone eagle, lone wolf, loner, pioneer, Daniel Boone, free thinker, self made man, live wire and go-getter are favorably rated (also feminine types like bachelor girl and coed with connotations of making one's way alone in a man's world). A diehard may be seen as having courage to stand against the crowd. One finds subdued admiration for rebels, revolutionaries, even hermits like Henry David Thoreau, who have "the courage of their convictions."

Asked to name an independent spirit, Americans are apt to think of Charles Lindbergh, Abraham Lincoln, Albert Schweitzer, Harry Truman, Frank Lloyd Wright, Socrates, Teddy Roosevelt, General MacArthur, Henry Thoreau, Tallulah Bankhead, Robin Hood, Boris Pasternak, Billy Mitchell, Martin Luther, Hamlet, Errol Flynn, Marlon Brando, James Dean, G. B. Shaw, Patrick Henry, Orson Welles, Ben Franklin, Ed Murrow, Sam Rayburn, Carl Sandburg, or Marshal Tito. Americans are impressed not so much by the greatness of achievement as by the ability or will of these heroes to be different and follow the solitary path. It was not so much *what* Lindbergh did as the fact that he did it *alone* that most impressed Americans (after all, the Atlantic had already been flown). The pathos of aloneness explains the appeal of many heroes of literature and life who stand, fight, succeed—or, it may be, fail and die—alone. The Message to Garcia was carried alone, Byrd stayed at the South Pole alone, Roland made his last stand alone, Floyd Collins died in a cave alone. Harry Truman was a good Joe in some ways; but his unexpected election in 1948 illustrates the role of the independent spirit, when, deserted by his party and ridiculed by much of the press and public, he went on to campaign alone.

The *bohemian* is interesting in this connection. At first glance, he is mostly a fool, belonging with beatniks and other eccentrics. His rating was: *Unfamiliar,* 22; *Hero,* 15; *Villain,* 18; *Fool,* 54; *None of these,* 85 (184 raters). But if three common meanings of bohemian are distinguished, then raters give different reactions, for example:

	Unfamiliar	Hero	Villain	Fool	None of These	Number of Raters
1) a person who follows the bohemian style of life as a *kind of fad* in imitation of others	0	4	0	54	9	67
2) a person whose bohemian way of life reflects *creativity*	0	35	1	7	24	67
3) a person whose bohemian way of life is a *rebellion* against pressure to conform	0	8	10	23	27	67*

* It was permissible to class a bohemian in more than one category.

In other words, when a bohemian is peculiar because of creativity, he seems heroic to many. He is a fool when simply imitative or a rebel against convention. Willingness to depart from the common path is appreciated when for the sake of something worthwhile—even if not an outstanding success. I think the public is on the lookout for authentic cases that it can approve; but guards against pseudo-individualism (whether faddist or indiscriminate rebel) knowing well that beard, beret, and bare feet do not make a true individualist any more than they make a true artist. As a *conformist,* a bohemian looks poor indeed; he would probably do better as a regular fellow. If he can convince people that he is genuine and has a chance of being creative, they may see in his strange ways the courage and aloneness of the independent spirit.[19]

Other types—not necessarily heroes—have a part in what I would call the American reaction against conformity. One is the *jester,* sometimes a savage wit or acidly funny commentator who debunks the polite shams of

[19] The heroic side of eccentricity is visible in many "characters" who dare to be different. See Irving Wallace, *The Square Pegs* (New York: Alfred A. Knopf, Inc., 1957) or Gerald W. Johnson, *The Lunatic Fringe* (New York: J. B. Lippincott Company, 1957); especially John F. Kennedy's study of American leaders who had the courage to stand against the majority, *Profiles in Courage* (New York: Harper & Brothers, 1956).

good-Joe-manship (Oscar Levant, Groucho Marx, Pamela Mason, Fred Allen). George Bernard Shaw once remarked that American audiences liked him best when he insulted them. Another version is the *angry commentator* (Westbrook Pegler, Fulton Lewis, Father Coughlin), whose indignation serves as a contrast to blandness; people get a "kick" out of agreeing or disagreeing with them. Such types get some appeal from the fact that they stand up and challenge the assumptions of a super-friendly world where it is hard to get openly mad at anybody. Getting mad in a world of good Joeism is like fighting in mush; soothing softness smothers the fellow who wants to "have it out"; he finds some relief in vicarious violations of the "social ethic." The Western hero rides off alone on his horse or individually settles issues with the bad guy, while in real life people are expected to be organization men and make decisions with the approval of committees and families. Modern man is caught in a dilemma between two ideals, standing on his own feet (according to the Protestant ethic), and complying with groups. The independent spirit helps solve this dilemma. Working counter to the good Joe, he maintains a balance between contradictory ideals. Some people who admire the independent spirit are really one thing but vicariously another. Certain conservative colleges maintain one "radical" just to prove to themselves that they are liberal.

Another way of adjusting to such a dilemma is to be really one thing but overtly *imitate* the other. Suppose a man wants to be *both* fashionable and "different." He adopts a pose that will give him the credit for being a "character" but is careful to choose something in style. Russell Lynes notes the use of pipes, charcoal-gray suits and other fashionable props to achieve "mass-produced eccentricity." Movie actors often (on the advice of press agents) adopt some style of life that will make them "glamorous," "colorful." It seems clear that such pseudo-individuality enables people to play at being individualists when they are in fact conformists; so, they eat their cake and have it too.

Vicarious and imitative individualism reflect a world where conformity is uncomfortable. People are tired of roles and welcome a vacation, as it were, in the pose or hobby of "being yourself," yet are not ready to break away. It seems reasonable that independent spirits in our society function more as compensation than as an expression of individualism.

Group Servants

He will avenge all your wrongs;
he will give combat at your fords;
he will decide all your quarrels.
"The Saga of Cuchulain"

> If any in distress did pass, to them he
>   was so kind,
> That he would give and lend to them, to
>   help them in their need:
>   "The Ballad of Robin Hood"

The last group of heroes come closest, perhaps, to the traditional picture of what a hero should be—a person with a strong arm and a heart of gold, tirelessly serving his group. Compared with the glamor girls, big wheels, smart operators, and smoothies of American society, they are the social workers, as it were.

Defenders enforce laws, right wrongs, protect ramparts, save people in trouble, arrive in the nick of time to rescue the weak from the strong (ogre, persecutor). Carrying such an image are names like:

G-man, cop, gang-buster, Lone Ranger, emancipator, protector, savior, deliverer, dragon-slayer, Galahad, Saint George, Sherlock, investigator.[20]

Asked to name a defender, Americans mention: Lincoln, Moses, Washington, Clarence Darrow, Perry Mason, General Wainwright, Fidel Castro, Saint George, Joan of Arc, J. Edgar Hoover, Émile Zola, Jack Webb (Sgt. Friday of "Dragnet"), and Winston Churchill.

Another group of heroes may be called *crusaders,* who try to bring in a new order or carry the cause forward—indicated by terms like reformer, trust-buster, dragon-slayer, Quixote, Galahad, and, in one sense, missionary. Asked to name a crusader, Americans are apt to think of Richard the Lion-Hearted, Billy Graham, Carrie Nation, Fidel Castro, Samuel Gompers, Jackie Robinson (a colored man in a white sport), Margaret Sanger, Martin Luther King. The crusader is marked by a militant highmindedness which sets him apart from defenders, who may be content to let well enough alone. If the cause for which he fights is not recognized, however, he may seem a fool, even villain. The case of Woodrow Wilson illustrates this vulnerability of the high-minded crusader. On the other hand, the rise of Huey Long was helped by his role as a "David" who challenged the Goliath of Standard Oil in Louisiana and his crusade to share the wealth and make "every man a king."

Martyrs make exemplary sacrifices for group causes. What they seem to symbolize above all else is loyalty. As martyrs, Americans mention Joan of Arc, Jesus, Gandhi, Lincoln, St. Stephen, Nathan Hale, Sacco and Vanzetti, General Custer, General MacArthur, Billy Mitchell, St. Peter, Socrates, and the Unknown Soldier. The ideal is often extended beyond

---

[20] Of 225 raters, 135 thought of investigator as a hero, 43 as a villain, 17 as a fool, 56 thought of him in a neutral category.

supreme sacrifice to people who have suffered for worthy reasons, even pacifists and conscientious objectors are martyrs to some people. However, a distinction should yet be made between martyr, victim, and scapegoat, since the latter two lack heroic rating.[21] Martyrdom has dramatic characteristics which mark it off from passive suffering, however undeserved: it is plainly for a cause and voluntary, proving the loyalty of the sufferer. It is a powerful symbol for stimulating morale and social movements.[22]

From cases like Sacco and Vanzetti we learn that the martyr is not narrowly ethnocentric but able to appeal beyond his group, uniting large numbers of people sentimentally.

To about one out of four raters, however, the martyr is a fool—a dupe, fall guy, fanatic, gloryhog—possibly a neurotic who gets satisfaction from suffering. General Custer is a hero with the underside of a fool. Unless people are involved in a conflict, it is difficult to appreciate an act like martyrdom. In the perspective of comfort and pleasure-seeking, such a course seems only gruesome. Some feel that no cause is worth dying for, that anyone who gets into such a jam has only himself to blame—these, however, are alienated and anomic perspectives that deserve treatment in another chapter.

Benefactors exemplify tireless work for the public in nonmilitant ways. Americans mention: Lincoln, Jonas Salk, Curie, Schweitzer, Nobel, Carnegie, Rockefeller, Ford, Edison, F. D. Roosevelt, Baruch, Gandhi, Wilson, Hoover, Franklin, Jefferson, Eisenhower, Einstein, John L. Lewis, Florence Nightingale, William Booth, and—in a somewhat different sense—Robin Hood. A benefactor is conceived as having a heart of gold, working without reward to bestow gifts on society. In highest conception he is a kind of light-bringer or Lycurgus, close to the culture hero of mythology.[23] *Great benefactors* are indicated by titles like great man, founding father, genius, prophet, messiah, father of his country. On a smaller scale are *do-gooders,* who do not quite have the stature of nearly magical philanthropy —ordinary persons working in the ideal of service—not a Prometheus bringing light, but perhaps a social worker with a relief check. Asked to

[21]

	U	H	V	F	X	N
martyr	4	103	6	39	19	159
victim	3	21	6	19	121	155
scapegoat	6	3	8	20	41	70

U = unfamiliar, H = heroic, V = villainous, F = foolish, X = none of the preceding, N = number of raters. Raters were allowed to place a type in more than one category if they desired.

[22] See Donald W. Riddle, *The Martyrs, A Study in Social Control* (Chicago: University of Chicago Press, 1931), for some evidence of the power of the martyr pattern.
[23] See A. Van Deurson, *Der Heilbringer* (Groningen: J. B. Wolters, 1931).

name a do-gooder, Americans mention a list overlapping with benefactors, such as Eleanor Roosevelt, Carrie Nation, Florence Nightingale, Carnegie, Eva Perón, Robin Hood, Conrad Adenaur, Norman Vincent Peale, Hoover, Pollyanna, the Salvation Army, Schweitzer. Many do-gooders have an effect on popular ideals without being famous. The typical one is an ordinary person (usually a woman) who gives much time to voluntary work in churches, hospitals, women's organizations, civic associations, social agencies, and such.[24] She is not a Lady Bountiful (stepping out of a limousine with baskets for the poor) but a middle-class woman whose motives might be religious sentiment, plain good-heartedness, the wish to join something, social climbing, or simply desire for a leisure activity with overtones of "help" and "work" instead of "fun."

The do-gooder is more ambivalent than the martyr (out of 200 raters, 95 said hero, but 68 said fool). Because of this, a person who works for worthy causes may wince when told that he is a do-gooder. But it is hard to think of a better name for him. Terms like dollar-a-year man, Uncle Bim, Lady Bountiful, good Samaritan, boy scout, angel (backer), or big brother are hardly better, though predominantly favorable in rating. We cannot ignore the negative undertones—meddler, buttinski, bleeding heart, eager-beaver, fanatic, Quixote, bigot, prude, hypocrite, "holier-than-thou," flat-heel (a grim professional social worker).

As a whole, group servants symbolize solidarity. If most people were do-gooders, we would have a world very much like a beehive—the collectivistic ideal of service and sacrifice. As with the other models, Americans approach them only occasionally. Our model system is inconsistent enough to make them seem unrealistic against a background of opposed types. They are an important—but a single—part of the American character. Derisive undertones of "do-gooder," "martyr," and our survey of American hero types show that people are striving in other directions and will not commit themselves fully to the ideal of service. Business, for example, has little place for the do-gooder, unless it is in the philanthropy that earns tax reduction. Just as in the language of soldiers, "hero" doesn't mean the winner of the Congressional Medal of Honor, it means someone who sticks his neck out. Group servants do symbolize solidarity, but the derisive undertone of the term shows some alienation. We must also consider the possibility that their function is compensatory—to make people feel better about what they are doing, or not doing.

---

[24] Clarence W. Hall, "America's Amazing Women," *Readers Digest,* July, 1955, p. 17-22. The clearest portrait of the American do-gooder is probably that supplied by Pitirim Sorokin, *Altruistic Love* (Boston: Beacon Press, 1950).

Conclusion

The existence of these types and celebrities states for us as a people what we seem to the world and, in some measure, what we are.

Seeing inconsistencies, let us note that some compensate one another. We observed, for example, that an independent spirit can provide a relieving contrast to conforming models and make people who have to conform "feel better" because somebody—some "character"—has the courage to be different. Do-gooders and good Joes can make people feel good in a world where egoism and ruthless competition may be the "facts of life." The two-gun-man in Western dramas is an image of self-reliance in a world of organization-men. Such compensatory types can help people put up with a reality which is different from the ideal, by masking and euphemizing it or by providing relief and escape from it—perhaps by alternative roles in avocation, play or fantasy. It may be that many apparently inharmonious types in American culture work together in this way: to provide alternative versions of reality or of the ideal; when people get sick of A they turn to B; and when they get sick of B they turn to A.

But we have looked at only a third of the picture. There are also the antagonists. Villains and fools are often negative counterparts of the very situations and roles represented by heroes. Before commenting further on heroes, let us turn to villains.

CHAPTER 2

VILLAINS

Billy the Kid did not make a good villain because he was blonde, blue-eyed, well built, and rather handsome; women fell for him. He was brave and a square shooter. Such discrepancies in the character of a bad man made him resemble others (Robin Hood, Don Juan, François Villon, Pancho Villa) who perhaps should have been villains but were not. A pure villain lacks redeeming traits that confuse him with a hero (as in the *Song of Roland* where a Saracen, is referred to as all compact of evil and as black as melted pitch). Popular speech provides unambiguous images of hatefulness, also literature (Judas, Benedict Arnold, Simon Legree, Uriah Heep). A proper villain has the opposite traits of a hero and threatens the group the hero serves.

For all this, paradoxically, he is a popular favorite. One TV serial, Captain Video, dispatched over three hundred evil-doers in seven years for the pleasure of viewers. Some sports cast certain athletes as bad actors (bullies, cheats, poor sports, sadists, and the like) because of the marked drawing power of such types. Movie stars have made reputations playing villains—Lon Chaney, Noah Berry, Eric von Stroheim, Boris Karloff, Ernest Borgnine,[1] to name a few. The villain may be institutionalized in festivals. In Mexico, for example, Judas is celebrated on *Sabado de Gloria* by effigies garlanded with exploding firecrackers. The villain is a functional character, and ritual is a social device for repeating his functions again and again. He often serves society, for example, as a scapegoat or safety valve for aggression, or as a perfected hate-symbol building morale for law enforcement and other actions. Oddly, he serves society by deviating from its mores.

Are there signs that the number of villains in America is increasing or decreasing? One would think that when people are prosperous and well-educated they would be less aggressive and need fewer villains. The unrealism of this assumption is evident in the mounting crime rates and other signs of disorganization. True, villains, particularly the old-fashioned, moustache-twisting variety are out of date; nineteenth century audiences gobbled up melodrama that by today's standards would not even get printed.[2] The Devil is disappearing too; though, in the opinion of some, such as C. S. Lewis and Denis de Rougemont, he has just gone underground. Witchery surely has little place in modern life. Also, juries seem less willing to pin down guilt and demand harsh punishments. Finally, education has helped to explode some of the cruder ethnic and national stereotypes. Yet, on the other side of the balance, erasing these reasonable considerations, is the dismaying amount of aggression that the twentieth century has generated—a moral cruelty that has not been surpassed in any era of which I am aware. *Moral* aggression is the self-righteous kind that names the other as villain.

This survey supports the view that vilification is not dying out, and may be increasing. Our language is rich with vilifying terms and we readily use them. Nor is this surprising when we consider: (1) the diversity of the role structure and the likelihood of playing the wrong role—suffering and causing frustrations; (2) conflicting group standards, absence of a sovereign morality accepted by all Americans (rather, we have situational rules of the game in which heroes of one game may be villains of

---

[1] His first fame came from his role as the sadistic Fatso Judson in *From Here to Eternity*. It came somewhat as a surprise that he later broke out of the villain type by his sympathetic role in the Academy Award-winning *Marty* in 1955.

[2] Mary Noel, *Villains Galore, the Heyday of the Popular Story Weekly* (New York: The Macmillan Co., 1954.)

another); (3) a high rate of deviation from all kinds of rules—legal, moral, customary (polls show that the average American has committed felonies at some time); and (4) the sheer amount of vicarious and actual aggression and scapegoating.

In sorting types for this survey, I found certain dimensions useful. One is degree of *visibility,* whether a type is out in the open or under-cover. Another is the *kind of threat* a type poses to a system, for example, breaking laws or mores, abusing status, parasitism, invasion from outside or disloyalty from within. Also the *social position* of the type (insider, outsider, stranger-within, subordinate, superordinate). Finally, *serious-ness* of attitude toward the type, ranging from tolerance of a scamp to loathing toward a monster. The main categories are: (1) types violating order or status (desperado, rebel, flouter, rogue, and trouble-maker); (2) types usurping power, authority, or status (oppressor, authoritarian, selfish grabber); (3) villainous strangers (intruder, suspicious isolate, monster); (4) sneaks and traitors representing disloyalty, both flagrant and secret; and (5) miscellaneous social undesirables.

Villains Symbolizing Threat to Order and Status

Let us begin with the *desperado,* who symbolizes lawless force and violence used to upset the social order. Were all like him there would be anarchy. Such roles are given the names:

> bad man, outlaw, bandit, two-gunman, tough guy, gangster, gunman, gun-moll, trigger man, mobster, thug, high-jacker, vandal, hoodlum, (some senses of) zoot-suiter,[3] underworlder, public enemy.

Here we see the strong man using his power to harm rather than serve people. Asked to name a desperado or outlaw, Americans frequently mention Billy the Kid,[4] Jesse James, John Dillinger, Al Capone, Pancho Villa, Robin Hood, Emiliano Zapata, and Baby-Face Nelson. It is possible to romanticize a desperado as a kind of heroic berserk, an independent spirit who cannot be restrained, but to most people he is more like a mad dog, epitomized by the career of Charles Starkweather.

In some situations, the hero must act much like a desperado, hence, the ambivalence toward such types. For example, the fighting fury of a

---

[3] Zoot-suiter, from an ambivalent symbol for Mexicans, turned into an image of hoodlumism and violence during the period of the zoot-suit riots. See Ralph Turner and Lewis Killian, *Collective Behavior* (Englewood Cliffs, N.J.: Prentice-Hall, Inc., 1957), p. 127.

[4] Of 79 people rating Billy the Kid, 37 said he was a hero, 42 villain, 6 fool, and 6 none of these. Some people rated him in two categories.

berserk in Icelandic saga—the gunman in the Old West—some of the glorified Indian-fighters—battle heroes who get decorated for running amok. The indifference of some Americans toward gang killings sometimes turned into admiration for the battle-scarred champions who emerged from gang wars as big shots. In other words, in an area where the public "doesn't care" or where violence is expected from good guys too, the ruthless killer has a good chance to emerge as a hero who goes the good guy "one better." At the other extreme, when lines are tightly drawn and society is staid, even a tavern roisterer can seem like an outlaw.

The *rebel* is more pointed in his attack on authority, since he deliberately aims to overthrow it. Names like radical, revolutionary, red, bolshevik, subversive, usurper, mutineer, and anarchist carry such connotations. The American attitude toward the rebel is mixed, as shown by the fact that he is somewhat more often rated heroic than villainous; also by the people mentioned as rebels: Earl Browder, Fidel Castro, James Dean, Marlon Brando, Jefferson Davis, Tito, Thoreau, Eugene Debs, Dennis the Menace, John Brown, James Hoffa, Senator Wayne Morse, Thomas Jefferson, John Brown, Robert E. Lee, Patrick Henry. This admiration for the rebel is understandable in the light of the independent spirit as a hero type, American revolutionary history, and the dislike of authoritarians (almost anyone who opposes them becomes popular). To find "rebel" meaning a sheer villain one might have to go back to the "Johnny Reb" of Civil War days. The American social structure is too varied to condemn rebels consistently. To see a rebel always as a villain requires unified authority and what might be called a Tory point of view.

Another type about whom Americans are ambivalent is the *flouter*. Less pointedly subversive than the rebel, not so violent as the outlaw, he seems to thumb his nose at the social order by scandalous misbehavior. Words like profligate, debauchee, wastrel, reprobate, harlot, Jezebel—even jay-walker, speeder, speed demon, and hotrodder (screeching his wheels outside a police station)—convey an image of one who not only misbehaves but seems to flaunt it before the world. The perfect flouter is a reprobate whose ideal end is shame, poverty, disease, delirium tremens, and death (Hogarth's "The Rake's Progress" depicts his downfall). A self-conscious flouter may be so expert in his exhibitions that he becomes the talk of the town; he may agree with Oscar Wilde that "there is only one thing worse than being talked about, and that is not being talked about." In this respect he is a perverse splendid performer. As moral flouters, Americans may mention: Tommy Manville, Mickey Jelke, Pope Alexander VI, Henry VIII, King Farouk, Ingrid Bergman, Sadie Thompson, Errol Flynn, Charlie Chaplin, Rabelais, Elizabeth Taylor, Madame Bovary, Mike

Hammer, Rafael Trujillo, H. L. Mencken, G. B. Shaw, Jean Paul Sartre, Alfred Kinsey. Like rebels, flouters can become heroes if the public sees them as champions of a cause—two cases in point would be Bertrand Russell championing "free love" and Mae West as an exponent of "sex."

Even more ambivalent is the *rogue,* a complex character who enjoys the distinction of being at the same time hero, villain, and fool—often given the names rascal, scalawag, scamp and hell-raiser. Such types have a mixed rating in which villain is first, fool next, and hero last. Figures like Tyl Eulenspiegel, Robin Hood, François Villon, and Pancho Villa have made the rogue famous. Criminal, amusing fellow, and champion of freedom combine to form the curiously mixed status often held by the rogue. The public is likely to be indulgent towards him (possibly with a "boys will be boys" attitude); a criminal defined as a rogue may be acquitted before he gets to court—if he ever gets to court. Asked to name a rogue, Americans are likely to say: Errol Flynn, Robin Hood, Falstaff, Huey Long, Dennis the Menace, Sir Francis Drake, François Villon, Sergeant Bilko, Maverick, Rubirosa, Long John Silver, Marlon Brando, Doug Fairbanks Senior, Mark Twain, Tom Sawyer, Casanova, Don Juan, Groucho Marx, Rafael Trujillo Jr.

Finally, we come to a type on whom Americans agree negatively— the *troublemaker.* He stirs up trouble and makes life difficult. He has names like:

> bad apple, smart guy, wise guy, upstart, sorehead, agitator, rowdy, rough-neck—also labor-baiter, red-baiter, rabblerouser, muckraker, warmonger, munitions-maker.

If he were not around things would be all right. His typical mischiefs are to arouse discontent and conflict, disturb status, "rock the boat," and make a nuisance of himself. Often his offense is not so much *what* he does as going about it in the wrong manner (another might do the same thing smoothly without being labeled as a troublemaker). Or, he might be a newcomer unwilling to accept procedure established by tradition or authority (I think of some who were fired for trying to reorganize a department they were not in charge of). He is the serpent who introduces sin into paradise. He is active, unlike the passive "hot potato" who through no fault of his own is embarrassing or troublesome to deal with. He is the opposite of the smoothie and good Joe, doing the very things they would avoid. As troublemakers Americans mention: Nikita Khrushchev, Senator McCarthy, Governor Faubus, Eddie Fisher,[5] Elizabeth Taylor,[5] John Kasper, Cassius, Iago, William Randolph Hearst, John

[5] Parties in a famous love triangle in 1959.

Brown, James Hoffa, Gerald L. K. Smith, Nasser, and Batista, among others.

These five general types symbolize a threat to social order. A society that strongly and uniformly disapproves them is pretty well settled and has established routines and status. But our pluralistic and inconsistent society does not present such a united front against those who threaten order and authority. Ambivalence toward such types might well be a sign of conflict, if not the breakdown of orders and authorities. It might possibly be a sign that people feel insecure and defensive, or alienated and offensive, toward the order of which they are part. The troublemaker seems to have a significance different from the other four villain types. I would say he stands for a judgment on the basis of *expediency* (let's not make trouble), whereas hating a flouter, rebel, outlaw, or rogue is an indignant reaction against the shock they give to absolute moral rules. If Americans unite against a troublemaker easily, is it not because they can dislike this kind of person without being committed to absolute rules or in agreement with others about them? One can hardly say "flouter," "rogue," "rebel," or "outlaw" without a strongly negative moral connotation, but one can say "troublemaker" and mean it.

Usurpers and Abusers

Several important kinds of villain grab more than their share, or use power improperly. Unlike outlaws and troublemakers, they may be firmly entrenched in positions of authority. They do not threaten order but may usurp or abuse status—take more than they are entitled to—grossly enough to arouse outrage.

Most obvious are the *oppressors* who misuse power over weaker rivals, subjects, and victims. This villain has names like bully, persecutor, tyrant, despot, Simon Legree, inquisitor, Nero, Bluebeard. He might be a wrestler twisting the ankle of a helpless opponent, a love despot or Svengali, a Biblical Pharaoh or Roman emperor, or Simon Legree in *Uncle Tom's Cabin* pursuing his victims across the ice with bloodhounds. Ideally he should be proud, powerful, cruel, unfair, and relentless. Harriet Beecher Stowe found her model for Legree in a brutal overseer on a New Orleans boat who, displaying a fist as hard as an oak burl, boasted he "got that from knocking down niggers." [6] A special type, to be distinguished from the ordinary tyrant or bully, is the *moral persecutor* (embodied in characters like Javert in *Les Miserables* or Cotton Mather in real life) whose

---

[6] Forrest Wilson, "The Book that Brewed a War," *Reader's Digest* (May 1941), p. 105.

relentlessness is a part of their moral zeal. This difference, however, may not be important to the victims.

Among the oppressors often named by Americans are Stalin, Khrushchev,[7] Hitler, Mussolini, Governor Faubus, Batista, Goliath, Henry VIII, Senator McCarthy, Simon Legree, Perón, Himmler, Hoffa, Franco, Goering, Capone, and Bluto (the big guy who fights Popeye). This kind of villain is the top dog at his worst. In America where there is much sympathy for the underdog, it is comparatively easy to become an oppressor by abuse of authority. General George Patton was called an oppressor, for example, for "slapping" a soldier in a hospital in Italy during World War II; a Marine Sergeant, Matthew McKeon, for ordering a night march into a swamp that resulted in the drowning of six men; television showed Senator McCarthy scowling and bullying witnesses. This is the way the oppressor's image is made.

Closely related to the oppressor is the *authoritarian*, popularly conceived[8] as a bigoted, narrow-minded person so sure he is right that he does not hesitate to impose his ideas on others, even at the expense of their freedom. Out of 130, 55 rated him as a villain. Unlike oppressors, who can be found anywhere, this type seems indigenous to liberal countries which recognize the *right* of an individual to his own opinion. Otherwise it does not make sense to dislike someone who imposes authority, curtails debate, or tells people what to do. After all, what are top dogs for?

Names like dictator, autocrat, fuehrer, fascist, fanatic, censor, bigot, reactionary, philistine, and disciplinarian convey an authoritarian image to many Americans; so, to some extent, does bureaucrat—meaning a petty despot. Asked to name an authoritarian, Americans mention: Hitler, Khrushchev, Fidel Castro, Franco, Stalin, the Pope, Peter the Great, Franklin D. Roosevelt, Tojo, McCarthy, Nasser, Bismarck, Governor Faubus, and the leaders of the Inquisition.

What kind of situation promotes the existence of the authoritarian as a type? It seems to me that you have to have (1) a liberal ideology (saying opinions are equal and providing rules of the game which a villain can violate), (2) a lack of general consensus and uncertainty about authority,

---

The American image of Khrushchev found by the Gallup Poll (Sept. 11, 1959) was not so much of a ruthless, cruel, domineering despot as a two-fisted, hard driving business man; bitter criticism of him as a gangster or butcher came from relatively few. Many expressed admiration for him, albeit grudgingly in terms like "a cutthroat with a sense of humor," "a shrewd businessman," "a pretty hard egg."

[8] Efforts by psychologists to determine the actual traits of the authoritarian personality are not directly relevant to our investigation of the social type as a form of consensus. See T. W. Adorno, E. Frankel-Brunswik, D. J. Levinson, and R. N. Sanford, *The Authoritarian Personality* (New York: Harper & Brothers, 1950).

and (3) a pluralistic structure in which some subgroups give members confidence to claim authority. In such a situation various people assert authority and come into conflict. Part of the population stands back from these conflicts (seeing them as merely matters of opinion) and defines as authoritarian anyone who speaks too confidently about them—perhaps using such terms as bigot, dogmatist, puritan, prejudiced, philistine. In other words, people who are insecure about authority use "authoritarian" as a tool against authority to prevent it from concentrating in the wrong hands—usurpers and pretenders—not against authority per se. In a society where authority was firmly concentrated, there would be no place for such a villain because the "right" people would have authority and there would be no pretenders to dismiss. At the opposite extreme, if there were no authority—complete equality of opinion—then there would be no authoritarians because no one would be sure enough of his opinions to assert them with sufficient firmness to be called a bigot.

Another type arrogates not authority but privilege; I shall call him the *selfish grabber* (road hog, fish hog, land-grabber, spoiler, plutocrat). This fellow ignores the rule of equality and takes too much for himself. The rate-buster (job-killer) is an industrial workers' version; he is so anxious to make more for himself that he raises the quota and makes it harder for others.[9] Asked to name a selfish grabber, Americans mention Dave Beck, James Hoffa, Rockefeller, Vanderbilt, Leland Stanford, Napoleon, Scrooge, Batista, Genghis Khan, Louis Wolfson, also certain movie stars who have taken spouses away from somebody. It may be noted, in passing, that the grabber is the opposite of the benefactor (hero type).

The *snob* is another claimant of undue privilege; he sets himself above others on the basis of presumed better social class. He may be a successful climber who has made his new status a little too obvious. As with the authoritarian, one cannot explain the snob away as a sign that people hate high status. People like high status but hate those who have no right to it or are too crude in their methods of claiming it. Ordinarily, it is the climbers, envious of high status, who use the term snob. In a fixed caste system, on the other hand, there is no place for a snob. When Americans name snobs we can see that some celebrities carry a debit of ill will: Grace Kelly, Elizabeth Taylor, the Duchess of Windsor, Queen Elizabeth, Hedda Hopper, Ingrid Bergman, Elsa Maxwell, Mike Romanoff, Amy Vanderbilt, Zsa Zsa Gabor, Alexander Hamilton, Prince Rainier, Katherine Hepburn, Barbara Hutton, Greta Garbo, Dorothy Kilgallen, Betty Davis, Emily Post. Even the modest Lindbergh was called a snob when he

[9] See Melville Dalton, "Worker Response and Social Background," *Journal of Political Economy*, LV (1947), 323-332.

claimed privacy, refused to give interviews, and accidentally splashed mud on people once when landing his plane.

Villainous Roles of the Stranger

We turn now to a dimension of villainy that centers on the one who doesn't belong, the stranger, the outsider who, when inside, is felt to violate the unity of the group, even threaten its security.

We may designate the *intruder* as an unwelcome stranger who pushes his way into a status system. A variety of American labels indicate uninvited entrance: invader, crasher, gate-crasher, claim jumper, snooper, meddler, climber, foreigner (and various ethnic labels that ask, in effect, "Why are they here? Why don't they go back where they came from?"). Even mother-in-law connotes a meddler who spoils marriages. Americans may show animosity toward intruders because of the way they have crashed in or what they may do after they are in.

Similar are *suspicious isolates,* whose strangeness and detached or marginal position mark them as not belonging and arouse suspicion of what they may be up to. Terms such as queer, creep, prowler, half-breed, some ethnic labels, even stranger, convey such a notion. Anti-semitic agitators claim that the Jew is "by nature unassimilable," that he has an "indefinable foreignness" even when his race is not given away by names like Blum and Finklestine.[10] Suspicious isolates are mistrusted not because of how they crashed in or where they came from, but rather because they are too queer to fit in and be trusted. They remain vulnerable to scapegoating as long as they remain isolated and visible,[11] at least until they define their role clearly.

A third class of strangers are so utterly beyond the pale that they seem alien not only to the group but to the human species. I refer to *monsters,* indicated by names like:

pervert, degenerate, moron, psychopath, sadist, fiend, demon, devil, witch, vampire, ghoul, ogre, Jack-the-Ripper, Bluebeard, Nero, hell-cat, dope fiend, hophead, firebug, bloodsucker.

The attitude toward monsters is not just hatred and fear, but horror. A military enemy is calculable—even a Judas or Creon acts from certain low but familiar motives; but there is a point where the doing of evil passes

---

[10] Leo Lowenthal and Norbert Guterman, *Prophets of Deceit* (New York: Harper & Brothers, 1949), pp. 73-78.

[11] See Gordon Allport's comments on visibility as a factor in scapegoating. *ABC's of Scapegoating* (New York: Anti-Defamation League of B'nai B'rith, 1948).

comprehension and gives a creepy feeling associated with werewolves and vampires. At this point people call into service the concept of the monster. Though the monster belongs to folklore, many real people have contributed to the concept (the Marquis de Sade, Winnie Ruth Judd, William Heirens, Loeb and Leopold, and Ilse Koch, the "witch of Buchenwald," who made lampshades out of men's skins), also fiction like *Dracula, The Bat, The Phantom of the Opera,* and *Frankenstein.* Asked to name a monster, Americans mention by far most often Mary Shelley's creature, Frankenstein, and after that, Himmler, Beria, Stalin, Tojo, Goebbels, Genghis Khan, Robespierre, General Sherman, Bela Lugosi (*Dracula*), Boris Karloff, Lon Chaney, Claude Rains (*Dr. Jekyll and Mr. Hyde*), and "King Kong."

We may suppose that the kind of society which favors the stranger as villain would be the same that favors conformer-heroes rather than independent spirits—namely, a closed society[12] with high unity, though subject to invasion by outsiders. Belief in superstitions such as witchcraft would, of course, help in the defining of certain kinds of villains. On the other hand, if there were too many strangers and much mobility, the closed system would probably break down in favor of a pluralistic society where different people were accepted. As mobility increased, the society would approach a point at which it would be impossible to define the stranger as villain—everybody would be strange and the feeling of unity would be too weak for people to defend. What I am suggesting is that the definition of the stranger as villain should thrive in societies where group unity is high and *at the same time* where there is invasion and some kind of crisis to social structure.[13]

Traitors and Sneaks

Two kinds of villainy often go together: cowardly underhandedness and disloyalty. All of the following, except the first, have to be detected or "flushed out." They sap the strength of the social organization by activities ranging from parasitism to treason.

In a conflict where group lines are sharply drawn the *renegade,* publicly, even flagrantly, goes over to the other side. Such an action is not only a loss of strength to the society but a kind of treason, the worse because it makes for bad publicity. Names like turncoat, Benedict Arnold, scab,

---

[12] See Karl Popper, *The Open Society and Its Enemies* (London: Routledge and Kegan Paul, Ltd., 1952).

[13] Compare E. S. Bogardus' conception of the "Race Relations Cycle," *American Journal of Sociology,* 1930, 35:612-617.

company man, nigger lover (and other kinds of lover) may be applied to such a role.[14] When Americans are asked to name a renegade, Arnold is by all odds the winner (he not only went over to the other side, but flagrantly gloated over it and was never punished); after that come others such as Paul Robeson, Quisling, Geronimo, Rudolph Hess, Sir Henry Morgan, the Rosenbergs, Earl Browder, Mata Hari, Judas, Tokyo Rose. Certain Americans who conspicuously showed a liking for another country (Charles Chaplin, Robeson, Ezra Pound) acquired the flavor of renegades; even Lindbergh fell under the "shadow of treason" when he accepted a medal from the German Air Force in 1938. When a celebrity goes to the other side it is particularly shocking because one is afraid that others may follow his example. The conversions to Communism of American prisoners-of-war in Korea also produced a shock. On the other hand, turncoats from the other side (confessing communists, ex-Nazis) reverse some of the symbolism of the role; they are welcomed as a contribution to solidarity, encouraged to publish their memoirs; some even get to be celebrities.

Villainy drops underground with *hidden traitors* who sell out or bore from within while in a position of trust. Knowledge of what they are up to often comes too late. Dante gave the lowest place in Inferno to traitors. Two images compete for vividness in this category: Arnold (a secret traitor before he was an open renegade) and Judas. Other names associated with them are Aaron Burr, Quislings, MacBeth ("false heart must hide what the false heart doth know"), Alger Hiss, Brutus, the Rosenbergs, Claus Fuchs, Mata Hari and other spies, Delilah, Uriah Heep, double-crosser, informer,[15] tattler, party-liner, communist,[16] Reds (regarded as termites in the American social structure; a similar role was imputed to Jews in Nazi Germany). The fear of hidden traitors easily becomes hysterical, almost paranoid, especially in crisis, perhaps because they teach the alarming lesson that even the weakest person, if unknown, can throw a monkey wrench in the works.[17]

Deceivers can be defined as con-men who put something over on people

---

[14] See also Goffman's discussion of renegades from colleagueship, *op. cit.*, p. 164.

[15] A film classic, *The Informer,* starring Victor McLaglen, shows this role in clear sociological outline.

[16] A Gallup Poll of May 23, 1948, showed that most Americans (65%) thought American members of the Communist Party were loyal to Russia.

[17] The history of treason in America and its disastrous political effects have been detailed in studies such as: Nathaniel Weyl, *Treason, the Story of Disloyalty and Betrayal in American History* (Washington, D.C.: Public Affairs Press, 1955); and Rebecca West, *The Meaning of Treason* (New York: The Viking Press, Inc., 1947); and Morton Grodzins, *The Loyal and the Disloyal, Social Boundaries of Patriotism and Treason* (Chicago: University of Chicago Press, 1946).

from the outside rather than insiders who betray a position of trust.
Americans designate them by names like:

> hypocrite, phoney, liar, fraud, fast talker,* con-man, gyp, cheat, slicker, wolf,
> fox,* crook, quack, charlatan, Ananias, huckster, faker, sharpie,* tout, heart-
> breaker,* two-faced, two-timer.

A deceiver is not as bad as a traitor: he may sell goods by fraud, break
promises—even hearts—bamboozle people, masquerade under false pre-
tenses, but he does not strike as deep a note of alarm, or menace internal
security as much as the traitor. Compare the attitudes toward a swindler
and a traitor. The deceiver, being basically a stranger, is not under the
same obligation as a kinsman, a close friend, or a soldier under oath of
duty, whom one has a *right* to trust; indeed, in a swindle, there may be a
feeling that the victims "had it coming" to them (why did they trust him
in the first place?). A deceiver invites trust by misleading overtures—his
fault is a lie, but treason is too strong a word; one has no right to expect
deep loyalty from him. He is a villain who belongs in the world of *Gesellschaft*[18]—you have to watch out for him all the time; it is no surprise to
be gypped; almost anything can be faked, a smile, a credit card; the
deceiver's philosophy is *caveat emptor*. Consistent with this is the fact
that some deceiver types (marked above with an asterisk) show ambivalence—some are even admired[19]—whereas no traitor types get any sympathy. The deceiver has been used as a damaging tag for ethnic groups
such as Orientals and Jews.[20] People named as deceivers or frauds vary
greatly in valuation: "Prince" Mike Romanoff, Ivar Krueger, Samuel
Insull, Dave Beck, Sherman Adams, Sergeant Bilko, Batista, Huey Long,
Iago, Judas, G. L. K. Smith, Prophet Jones, Father Divine, Billy Graham,
Khrushchev, Mussolini, Mata Hari, Satan.

A *sneak attacker* is another kind of surreptitious villain who strikes in
a cowardly fashion using secrecy or surprise. Any burglar or assassin pos-
sesses all the necessary qualities for the role. Conspicuous examples have
been provided by the "black hand" terrorists, hooded lynchers, "rat
packs," "mad bombers," and "phantom snipers" publicized in newspapers

[18] A sociological term first employed by Ferdinand Tonnies to describe the kind
of society where relationships are impersonal and people try to manipulate each other;
opposed to *Gemeinschaft* in which association is intimate and for its own sake.

[19] It may be added that certain kinds of lying are condoned, even encouraged, by
our society—for example, deceiving the enemy, deceiving people "for their own good,"
"blowing up" a product one wishes to sell, or "getting the best of" other deceivers.

[20] Angus Cambel, "Factors Associated with Attitudes Toward Jews," in G. E. Swanson,
T. E. Newcomb, and E. L. Hartley (eds.) *Readings in Social Psychology* (Henry Holt,
1952, 2nd ed.) p. 604; Daniel Katz and K. W. Braly, "Verbal Stereotypes and Racial
Prejudice," *ibid.*, p. 70; and Lowenthal and Guterman, *op. cit.*, pp. 24, 84-85.

—though no image in America overshadows that of John Wilkes Booth. Also vivid is the attack on Pearl Harbor engineered by Tojo. Names such as:

> snake-in-the-grass, sneak, backbiter, mudslinger, gossip, cat (catty), eavesdropper, black-hander, poison penman, weasel, thief, assassin, spy, and (a certain sense of) sharpshooter,[21] are used for people who play such parts.

In legend the villain stabs the hero in the back, shoots him in the heel, or catches him while asleep—"a good man is never in danger but when he is in danger from a coward," says Sir Lancelot.

Chiselers and *parasites* sap social organization by exploiting an advantage or by going along for a free (often a first-class) ride. How large their number may be is suggested by Wyatt Marrs, *The Man on Your Back.*[22] It might include whole areas of business, professions, politics (whitecollar crime). Almost anywhere one can use words like:

> chiseler, freeloader, parasite, sponger, leech, golddigger, alimony artist, ambulance-chaser, racketeer, shyster, loan shark, black-marketer,[23] bootlegger, grafter, five-percenter, ward-healer, (dirty) politician, lobbyist, spoilsman, fat cat, profiteer, munitions-maker, tax-dodger, expense account aristocrat, boondoggler, inside-dopester, carpetbagger (obsolete), moocher, panhandler, scrounge, pimp, kept woman, extortionist, bloodsucker.

Chiselers and parasites pursue their objectives by sly, petty, camouflaged means, for they are often too weak to get what they want openly. They are status-exploiters who abuse a position by using it as a front for covert activities made easy simply by the nature of the position rather than by any special privileges of the position. Society would not allow such exploitation if done openly (for example, a political official giving out tips, expanding a legitimate project into a boondoggle, or free-loading while guest at a party). It is not very clear what Americans want to do with all these chiselers; the attitude toward them varies greatly in spite of formal disapproval by the majority.[24] Sometimes, during a speculation boom or a rush for war contracts, we look almost like a nation of freeloaders.

While parasitism and chiseling are not very visible, some have overdone it enough to get newspaper publicity. Often mentioned in such a

[21] The often observed hatred of snipers—even by their own armies—is probably due to the sneaky manner of attack; an example is given by Bruce Catton, *A Stillness at Appommattox* (Doubleday & Company, Inc., 1953), p. 189.

[22] Subtitle: A Preface to the Art of Living Without Producing in Modern Society (Norman, Okla.: University of Oklahoma Press, 1959).

[23] See Marshall B. Clinard, *The Black Market* (New York: Rinehart & Company, Inc., 1952).

[24] Erwin Smigel "Public Attitudes toward 'Chiseling' with Reference to Unemployment Compensation," *American Sociological Review*, 1953, 18:59-67.

category are: James Hoffa, Mickey Cohen, Frank Costello, Mike Stom-panato (slain lover of Lana Turner), J. P. Morgan (typifying the profiteer), Boss Tweed, Barbara Hutton (an heiress epitomizing idle wealth to many Americans), Father Divine (thought of as a cult racketeer, whose followers often turn their property over to him); certain literary figures, such as Shylock, Tartuffe (religious hypocrite), and Wimpy (moocher of "Pop-eye" cartoons).

Like parasites, *shirkers* fail to do their share, but in a specific role rather than the whole life pattern. Evasion of an important obligation is in-dicated by names like:

> slacker, quitter, draft-dodger, deserter, coward, chicken, yellowbelly, hit-and-run driver, fly-by-night, ingrate, welcher, Indian giver, loafer, corner loafer, deadbeat.

In some the offense is as serious as treason, but in all cases it is better described as nonperformance of duty because of a personal fault (laziness, selfishness, cowardice, dishonesty, negligence, or simply lack of motivation, such as low morale). Shirkers are more conspicuous than parasites, be-cause their role failure arouses outrage, whereas the tapeworm in the body politic might be there for years without being felt. Examples of the shirker mentioned by Americans include: Arkansas' Governor Faubus (failure to integrate the schools), President Harding (Teapot Dome scandals), King Edward VI, Pontius Pilate, Eddie Fisher (desertion of Debbie Reynolds—a scandal that much occupied the public in 1959), and people who abscond with funds or evade military service.

Last are *corrupters* who exert a poisonous or demoralizing influence. "Bad apples" spread discontent in a work organization, bribers weaken men in public office, agitators spread seditious doctrines, teachers are required to sign loyalty oaths to avoid suspicion of propagandizing. Socrates was convicted of corrupting the young. The astonishing vilifica-tion of Oscar Wilde in England seems in part due to such a conception of him. A corrupter may be thought of as a serpent in the Garden of Eden, a kind of spider entangling people, an octopus,[25] a festering infection,[26] a sorcerer casting a spell. Famous corrupters in literature are Fagin in *Oliver Twist*, Lady MacBeth, Iago, Circe, and the evil governess in Henry James' *The Turn of the Screw*.[27] Words conveying such an idea include:

---

[25] During Rasputin's sway as a power-behind-the-throne in Russia, cartoons in America depicted him as an octopus holding the entire Russian Empire in his tentacles, or as a puppeteer with the Czar and Czarina on his knee.

[26] Exemplified by the role of the Comintern; Russia is conceived by many Americans as a vast citadel of corruption, spreading its poison throughout the world.

[27] See the "golden fly" theme, David Malcomson, *op. cit.* pp. 201-232.

bad apple, seducer, debauchee, degenerate, fast crowd, fast woman, vamp, siren, Fagin, Rasputin, pusher (of drugs), reefer man, agitator, propagandist, pink.

"Guilt by association" is based on the presumed effect of long association with corrupters ("birds of a feather"). Persons named as corrupters include: Dave Beck, Al Capone, Iago, Big Bill Thompson, G. L. K. Smith, James Hoffa, Joseph Goebbels, Fagin, Frank Costello, Don Juan, Loeb and Leopold, Satan, Hitler, Mussolini, Boss Tweed, Mickey Cohen, Perón, Mickey Spillane, Nero, Goldfine, Elizabeth Taylor, Rasputin.

The types just reviewed—renegade, traitor, deceiver, sneak attacker, chiseler, parasite, shirker, corrupter—invert four main traits of the hero: loyal service, courage, fairness, and honesty. Were such villains rare, the world would approximate perfect morale: everyone doing his part, no shirkers or parasites, solidarity unbroken. On the other hand, the presence of many chiselers and parasites and the lurking approval for deceivers indicate weakness in society: deviation from norms (honesty, loyalty, courage, fairness), exploitation, alienation, anomie, and possibly failure of the social bond.

Social Undesirables

Last in this survey are villains whose role is not always specified by their labels, though it is plain enough that society wants to be rid of them.

Pariahs are so disreputable that it is damaging to associate with them and they are viewed with antagonism. Lacking responsible positions, often with suspicious leisure and mobility, they are suspected of various villainous roles; yet the general fault is low status, *regardless of acts* committed; they are called:

no-good, blacksheep, bad penny, bum, tramp, vagrant, skidder,[28] skid row, floater, derelict, low-lifer, bar-fly, boozer, floozy, loafer, corner loafer, poor white, underworlder, convict, gypsy, scum, outcast.

From such names together you get the picture of a hierarchy which penalizes status failures—persons unable to maintain responsible positions and good reputations. As debits, there are the damage from associating with them, injury to dependents, cost of supporting them, question of what they are up to, and sheer embarrassment from having them around. Thus, there is a pressure to get rid of them regardless of any specific acts

---

[28] A study of skidders, however, shows that they do not conceive of themselves as disreputable. H. L. Wilensky and Hugh Edwards, "The Skidder: Ideological Adjustments of Downward Mobile Workers," *American Sociological Review*, 24 (April 1959), 215-231.

for which they may be accountable. The concept of the "no-good" is a considerable obstacle to social work.

Remaining is a collection of *ambiguous vilifying epithets* consigning someone, without nice discrimination, to the entire category of villain: rat, louse, skunk, dog, s.o.b., bastard, rotter, heel, sidewinder, bad nigger, damyankee, enemy. They tell little about the villain's role but serve as a kind of bomb to explode him from the social order.

Conclusions

These are the faces of the bad guy repeatedly photographed by American popular language. The celebrities mentioned are not the main focus, indeed their connection is often accidental—an unfortunate episode that linked them with a villain type in the popular mind. The main thing is generalized forms of deviant behavior that have structural significance in American society.

The survey suggests that, far from declining, the villain is actively with us, his deeds are many and his kinsmen legion, as shown by a rich and growing vocabulary. The main kinds are: *enemies of law and order* (desperadoes, rebels, flouters, rogues, troublemakers), *status abusers and arrogators* (oppressors, authoritarians, selfish grabbers, snobs), *villainous strangers* (intruders, suspicious isolates, monsters), *disloyal and underhanded* types (renegades, traitors, deceivers, sneak-attackers, chiselers, shirkers, corrupters), and miscellaneous *social undesirables*.

What is one to judge from these bad actors? It seems to me that they make certain structural features of American life more visible, for example, the shabby side of status climbing (snobs, crashers, selfish grabbers, who flout rules of discreet climbing and the ideology of equalitarianism). Types like oppressor and authoritarian do not prevent oligarchy but check improper claimants from asserting themselves too freely. Other types reflect in-group thinking in a society predominantly pluralistic and secondary (mistrust of squares, creeps, and isolates and corresponding approval of conformers and good Joes; outrage at flouters, traitors, subversives). A type like the troublemaker suggests a wish to keep things as they are which is based not so much on mores as prudence (people who make too much fuss about anything—even morals—are bad for organization). Such a villain works for a kind of expedient conformity. Yet I do *not* see overwhelming conformity reflected by the great number of American villain types: besides outlaws, rebels, and flouters, we have many chiselers and parasites—chronic abusers and evaders—built right into the structure as institutionalized deviations. Our society's structure and role-playing are so elaborate that there can be deviation by and within conformity, as well as outside it. Rather than a triumph for conformity, the array of villain types, to me, portends a weakening of control—possibly anomie— at many points.

On this question, of whether many villain types indicate a victory for conformity, I would offer the hypothesis that: the more names for villainy and the weaker the disapproval expressed, the greater the amount of deviation. Conversely, the fewer names for villainy and the stronger the disapproval, the rarer is deviation. The reasoning here is that frequency of actual behavior increases the need for naming it in various situations. At the same time, people become sophisticated and cannot be shocked as they would be if it were rarer. While I do not have information to test this hypothesis, it seems to me that the large number of American villains and the ambivalence toward some argue more that villains are loose than that control is strong. The barn is being locked too late, as it were.

Another peculiarity of villain types is that many support the same value themes as heroes. There is a kind of teamwork between heroes and villains (this is not saying that all themes and types are consistent). It is reasonable that the "act" of hero versus villain is a kind of conspiracy to make everything come out all right in support of a value. With this thought, I have tried to match up some heroes with corresponding themes and with villains as supporting characters for the same dramas. That is, if Americans favor hero X to realize a cultural theme, then they will penalize villain Y who violates this theme and try to make the show come out so he doesn't win.

Hero types	Corresponding theme	Corresponding villains
good Joes, charmers	belongingness and acceptability	strangers, isolates, monsters, troublemakers, deceivers (false friends)
conformers (moralists, smoothies)	conformity	outlaws, rebels flouters, corrupters, troublemakers
group servants (benefactors, defenders, martyrs)	cooperation and solidarity	shirkers, loafers, quitters, parasites, chiselers, traitors, cowards, renegades
winners (strong men, top dogs, brains, smart operators, great lovers)	getting what you want and beating others (fairly)	selfish grabbers, cheaters, bullies, cowards, authoritarians, oppressors, criminal masterminds, conmen, wolves.

Such types seem complementary, working hand-in-hand to support the same ideals. At the same time it is plain that some American heroes and villains are at war in a way different from the ritual drama. In some cases the resemblance is confusing; for example, a smart operator looks so much like a con-man that it is hard to tell who is which, let alone who is defeating the other. It may weaken a value to have contradictory (hero, villain, fool) types apply to the same kind of behavior; for example, a creative artist as both an independent spirit and a suspicious isolate or pariah. Such resemblances and ambivalences probably show conflict in the social structure; it may be dysfunctional to have heroes and villains who are not on the same "team" (cast), who divide audiences of the same dramas—that is, break down consensus.

It is reasonable to suppose that the normal function of villain and hero types is to drive the bad guys into a corner and to encourage the good guys to come out. This survey shows that the bad guys are definitely not in a corner. We have a picture of what types of bad guys there are and what they seem to be doing; further, this survey indicates that detailed studies are needed of many types of villains to elucidate their functions and the structures reflected by those functions—underworld organization, *sub rosa* deviations under cover of conformity, and so on.

CHAPTER 3

FOOLS

Ridicule and wit make plain to us the folly, humbug, and incompetence of the social structure. For this kind of truth (consensus) the fool is institutionalized.

Take that interesting American ceremony known as the Gridiron Club Dinner, given annually by newspapermen in Washington, D.C. The guests of honor are usually the President of the United States and several hundred VIPs who come with mingled glee and dread, for the main informal function of this banquet is to lampoon politicians. The *pièce de résistance,* is a carefully prepared program of songs and skits, ranging from harmless witticisms to heavy satire which could conceivably endanger a career. Despite this rather forbidding bill of fare, guests are eager to come. First, there is an "off the record" rule. Secondly the social distinction is so great that people will wangle invitations even when they know they may be mocked. Also there is the idea that making a fool out of big shots is good for American democracy. A public man must show he can "take it," be a good sport and not a sorehead, and give reassurance that he is not above criticism. Consequently, since the Club was founded in 1885, every president except Grover Cleveland has attended its dinners.

Clowns play a similarly important part in the life of the Hopi Indians. Normally, the Hopis are sober and decorous and deem immoderate laughter a disgrace; but during the sacred Kachina ceremonies, clowns represent everything that a Pueblo Indian is not supposed to be—filthy, idiotic, deformed, bad mannered, obscene, gluttonous, silly, talkative, uproarious, malicious, violent, cruel. They jibe at tribe-members with great freedom—bringing out thiefs, sluggards, and lovers. Far from being a nuisance, they have a very important role—to act out the suppressed side of the Pueblo personality; more important perhaps, they function as a social conscience which sees into every fault.

Anthropologists have found that institutionalized clowning is well developed in all the major cultures. Every kind of society seems to find fool types useful in: sublimation of aggression, relief from routine and discipline, control by ridicule (less severe and disruptive than vilification), affirming standards of propriety (paradoxically by flouting followed by comic punishment), and unification through what Henri Bergson and Kenneth Burke have called the communion of laughter.

Particular types of folly indicate something about the prevailing character and structure of a group. It is possible to sort American fools into five major categories:

1) incompetents (clumsy, rash, simple, weak) who illustrate and penalize ludicrous role failures;
2) types which discount people who claim more than they have, thus correcting certain status-abuses and pretensions;
3) non-conforming types which ridicule deviants and outsiders;
4) overconformers who suffer comic rebuke because they have been too enthusiastic in complying with group standards; and
5) certain types (especially comic butt, clever fool) having conspicuous functions as outlets for aggressive tension.

These categories are not exhaustive, nor are they strictly exclusive, but they do conveniently group many American types.

Ludicrous Role Failures

By giving a person a fork that bends or a glass with a hole in it, a practical joker can make almost anyone seem incompetent. Ludicrous role failures are usually fiascoes, such as the battleship Missouri running aground in her home waters in Chesapeake Bay in broad daylight. In this particular case, the role failure is that of the *clumsy fool*, who proves himself disgracefully inept in carrying out roles required of the average member or status incumbent. The clumsy fool is given names like:

> lummox, boor, dub, duffer, dud, stumblebum, Ichabod, tanglefoot, butterfingers, landlubber, fuddyduddy, wallflower, wet blanket, spoilsport, ham, sloppy Jane, litterbug, crumb, lout.

Certain situations can force even a capable person into this part, for example, the *faux pas* of the *nouveau riche* in high society. Where a polite lie is the only graceful thing, honesty makes Moliere's "misanthrope" a boor. Those whose unfamiliarity with situations causes them to act clumsily might be called *naïve newcomers,* this term includes novices, greenhorns, and rustic[1] fools (yokel, rube, hick, peasant, hayseed, clodhopper, apple knocker, hillbilly). High standards of performance tend to make clumsy fools: professionals are more vulnerable than amateurs in the same game; statesmen are continually being criticized for bungling that would be ignored in an ordinary man. Clowns achieve by miraculous timing and hidden grace the ability to do things in the most awkward possible manner (oddly, too much grace could make him a fool to his fellow professionals).

Asked to name a clumsy fool, Americans think of Jerry Lewis, Jackie Gleason, Red Skelton, Stan Laurel and Oliver Hardy, Charlie Chaplin, Buster Keaton, Lou Costello; Humpty Dumpty, Gargantua, Don Quixote, Ichabod Crane, the near-sighted Mr. Magoo, Goofy (Disney), Joe Palooka; Warren G. Harding, and Benito Mussolini.

Dumas was probably thinking of the *rash fool* when he wrote: "les fous et les heroes . . . deux classes d'imbeciles qui ont beaucoup de choses en commun." Certain kinds of role-failures come from courage, overenthusiasm or bad judgment carrying a person to a reckless extreme, for example, the charge of the Light Brigade. Types prone to this sort of thing include:

> daredevil, flagpole sitter, stunt artist, barnstormer, speed demon, joy rider, dragracer, hotrodder, jay-walker, highroller, plunger, wastrel, ne'er-do-well, prodigal, coquette, flirt (reckless with hearts).

Though daredeviltry is an established tradition in America,[2] it is not,

---

[1] A type probably destined to disappear from America as urbanization proceeds.

[2] Sam Patch was a quasi-legendary figure who is said to have popularized taking break-neck risks; he was followed by Steve Brody, with his famous leap off the Brooklyn Bridge, Harry Houdini with his underwater escapes, and a whole cavalcade of balloonists, aviators, channel-swimmers, delayed parachute jumpers, racing motorcyclists, human flies, acrobats, jalopy-racers, auto-crashers, people going over Niagara in a barrel, and so on.

on the whole, viewed as heroic; most people don't see any sense in sitting on a flagpole[3] or going over Niagara in a barrel, even if it does bring notoriety and money. Of course they would approve reckless extremes in a soldier or fireman. Certain historical episodes stand out: Custer's last stand, Woodrow Wilson's mission to Versailles, Henry Ford's "peace ship." During the Great Depression the Chicago Civic Opera House was referred to as "Insull's Folly." Individuals mentioned as rash fools include: Dr. Kinsey, King Farouk, Rafael Trujillo Jr., Harry Truman, Senator McCarthy, Governor Faubus; in literature Don Quixote, Romeo, Othello, Cyrano de Bergerac, Clyde Griffiths, King Lear, Madame Bovary.

The *simpleton,* who makes absurd mistakes and is easily taken advantage of, may be the prototype of fools. Folklore is full of people who, as the saying goes, don't know enough to get in out of the rain. American slang gives them names like:

> goof, sap, nitwit, dumbbell, dumb Dora, Jackass, boob, moron, mutt, ignoramous, simp, blockhead, bonehead, knucklehead, knothead, squarehead, chowderhead, pinhead, Li'l Abner (strong but dumb), chatterbox, and flapper (lightheaded females).

Americans mention: Stan Laurel and Oliver Hardy, Mr. Peepers, Simple Simon, Mortimer Snerd, Dopey (a Disney dwarf), Red Skelton, Andy of "Amos and Andy," Li'l Abner, Daisy Mae, Marilyn Monroe, Gracie Allen, Bottom, Sancho Panza, Harpo Marx, Jerry Lewis, and Lennie (Steinbeck's *Of Mice and Men*), among others.

The *dupe* (often played by simpletons) is known in America as the chump, fall guy, easy mark, pushover, sucker, cuckold, sugar daddy. He is easily taken advantage of (not just by smart operators). Because his gullibility is a fault, he gets little sympathy; in the eyes of the world he has no one to blame but himself. Some public roles can make people look gullible even when they are not so, for example, Chamberlain's pact with Hitler at Munich, Wilson's negotiations with the French and British, Henry Wallace's candidacy for the Presidency in 1948 in which he was reputedly used by Reds.

Weak fools are indicated by names like:

> sissy, mollycoddle, pantywaist, dude, Fauntleroy, creampuff, mama's boy, nambypamby, clinging vine, softy, weakling, weak sister, sob sister, bleeding heart, sentimentalist, crybaby, calamity howler, jellyfish, backslider, lush, tosspot, yes-man, straddler, pussy footer, Milquetoast, pacifist, chicken, crooner (as a sissified singer of love songs).

[3] An illustration of the public attitude toward daredevils is given by "Shipwreck" Van Nolen, a flagpole sitter, who, during his seventy days aloft was continually asked by passers-by if he was "nuts"; some even threw bottles at him. After such experiences he began to doubt his own sanity: "I got to thinkin'—How do I know I'm not (insane)? Maybe I'm just a smart paranoid."

What is common to these types is the implication that they can't "take it"—are soft, break down, give in too easily—cannot carry out a role requiring a certain amount of toughness. Certain psychological traits lead to a weak fool's role (neuroticism, effeminacy, over dependency, soft-heartedness, etc.). One classic picture has been given in H. T. Webster's cartoon character Caspar Milquetoast. James Thurber's males are woman-dominated and timid—as E. B. White says, "frustrated, fugitive beings" who "seem to be trying to get out of something (a room, a situation, a state of mind), at other times they are merely perplexed and too weak or humble to move." [4] An important early literary source of the weak fool image was a magazine serial about Little Lord Fauntleroy, written in 1885 by Frances Hodgson Burnett. The serial became fashionable among American women and caused the attempted sissification of a generation of middle-class males. The American man's fear of being sissified (pointed out as a national character trait by Geoffrey Gorer in *The American People*) has not lessened with new sources of insecurity such as the decline of the double standard. Certain celebrities have epitomized the sissy to the public: Rudolph Valentino was sneered at as a "powder-puff hero"; for a time some suspected Frank Sinatra of being a sissy, until his fistic prowess dispelled this notion; Liberace, a wavy-haired television pianist, accepted the role of public sissy with his remark that the mean things people said about him made him "cry all the way to the bank." Asked to name a weakling or sissy, Americans mention Liberace, Milquetoast, Fauntleroy, Walter Mitty, Wally Cox, Mr. Peepers, Lord Byron, Oscar Wilde, Quisling (weakness leading to treason), President Harding (as a yes-man), rock-and-roll singer Elvis Presley.

Sometimes an approved role can look like a weak fool—a good-hearted person who "turns the other cheek"—a liberal who gives ground or permits an enemy of liberty to speak freely—a humanitarian who is accused of wanting to "coddle" criminals—a good Joe who wants to get along with everyone and begins to look like a yes-man. These observations make one wonder if there are not pressures within the American ethical code (reflected by appropriate hero types) that urge people to play a role which non-Americans see as the weak fool.

A *coward* is not simply a fool, though plainly akin to the weaklings just discussed. The implications of his role are too serious to make it consistently comical. He is rated equally as villain or fool. As a villain, he is a shirker—almost a traitor. True, in comedy the buffoon often runs from duels and quakes at the slightest danger, but in real life the same

4 James Thurber and E. B. White, *Is Sex Necessary?* (New York: Harper & Brothers, 1929), p. 196.

role might not seem at all funny. A public figure's prestige is damaged by cowardice, for example, Mussolini's running away.

Clumsy, rash, simple, gullible, weak, and cowardly types reflect the demand of the group for competence in its members. They are protected from more severe blame only because their failure is not of serious consequence to the group and is caused by inadequacy rather than malice. No doubt varying conditions affect what kinds of incompetence are recognized and how they are regarded. If life were a kind of *Nibelungenlied*, weaknesses ordinarily not penalized in our society would be regarded as cowardice and there would be less place for a rash *fool*. In very sharp competition, the number of suckers increases and more foxes shift from villains to smart operators, because there is a premium on shrewdness and a contempt for gullibility. If manners are very nice and social protocol rigid, there are more clumsy fools—there is a sharper discrimination in the ways a person can fail. Consistency of hero types also affects the number of fool-types. Where, say, the good Joe and the tough guy are both admired, the people trying to live up to the good Joe may look like softies to the devotees of the tough guy; again, followers of the smart operator ideal would regard as suckers those who followed the good Samaritan ideal. Success in achieving one heroic ideal can look like role failure in another perspective (Albert Schweitzer is a case in point).

"Discounting" Types

Role inadequacy is not always obvious. Discounting types function to detect subtler forms of incompetence and to correct judgments of status— to take down people who claim too much. They are used as a hidden price-tag to inform people that this person may be dealt with at less than face-value. Discounting is not outright rejection but, as Kenneth Burke has put it, "making allowance for the fact that things are not as they seem" and going along on this basis; "by proper discounting everything becomes usable." [5]

Discounting is important in a society where there is much alienation and false front.[6] You have to come to terms; people are making claims that can't be openly challenged (nor proven)—there is neither time nor

[5] Kenneth Burke, *Attitudes Toward History*, Vol. II (New York: The New Republic, 1937), pp. 112-113.

[6] Beyond Ferdinand Tonnies' basic analysis of the inherent hypocrisy of *Gesellschaft*, see Erving Goffman's interesting account of the manipulation of front in modern institutional settings, *op. cit.;* also the humorous side of such strategies in books like Stephen Potter's *Gamesmanship* and Shepherd Mead's *How to Succeed without Really Trying.*

justification for calling everybody's bluff—life must go on. Discounting puts it all on a safer basis; nobody is offended—but nobody gets full credit either. Discounting is also important in a mobile society. The more people move, the more they get out of place and need to be put into their place (climbers may claim too much, top dogs lose competence or be outshone). Such facts are stated by discounting fool types, which help people to deal informally with the realities of a changing, pretending, and pretentious society.

As an example of how discounting fool types work for informal status adjustment, take the boss who has come to be regarded as an old "fuddy-duddy" by employees (he is joked about, his orders are modified, advantage is taken of his weaknesses and prejudices). Yet he stays boss—employees not only obey him but even "cover" for his mistakes. Such informal arrangements are a kind of cushion making a more comfortable fit between the requirements of formal structure and facts of personality. The fool type "old fuddyduddy" helps people remember the limitations of the status occupant and lets them know when to take him with a grain of salt. Thus it contributes to the efficiency of an organization. This is the status modifying function of fool types—to put a tag on a status: X (the face-value) minus Y (the negative type). Innumerable positions are so modified—mother-in-law, father, politician, minister, professor, psychiatrist, cop, plumber, to name a few that carry, so to speak, comic ballast. Comic ballast holds down various status groups, slows upstarts, and checks those in high places.

Let us consider six kinds of discounting types in American society. The first devalues age or antiquated notions. In a society with both an "accent on youth" and an increasing number of older people, it is not surprising to find an important part played by the *old fool*—times have changed and left him without a role, or age has crept up and robbed him of abilities—he is not a "grand old man" but a fuddyduddy, a fogey, a dodo, a duffer, a mossback, a dodderer, in second childhood, deadwood, corny, or a cornball. As old fogeys, some Americans think of: Herbert Hoover, John Foster Dulles, Methuselah, Polonius, Scrooge, the Archbishop of Canterbury, Queen Victoria, Emily Post, George Bernard Shaw (!), Eleanor Roosevelt, and William Jennings Bryan; in television roles Frank Morgan and Charlie Weaver. There is some of the old fool in the superannuated playboy who tries to act the lover or sugar daddy. Men past fifty feel the pressure of discounting by younger men, urging mossbacks toward a less active part.

Another way to discount subtly is to imply that a person is a *second-rater*, out of his class—a small-timer among big-timers, a bushleaguer among major leaguers, a hack among fireballs, a palooka among champs. A highly competitive system uses such discounting to kindle the ambition of hopefuls and eliminate the unnecessaries ("has-beens," those who are slipping, flashes-in-the-pan who haven't made the grade). A "comer" by contrast, is a contender of promise, a dark horse to be watched out for.

No account demotes several steps lower. Names like nobody, punk, jerk, drip, twerp and squirt, imply that he is so insignificant that it is unnecessary to consider him at all (unless as flunkey or stooge)—he is not listened to, indeed, it may seem as though he were not there.[7] Organizations use such types to confine individuals and even whole classes to small influence (Okies, Arkies, crackers, poor whites, hillbillies, shanty Irish, ragamuffins, lowbrows). The no account type robs newcomers who have not managed to stake out a claim to legitimacy: "Listen to me, I am important." [8]

Another discounting type implies poverty of spirit; it names people who are incapable of carrying off roles in a grand manner. Aristotle in his *Ethics* referred to it as "littleness of soul"; let us call it the *small-minded fool:*

cheapskate, tightwad, skinflint, small timer, piker, piddler, small potatoes, tinhorn, gossiper, tattler, toady, stickler, jerk, and schlemihl.[9]

Character and attitude as well as ability are in question here. The small-minded fool is a "little man in a big pair of shoes." Certain statuses have become associated with small-mindedness: the auditor (hunting for the last penny), bureaucrat, tightfisted legislator, drillmaster, and schoolmarm. A familiar representation is the "tightwad" character of Jack Benny. Parasites such as the boondoggler, goldbrick, and chiseler also seem on their comic side to be too small-minded to make a fair contribution. Such a fool is too petty to rise to the villainous stature of a wolf of Wall Street.

Trivial intruders may be called *nuisances,* because they are annoying but somehow comical (pest, buttinski, kibitzer, back-seat driver, ear banger, bore, wet blanket, spoilsport, pill). If villains, they would fall into categories like the intruder and troublemaker ("sorehead," indeed, is about equally villainous and foolish). Comic discounting works as an accommodation—a buffer—to reduce possible conflict: once a person has

---

[7] See Goffman's discussion of the jerk as a "non-person," *op. cit.,* p. 152.

[8] American jazz musicians have struggled to achieve respectability as a group, ultimately to appear in concert-halls, colleges, and conservatories. The very phrase "that jazz" still means something of no account.

[9] A Yiddish word that has become part of American slang. See Louis Wirth, "Some Jewish Types of Personality," *Proceedings of the American Sociological Society,* XXXII (1926), 90-96.

been so typed, we are forewarned to put up with—or escape from—his little failings.

We have looked at discounting types that put a hidden markdown on people (old fool, second rater, no account, small-minded fool, nuisance), lessening influence they would otherwise have by formal status. Let us now look at types which mark down a person more drastically. Let us call them *deflating types*. They are like darts thrown at a rising balloon; they keep people from getting too high; they bring down the stuffed shirt, the blowhard, the phoney, and the upstart.

Pompous fools have the fault of pride. They make an unsound, grandiose claim which is "shown up" by a squelch or hard fall. Episodes from literature which illustrate it: Humpty-Dumpty, La Fontaine's fable of Sir Raven (who lost his lunch by responding to the fox's flattery), Bruin the Bear's similar disgrace by Reynard, Malvolio's pose as a great lover in *Twelfth Night,* and the poem, "Casey at the Bat" (in which the proud hitter steps up to the plate, lets two good pitches go by with bases loaded, then strikes out). A *stuffed shirt* sets himself above others, takes himself too seriously—highbrow, highhat, brass hat, uppity, swell, snob, bigwig, big head, know-it-all, holier-than-thou—the stuffed shirt has been well portrayed in American comedy by Andrew H. Brown, of "Amos and Andy." Americans often think of the V.I.P. or brass hat not as a deserving top dog but as a stuffed shirt—perhaps a high-ranking officer who specializes in parade-ground maneuvers but is never seen at the front. The stuffed shirt claims too much, has a pose, which people see and feel a need to puncture. The reason for this pose is often vanity. Americans see the stuffed shirt in personalities as diverse as: Ed Sullivan, Arthur Godfrey, Queen Elizabeth, Lawrence Welk, Charles De Gaulle, Lord Beaverbrook, the Vanderbilts, Anthony Eden, Clement Atlee, Thomas E. Dewey, Senator Knowland, William Randolph Hearst, "Prince" Mike Romanoff, Pontius Pilate, and Richard Nixon.

The *dude* is a variety of stuffed shirt (dandy, fop, coxcomb, tophatter, fancy Dan, fashion-plate) who puts on fancy airs. Aggression toward him is epitomized by the snowball at the top hat; he seems to need a little mussing up, partly because he is presumed to be a sissy (therefore safe to muss up), but more important because the pride of his fancy manners is resented. The offense against equalitarianism is more important than the offense against masculinity. A dude is forgiven as soon as he shows he is a democrat and he-man. Some highly popular people in America have been fancy Dans—Mayor Jimmy Walker of New York, "Gentleman Jim" Corbett, Franklin Delano Roosevelt (with his cape and cigarette holder), General Douglas MacArthur (with his specially designed uniform and cigarette holder), General George Patton (with his riding crop and pearl-handled pistols). Celebrities whom Americans call dudes include: "Ruby" Rubirosa, Liberace, Adolph Menjou, the Prince of Wales, Beau Brummel, Bret Maverick, Ali Khan, Lord Fauntleroy, Ray Bolger, Maurice Chevalier, Dean Atcheson, Lord Chesterfield, Frank Sinatra, Bat Masterson, Diamond Jim Brady, Thomas E. Dewey.

Another aspect of the stuffed shirt is seen in the *boaster* (blowhard, loudmouth, big noise, Joe Blow), who inflates himself by his own pump. Similar is the *show-off*—who boasts by actions, gets out in front too often, tries to hog the spotlight. Americans may call him grandstander, gloryhog, headline hunter, sometimes prima donna. (These types are comic sides of a hero we have called the splendid performer.) Celebrities who push too hard to get in front of the public—perhaps by grotesque stunts—sometimes earn this reputation: "Gorgeous George" the wrestler, Elvis Presley, Zsa Zsa Gabor, Milton Berle, Jerry Lewis, Liberace, Jackie Gleason ("loudmouth"), Rafael Trujillo Jr. (playboy), Mike Todd, Mickey Rooney, "Shipwreck" Kelly (flagpole-sitter), Jayne Mansfield (prominent bosom), Archie Moore, P. T. Barnum, Errol Flynn, and Mussolini, are mentioned as show-offs.

Finally, the *great lover,* who on his comic side is a fellow with illusions about his charm and has claims to prowess he cannot earn. He is given derisive names like Casanova, Don Juan, Romeo, lady killer, lady's man, and lover boy.

Pompous fool types have an important part in a mobile society where many people make claims that have to be certified. Fear of seeming a stuffed shirt or a blowhard tightens up the game, makes one cautious in advancing claims—one plays cards closer to the vest, as it were, with smaller bets and fewer bluffs. Besides holding status claims to a minimum, pompous fool types help rectify mistakes in status allocation: demoting and checking those who have climbed too high. As leveling devices, deflating types reflect the view of the men below looking at the men above, who respect real top dogs but try to bring down the phoneys.

Now let us take the viewpoint of top dogs looking down at aspirants coming up. They recognize "comers" of merit but try to deflate false claimants (as well as some inconvenient comers of merit) by the type *upstart,* whose fault is presumption and getting "too big for his britches" (meaning in practical terms that he considers himself equal to top dogs). Labels like whippersnapper, pipsqueak, hotshot, smart guy, smart Alec, smartiepants, wise guy,[10] help cut him "down to size" by informing the

---

[10] Goffman mentions the wiseguy as one whose fault is status arrogation, he doesn't have the backstage information he claims, *op. cit.,* p. 148.

world that in the opinion of experts he isn't as good as he thinks he is. Of course, people below also can resent the upstart; they may be jealous or, in the larger view, trying to protect the integrity of the status structure by letting only genuine top dogs get to the top. In either application, the result is to impede the ascent of opportunists, climbers and "comers." (It is interesting to note that the upstart role was attached by some Americans to both youthful aspirants for the presidency in 1960, Richard Nixon and John F. Kennedy.) Such a type is unquestionably a handicap to any candidate for elective office. The upstart is, curiously, the underdog with reversed sign.

It may seem strange that the upstart should play an important part in a society that favors the underdog. You can't have Lindberghs, it seems, without Great Gatsbys. The status system tries to encourage meritorious climbers and at the same time to discourage improper ones. Were no upstarts weeded out, there would soon be few places left for underdogs.

Comic phoneys help prune a status structure of deceitful climbers. They are seen in a comic light because of the petty, it may be preposterous, nature of their fraud. They are given names like:

buffer, humbug, bunk-shooter, poseur, faker, crystal ball gazer, pundit, prophet (derisively), goldbrick, boondoggler, gladhander, softsoaper, apple-polisher, and ballyhoo artist.

Countless people pursue some small racket in order to get something for only the effort involved in deceit—the goldbrick working hard not to look like a loafer, the softsoaper "buttering up" everybody. If the fraud were serious, they would belong with villains like the con-men, the chiselers, and the Uriah Heeps. But, whether because the motive is petty, or damage is slight, or because they are easily seen through,[11] or are amusingly shown up,[12] they remain comic types. Ben Hecht's *Count Bruga* shows how far a phoney can go and still be funny. If such a type is amusing, it is also because he is a would-be con-man or smart operator who has ludicrously failed to make the grade. We must admit that the type does not control *all* smooth deceivers—only the unsuccessful ones. Tolerance, even affection, for the transparent humbug is shown when Americans mention that genial restaurateur "Prince" Mike Romanoff.

[11] One thing that helps make them funny is being able to see through their pose before being badly taken in by it; thus American audiences enjoy the transparent but elaborately concealed maneuvers of "Sergeant Bilko," "the Kingfish," or Charlie McCarthy. The late W. C. Fields was a master at playing a crafty rogue whose slightly battered appearance and shifty ways gave him the air of being continually on the lam.

[12] Ideally, comic phoneys end in a fiasco by which they are shown up and disgraced —for instance, *Tartuffe*, or Falstaff's lie about his fight with one hundred men being whittled down to running from two.

Such discounting types (old fool, second-rater, no account, upstart, pompous fool, comic phoney) show a world in which there is much puffing up and maintaining front—with corresponding need for seeing through poses and behind scenes.[13] People are insecure, and they bluff to hide weaknesses as well as petty, sometimes contemptible, motives. Society is like a poker game—there are always two sides to a role, what you let others see and the "hand" you cover up—where any visible gesture may be a bluff (if you underestimate it you may find yourself facing an overwhelming "hand" in the showdown). Discounting, then, is both a safeguard and a risk. Successful discounting prunes out the phoneys and the incompetents, or at least neutralizes them.

Types like old fool, has-been, second-rater, are parts of a competitive world where judgments are harsh and status insecure and consequently, poses are more desperate. In the "ratrace" there is little respect for the past—the important question is, what can you do now?—youth is impatient with age (dead wood)—knowing the ropes includes knowing whom to discount. It is a tournament of big-timers and champs, where anyone who isn't first rate looks bad, where you can be knocked down at any time; there is an intense struggle for identity (to be "somebody"). In such a game, the main parties are those coming up, newcomers who have just arrived, and old top dogs (some of whom are slipping) trying to defend their positions and put down climbers.

I think discounting types should also be interpreted as showing alienation in our society. It is one thing to discount a few phoneys; but discounting can spread to an entire system. A person who discounts everyone—his boss, his co-workers, all authorities—may show not so much incompetence of these persons as his own disaffection for the system. In other words, the use of discounting types may be a *language for beatniks and other alienated persons* in our society. (See the terms for overconforming fools to be discussed shortly.)

Finally, I would guess that discounting types in the long run favor a level conception of society rather than a hierarchical one, however real their services to the latter. The reason is that discounting tends to spill over—this one is an upstart, that one is a stuffed shirt—soon all are insecure. In a contest between vertical and horizontal discounters (those trying to maintain hierarchy by calling common men no accounts, climbers, and up-starts, against those trying to deflate top dogs and bring them down to their own level) the overall effect is likely to be an order in which no high status is completely valid, in which discounting has per-

[13] See Goffman's remarks on scene-management, *op. cit.*, as one of the realities of modern institutional life that must be continually taken account of.

meated the whole concept of hierarchy. Indeed, the very concept of man could become discounted and there would be a deterioration of the hero, the kind of thing lamented by Thomas Carlyle.

Nonconforming Fools

Every mobile society must deal with newcomers and deviants. When they seem harmless, though bizarre and outrageous, the mobile society usually classifies them as comic types, such as the deformed fool, character, strange fool, antic fool, or comic rogue.

A *deformed fool* may be called:

freak, misfit, shrimp, dwarf, midget, halfpint, squirt, slob, fatso, five-by-five, greaseball, Ichabod, babyface, schnozzle, eagle beak, plug-ugly, or ape.

Such names refer to a rather extreme physical departure, imitations of which are part of the clown's stock-in-trade. Every deformity is not funny, of course; but most comic deformities are extreme enough to startle the audience a little and set the person apart without offering any threat. Many comic deformities are signs of weaknesses or incompetence in playing a normal part ("babyface" has a hard time playing the man's role, big feet suggest tripping or stepping on others). Freakishness may be a debit in real life, but it can be an asset in the entertainment field if one may judge by celebrities in whom Americans see something of the freak, for example: Elvis Presley, Christine Jorgenson, "Gorgeous George" the wrestler, Primo Carnera, Jerry Lewis, Johnny Ray the "crying crooner," Liberace. Others mentioned as freaks (but not necessarily as fools) include: Toulouse-Lautrec, Quasimodo, Rasputin, Frankenstein, Tom Thumb, Cyclops; clearly the freak verges on the monster (dealt with among villain types).

The *character* has an important place in American life. This type is used by sophisticates to classify a person who is odd, colorful, or interesting. For example, a slightly crazed lady named "Rosie" used to come around the bright-light areas of Chicago selling flowers; police smiled when they saw her; nightclub habitués and cabdrivers greeted her. Almost every college has its "campus character." Famous people have been classed as characters, for example, George Bernard Shaw and Albert Einstein.[14] Calling a person a character does not imply ridicule or rejection, as in the

[14] Also Frank Lloyd Wright, Elvis Presley, Salvador Dali, Henry VIII, Bertrand Russell, Marlon Brando, James Dean, Pablo Picasso, Nero, Tennessee Williams, Liberace, Edgar Allan Poe, Greta Garbo, Vincent Van Gogh, Samuel Johnson, Jayne Mansfield, Oscar Levant, Ernest Hemingway, and Oscar Wilde.

case of "freak" or "screwball"; a smile often accompanies the word, even a suspension of judgment resembling the Samoan attitude *musu* described by Margaret Mead—acceptance of deviation, lack of curiosity about motivation, and in some cases respect.[15] The character type accommodates mobile and sophisticated people to a world where almost anything is likely; it is a catch-all category. Such a type suspends the primitive in-group tendency to ridicule and ostracize; the milder judgment "a character" means toleration with a smile.

A more primitive reaction to personality deviations is illustrated by *strange fool* types: oddball, crackpot, screwball, nut, gook,[16] goon, creep,* square, eccentric, misfit, crank*—along with special categories such as beatnik and bohemian (in a derisive sense), and pansy,* fairy, or fruit,* (those marked with an asterisk have strong villainous as well as comic connotations). I have no intention of lumping these kinds of people together, except that the popular types fall into the general category of those ridiculed for peculiarities of personality. The bohemian has been discussed as an independent spirit, but on the comic side he is an arty screwball, akin to the beatnik. The ordinary person does not slice very finely in such matters,[17] though cognoscenti who remember the vigorous bohemianism of the old days make a distinction.[18] As popularly conceived, beatniks are pseudo-intellectual crackpots and bums who make little contribution to the cultural life of America beyond a picturesque style of rejecting the "square" world in favor of pads, pot, and coffeehouses.

The *antic fool* is a more amusing non-conformer because of his role as:

cut-up, clown, life of the party, prankster, practical joker, funster, wisecracker, card, playboy, good-time-Charlie, (one sense of) party girl, ham

[15] Margaret Mead, *From the South Seas* (New York: William Morrow and Co., Inc., 1939), pp. 122-124.

[16] Gook was a term applied by American soldiers in Korea to Koreans, but it has the more general meaning of someone who is outlandish or queer.

[17] Persons nominated by Americans as bohemians include: James Dean, Marlon Brando, beatniks, Jack Kerouac (whose novel *On the Road* is hailed as the bible of the beat generation), Françoise Sagan, Jean-Paul Sartre, Van Gogh, Hemingway, Poe, Wilde, Max Bodenheim, Dylan Thomas, Salvador Dali, Charles Laughton, Henry Miller, Bertrand Russell, Dave Brubeck, Dizzy Gillespie, Henry Thoreau.

[18] "In the dark days of their arrival (on Grant Street in San Francisco) they were treated with the respect due for what people thought them to be: writers, artists, poets, musicians. But it was soon discovered they bore faint resemblance to their bohemian cousins. . . . With the intellectual range running from illiterate farm hands to alcoholic PhD's, the beats are involved in no way, shape or form with any brand of intellectualism. They have no intellectual discrimination. They are merely against the *status quo.* . . . The bohemians are the creative ones. They are too busy working to go the "drag" route. They have no time for the beatniks and their pseudo-intellectuality. There is a certain appeal about the bohemian. He has a quality of sentimentality. The beatniks do not." Jim Schock, *Life is a Lousy Drag* (San Francisco Unicorn Publishing Company, 1958).

(in the sense of overplaying for comic effects), Donald Duck, and Happy Hooligan.

He epitomizes the spirit of topsy-turvy: when he goes into action wigs are snatched, water is squirted, pants fall down, people are set on their rears; the author of such chaos seems like a human pinwheel exploding into comic pyrotechnics. His role is essentially a playful form of disorder (prank, cut-up, caper, frolic, high jinks) that disturbs decorum and dignity, hence furnishes the feeling that the rules are off for now. An antic must seem spontaneous, even be a little crazy. Americans see the cut-up in celebrities such as: Jerry Lewis, Red Skelton, Elvis Presley, Harpo Marx, Charlie Chaplin, Douglas Fairbanks Sr., Dennis the Menace, Errol Flynn, Milton Berle, Bob Hope, Frank Sinatra, Danny Kaye, Groucho Marx, General Rafael Trujillo Jr., John Barrymore, Lucy ("I Love Lucy").

What has been said about the antic applies all the more to the *comic rogue* (scamp, scalawag, prankster, rascal), who goes so far in mayhem that he almost joins forces with the villain. He is found in comic strip characters like Dennis the Menace, Krazy Kat, the Katzenjammer Kids, Little Kayo, Wimpy, and Happy Hooligan, Lying, stealing, and brick-heaving are his stock-in-trade. He approaches the flouter and deceiver among villains. Just as the antic fool suspends decorum, the rogue suspends *morality* in an unreal world of farce and outrageous situations (the clown burglars talking loudly as they climb through a window, the adulterer caught under a bed) that in real life might result in a riot or a call for the ambulance.

Such nonconforming types (deformed, strange, antic, rogue) provide a vacation from conformity but nonetheless affirm the order they seem to flout, though in different ways (deformed and strange fools by holding up negative models, antic fools and rogues by catharsis through vicarious misbehavior and the spirit of carnival).

Viewed as punishments, nonconforming types (unlike those that subtly discount without changing formal status much) highlight a person's peculiarities and set him on a lower status. Nonconforming fool types are mocking views of the independent spirit (they make his independence look like freakishness). Oddballs are excluded from the company of regular fellows, for they are in opposition to the well rounded personality of the good Joe. Such types (along with stranger villains) work in a team to support the good Joe complex; in other words, they give negative, anxiety creating images of what you may be if you don't try hard to be a regular fellow. The "character," however, is a civilized compromise which seems to say, "All right, if you want to be different, be interesting, and we'll forgive you." If a character displays qualities of a goodfellow he is quite tolerable. (I once heard a hotel barber put it this way: "He has his peculiarities but he's *all right*.")

The beatnik, unlike sheer oddballs, has acquired a rallying function for some deviants—he symbolizes the rejection of "square" models (smoothie, good Joe, moralist); his "cool" attitude negates the friendliness of the good Joe and the enthusiasm of the booster; his "beat" style of sloppiness rejects the smoothie and the entire world of fashionable and successful living. We shall consider him later under anomic types.

In general, nonconforming fool types raise a question similar to the one we ask of villains: do they indicate breakdown or control? It seems to me that the answer depends on the number of such types and the attitude toward them. A large number of oddballs, beatniks, and so on indicate the breakdown of conventional norms; but a small number, severely ridiculed, shows that society has quarantined them successfully. When people are blasé about "characters," it shows that the ridicule implicit in such a type is too weak to have much deterrent effect and that such deviations are quite common. I would judge that our American fool typology tends to be *blasé* and weakly controlling rather than severe and tightly controlling. The resentment of the beats, hepcats, etc. against the squares shows considerable rebellion against the makers of protocol and lack of effort to live up to the standards of the gray flannel suit. The retreatism of alienated persons—fool types like the beatnik, oddball, and character—might indicate severe *anomie*.

Overconforming Fools

The next collection of fools go too far in living up to group standards. Prudence recognizes that there are situations where conformity is the wrong thing and being too zealous in applying even good rules can get you into all kinds of trouble. Conformity is also mocked by individualists who admire the independent spirit; to them, someone who is timid or who sticks to the middle of the road may be a fool. Then there are alienated people ("out," socially or psychologically) to whom anyone who is "in"—who lives a conventional life—is "square," a fool. In all these ways the over-conformer is mocked.

I shall distinguish four main kinds of over-conformers, beginning with one who has a curious resemblance to the hero model of the smoothie. Let us call him the *yes-man,* the one who complies too readily—he is known by names like:

jellyfish, applepolisher, toady, party-liner, straddler (tries to agree with both sides), pussyfooter (tries to avoid disagreeing with anybody), clothes horse (wears anything that fashion imposes); joiner, Babbitt, and philistine (uncritical followers of convention).

Such a person lacks integrity, is too "easy," to manipulate, may even be a pushover; it is hard to tell where he really stands (or who stands behind him) because of his shifting position. One may be considered a yesman if he is tied so closely to a party or team that it is clear that his view is not his own. Many Americans mentioned "Ike" Eisenhower as a "top dog," but also as a "yes-man." This is understandable, I think, from his dual role, first as a military top dog, second as a middle-of-the-roader while President. Others mentioned as "yes-men" included: Harry Truman (as a party wheelhorse and loyal crony—somewhat peculiar in view of his later independent and outspoken role), Neville Chamberlain (pact with Hitler at Munich), Richard Nixon; the Russian Deputy Premier Anastas Mikoyan, Mayor Dail of San Diego, Mao Tse Tung (conceived as a Russian puppet), Governor Goodwin Knight of California, James Haggerty, and Sherman Adams; literary and popular figures such as Macbeth, J. Alfred Prufrock, Walter Mitty, Jiggs, Mutt and Jeff, Adam (talked into eating the apple by Eve), and "Chester" (of the TV serial "Gunsmoke").

A second group of conforming fools resemble the moralist hero type. *Rigid fools* have names like:

diehard, fanatic, single track mind, prig, prude, puritan, bluenose, old maid, stickler, corny, old fogey, some senses of gospelshark, holy Joe, and fundamentalist.

They stick to approved positions too long or carry them beyond the point where the majority, finding the position uncomfortable, bow out. The public may have the attitude, "that's all right as a general principle but don't carry it too far and don't apply it to me." Among persons mentioned as *"fanatics"* were: Billy Graham, Carrie Nation, Joseph McCarthy, Governor Faubus, Adolph Hitler, Father Divine, Aimee Semple McPherson, Robespierre, Mary Baker Eddy, John Wilkes Booth, Governor Pat Brown of California, Senator Robert Taft, Benarr McFadden, Gandhi, Billy Sunday, Nasser, and Dr. Townsend. The fanatic goes to extremes because of the intensity of his faith, and is likely to be involved in radical movements.[19] He is often a dupe of someone else's ideas (a cartoon by William Steig shows him in a weird costume, holding traces in both hands, with the caption, "Let the leader of the cult do the worrying"). A *diehard*

---

[19] Eric Hoffer's *The True Believer* (New York: Harper & Brothers, 1951) shows this side of the fanatic.

seems at times only an embattled fanatic who sticks it out to the bitter end, though sometimes Americans apply "diehard" to people who have just been around too long. Nominations included: Senator McCarthy, Adlai Stevenson, Governor Faubus, Thomas Dewey, General MacArthur, Mickey Rooney, Chiang Kai-shek, Truman, William J. Bryan, Carrie Nation, Karl Marx, Charles DeGaulle, Cromwell, John L. Lewis, Fulton Lewis Jr., Herbert Hoover, Winston Churchill, Senator Knowland, Norman Thomas, Bismarck, Caryl Chessman, Eugene Debs, and Eleanor Roosevelt. Another variant of the rigid over-conformer is the *prude* or *prig*, something of which Americans see in: Emily Post, Carrie Nation, Liberace, Eleanor Roosevelt, Queen Victoria, Dr. Richmond Barbour (a columnist giving advice to people in trouble), Margaret Truman, Amy Vanderbilt, Saint Paul, Queen Elizabeth, Juliet, Anthony Comstock, and Lord Fauntleroy. This is a comic view of the bluenose, not as a censor or authoritarian but rather too "nice" for the regular fellows.

A less moralistic over-conformer is found in the *faddist*:

> fan, autograph fiend, camera fiend, shutterbug, cigarette fiend, dance fiend, jitterbug, jazz fiend, zoot-suiter, bopster, rockhound, bridge shark, and hifi addict.

Except for derisive tone, such types markedly resemble the heroes of play discussed in a previous chapter. The energy of play generates much enthusiasm for extremes. A faddist seems a kind of weathervane in his style of life, switching from one thing to another (the word implies giddy-headedness, also that he is a dupe).

A fourth kind of over-conformer acts stupidly or blindly, albeit gallantly, because of high ideals. The *high minded fool* plunges into troubles that a more practical minded, down to earth person would avoid. His names include: Don Quixote, Candide, Pollyanna, romantic, idealist, do-gooder, and eager beaver. There is also an intellectual kind of high mindedness, in which a person is incapacitated by ideas (Plato's philosopher who stumbled into a well, Swift's learned scholars of Laputa lost in utterly useless researches). In America such a fool is indicated by names like egghead, bubblehead, star gazer, ivory tower thinker. When the morally high minded fanatic is in action, he is likely to be called crusader, Sir Galahad, or dragonslayer applied derisively. Certain episodes from American history illustrate such a role: Woodrow Wilson's mission to Versailles (indeed, the entire "war to end war") and the ill-fated "peace ship" of Henry Ford. Americans see something of the high minded fool in famous people like: Danny Kaye, Eleanor Roosevelt, Gandhi, Neville Chamberlain, Alexander the Great, Sherman Adams, John Foster Dulles, and Albert Schweitzer.

Such conceptions are a basis for the *mock hero*,—anyone referred to by a heroic title who is actually conceived as a fool. Almost any grandiose name such as dragonslayer, do-gooder, martyr, great lover, hotshot, big-shot belittles a person because it implies that he lacks those traits or that anyone who acts like that is a fool. A typical device of dramatic satire is to cast a high minded person in a situation where his idealism carries him to an absurd extreme. Mock heroes resemble the hero types of a culture (crusader, benefactor, brain, etc.), but are actually inversions of them. Without knowing the context, one cannot always tell whether a "hero" is being applauded or laughed at. This ambivalence applies with force to the "do-gooder" (listed under heroes in Chapter 1), since ratings indicate that about one out of three think him a fool. Unfortunately, a fellow trying to do a *really good* job may be stultified because he is typed as an eager beaver, that is, he exceeds the norm regarded as reasonable by his peers. Such is the rebuke of Sancho Panza to Don Quixote. Why people should be annoyed, even alarmed, by super-conformers will be analyzed in connection with alienation in later chapters.

Such conforming fool types (yes-man, rigid, faddist, high minded, mock hero) reflect several things about the society in which we live. First, the prudence of secular *Gesellschaft* (as Tönnies analyzed it), which does not demand like mindedness (perfect consensus) but only the surface of conformity. Absolute adherence seems fanatical; rules are not sacred but relative; the sensible person conforms "so much" and no more—"so much" being the amount of actual observance or lip service that others of prestige in that particular game are paying. A person who goes further seems a fool for *paying too much* for the privilege of playing the game (he is unlikely to make much at it even if not beaten badly). Hero, eager beaver, booster, prig, may be some of the titles he earns. Moreover, perceptive people can detect a false note in some overconformity, seeing behind "hero" and "eager beaver" other less attractive types: toady, flatterer, climber (in which case derision of a sincere striver paying "too much" changes to mockery to expose the phoney paying too little for some profit he is seeking). Cynical, alienated persons may see even sincere do-gooders as phoneys. So we see that *Gesellschaft* favors the perception of comic over-conformers in several ways.

Another thing which helps our understanding of overconforming fools is the conceptual scheme of David Riesman. It seems to me that yes-men represent the weakness of the other-directed character of modern times, as viewed by men of integrity (especially inner-directed ones who admire the independent spirit and think all who give in too readily are weaklings). But, in turn, inner-directed people, when they go to extremes

necessary to defend their ideals, seem diehards and fanatics to middle-of-
the-roaders and other-directed persons who regard dedication to principle
as folly. A society such as ours, filled with an anxiety to belong, is a
milieu for other-directed characters who go to extremes to climb, conform,
and belong and so seem like yes-men and faddists. The same milieu
shows inner-directed people and those raised in ethnocentric or sectarian
subcultures as diehards and fanatics.

Looking at another sociological theory, Robert Merton has pointed out
that bureaucracy emphasizes rules and discipline which become ends in
themselves; the person begins to judge himself by how punctiliously he can
remember and follow complex procedures. The rewards of bureaucracy
and entrenched in-groups favor (both by producing and selecting) a
person characterized by timidity, conservatism and technicism.[20] The
result is a man who will not stick his neck out, who looks sometimes like a
pussyfooter or a middle-of-the-roader, sometimes like a moralistic diehard
for principle (though his reason is not moral but simply the expediency
of getting on in a bureaucratic system).

Again, it is possible to relate overconformity to certain kinds of *anomie.*
For example, Merton called ritualism[21] rigid adherence to practices of
which the instrumental value has been lost (such as sticking to cash in a
consumption-oriented credit economy). Ritualism might indicate that
a person is maladjusted, his rigidity being labeled by types such as square,
corny, prig, or diehard. Another form of *anomie* would be viewing life a
game where one need not obey the rules but can manipulate them and
"con" his way, using legalism to cheat, press, or intimidate others. In
such an unethical situation—closely approaching *anomie* though out-
wardly formal—the person abusing the law the most might seem like a
stickler—a superconformer—who knows every cranny and loophole, and
speaks loudly in favor of law, namely of a game in which he has the aces.
Yet another expression of *anomie* might be that overconformity symp-
tomatizes a weakness of some kind—perhaps hostility, fear of rejection,
fear of being "found out"—of which compliance is the mask, that is, an
overconforming front hides the weakness in a role structure and alienation
in persons. In a coercive organization (perhaps penal, military, or
totalitarian) one would expect dislike of the system to be hidden under
compliance—the most assiduous boot-polisher might be a potential traitor.
Another anomic situation favoring certain kinds of overconformity is
sheer boredom and futility, where, to escape emptiness, people try anything for "kicks"; the result is various types of faddists and fanatics. A

[20] *Social Theory and Social Structure* (Glencoe, Ill.: The Free Press, 1949), pp. 151-160.
[21] "Social Structure and Anomie," *ibid.,* Ch. 4.

more extreme possibility is that moral crisis would be so severe that all values were thrown into question, all conformity seem overconformity, all heroes seem fools; in such case, pervasive mockery of conformers could indicate disintegration of the system. All I am trying to point out here is that overconformity may mean things very different from what it indicates on the surface (high morals in an individual and high morale in a society). We shall take this up again under anomic types.

Comic Butts and Jesters

Always the dulness of the fool
is the whetstone of the wits.
SHAKESPEARE

Last among major American fool types are two that serve markedly as outlets for aggressive tension (though all ridiculed types have some of this function).

The *comic butt* is indicated by names like Sad Sack, stooge, fall guy, henpecked, Jiggs, yes-man, low man on the totem pole, scapegoat, and buffoon. He may be found in almost any group as the one who bears the brunt of ridicule, the one whose position is so low that he habitually receives raw deals. Ethnic groups may have this role (in old carnival games, people used to throw baseballs at a negro to knock him into a vat of water). Individuals who receive such status may have some weakness which makes them incapable of fighting back (see weak fool types). However badly a butt is treated, people always feel that somehow he deserves it—his faults draw comic blame on him. By virtue of such faults a butt is an underdog viewed as a Sad Sack rather than a pathetic victim or plucky fighter. One reason he "deserves it" is that he doesn't fight back; indeed, he is the one in the group whose social duty, as it were, is to accept indignity. The circus buffoon takes pratfalls, lets others insult him, or insults himself. If he retaliates, he has only one comically correct course: to do so ineffectively—for yet another pratfall. This duty tells us that the butt, in dignity at least, is at the bottom of the status system; he has no honor to defend (indeed, it is impossible to insult a buffoon because, being as low as he can get, he cannot claim to have lost honor). The lot of the medieval buffoon, says Swain, "must have been a miserable one, however well he was treated in comparison with the other creatures in whose class he was supposed to be—the hounds and horses." [22]

[22] Barbara Swain, *Fools and Folly During the Middle Ages and Renaissance* (New York: Columbia University Press, 1932), p. 56.

Reciprocal to the butt is the *jester* as fool-maker, one whose privilege—even duty—is to make pointed fun of someone. The butt receives what the jester delivers, for example, a "hot foot" to a sleeping comrade. While almost anybody can play either role, the work is important enough for there to be a specialized functionary whose office is to release wit against plausible targets, for example, the medieval court buffoon. In America, various well known persons have had the informal part of national jester—Artemus Ward, Mark Twain, H. L. Mencken—even Lincoln—but none more plainly than Will Rogers, who was celebrated for his jibes at big shots. Groucho Marx has played a similar role on television. A jester may assume a pose of rusticity or ignorance, which says, in effect: "You can't blame me for making such a remark because I don't know any better" (Rogers pretended to be a half-literate cowboy, even avoided correcting his columns for grammar and spelling, though he was in fact expensively educated; nor can we forget the "ignorant" Socrates). Underneath such guises the sharpness shows; Shakespeare said, "This fellow is wise enough to play the fool and to do that craves a kind of wit." Thus, to call a jester a fool is rather a misnomer, for he is a fool-maker, too sharp to have much in common with his clownish cousins except that he dresses in their costume. Some writers have compromised by calling him the clever fool or the sage-fool.[23] In my opinion he might as well be described as a smart operator. Take that crafty simpleton, the "good soldier" Schweik, who carries on a game of his own under the protection of apparent stupidity: "I'm allowed to do that, Corporal, because I'm daft, but nobody'd think you could be such a fool." Here is a fool who is not as dumb as he looks; things are working out rather well for him. But, whether we call him "fool" or "hero," the jester performs his traditional mission, working hand in hand with the butt.

Such types plainly belong among the "safety-valve" mechanisms by which societies release tensions that might otherwise be damaging. Comic ritual projects possible insults of particular members into one vast and entertaining insult to a butt. The jester acts like a lightning rod. Were the butt to return the shock, he would fail in his function, might even change into a villain about whom something would have to be done, or split consensus by gaining sympathy as a victim or hero. (Certain things ordinarily prevent him from escaping from his role: his degraded status, which makes it hard for him to claim dignity, and the unanswerable cleverness of jest as the "last word.") When the jester and the butt play their parts properly, the group may get: accommodation of aggressive

[23] Enid Welsford, *The Fool, His Social and Literary History* (London: Faber and Faber, Ltd., 1935), p. 237.

feeling (catharsis in laughter and redirection against scapegoats), solidarity, and criticism or insight stated in the jest.

The presence of a butt is rather embarrassing in a democratic system where it is assumed that all are equal in dignity. It seems a kind of bullying to persistently mock the *same* person. A society such as ours checks this tendency by rotating the role, requiring that all "take a joke" in turn, and by the concept of "carrying a joke too far," namely that there are limits to what even Sad Sack must endure. If jest is chronically focused on one target, then it probably serves institutional and class rigidity. If it hits the wrong targets or roams aimlessly, it can divert criticism unproductively and dissipate group energy. Yet, when focused on stuffed shirts, snobs, diehards, and phoneys, it favors justice and reform. What mockery does for a society depends, then, on the conditions and forms of the mockery; it has a choice between equality or inequality, change or "things as they are." We can distinguish between dispersed and channelized mockery: the former ranging freely, the privilege (and burden) of everybody; the latter confined to certain forms, occasions, and targets. Dispersed mockery, it seems to me, favors an equalitarian and changing society. Though it risks dissipating criticism into irrelevant topics, it is free to range into dangerous areas and strike at things that count.

America has long been a land of dispersed mockery, where joking was the prerogative of everybody. We may ask at this point how it is going with this national asset. Many humorists have lamented the decline of "pointed" comedy in America. For example, Al Capp, the creator of "Li'l Abner," complained about the Pollyanna attitude of the American public. Another American cartoonist, Robert Osborn, observed that America has no rapier-like political cartooning comparable with that of England. "We . . . try to please everyone, to try not to hurt anyone's feelings." American humor seems to be sunk in an era of blandness.[24] Other American comedians (such as Steve Allen, George S. Kaufman, and Stan Freberg) have voiced similar views. If these comedians are correct, does the blandness they speak of mean that there is less aggressive tension and need for outlets? My answer would be that there is patently no decline of aggressive tension in America. So, if aggressive comedy is declining, it is not for lack of need but rather some combination of circumstances has stifled it. Fear of offending sponsors or buyers is no doubt important. But why are people so sensitive? Has insecurity of status increased so greatly that people are afraid to let fly a little dart for fear the bubble will collapse? I think Americans are trying to skirt certain dangerous, even

---

[24] "The Emasculation of American Humor," *Saturday Review of Literature* (November 23, 1957), pp. 16-17.

nerve wracking, facts by pussyfooting—somewhat like tiptoeing around
the house to avoid upsetting a bad tempered person. The kind of jesting
we welcome in such a frame of mind might be called good Joe comedy
("I Love Lucy") where nobody gets hurt and everybody is a swell fellow.
The good Joe is beginning to dominate entertainment; among his conquests, he has come into the Jester's act and said, "Let's cut out the rough-
house and be regular fellows." But a regular fellow today no longer has
to take a stiff jibe or hand one out; he is too thin skinned, circumspect,
and considerate for that. He is sensitive, perhaps, because he has things to
worry about that Mark Twain and Davy Crockett never heard of. Oddly,
our world has many crude outlets for violence and yet a lush, almost
feverish, good Joeism. We may as well, then, explore the possibility that
ratpack killings are some kind of payment for having displaced Touch-
stone from the jester's seat and enthroned King Joe.

Summary to Chapter 3

We have here looked at some types that reflect the society in which we
live. Five categories highlight some of their functions: 1) penalizing gross
incompetence and role failure; 2) discounting hidden weaknesses and
poses in a world of climbing and front, helping role discrimination, combing the social structure for certain kinds of parasites and free riders; 3)
setting non-conformists apart from regular fellows, to this degree favoring
like mindedness; 4) discounting overconformity and, maybe, providing
devices by which alienated people can spare themselves from commitment;
and 5) providing outlets for tension through the institutionalized roles of
jester and comic butt.

Such a survey shows certain aspects of American life in a comic light,
for example: growing leisure and enthusiasm for play, in faddist types;
inner-directed diehards versus other-directed yes-men; an equalitarian
effort to level stuffed shirts; insecurity of climbers in a game of pose and
discount, where people try to see through each other's "hands"; and (especially in mockery of over-conformers) alienation, a sense of not being
"with it," that runs counter to the impression created by good Joeism
(are we really a bunch of happy goodfellows or nervous ones keeping an
eye on one another and playing a game that is different from what it
seems?).

PART II

THE CHANGING AMERICAN CHARACTER

CHAPTER 4

IMPRESSIONS OF AMERICAN HEROES

At this point the emphasis of this book shifts from description to interpretation, though it is impossible to separate these neatly in any discussion of symbols. I shall try to read the types for what they tell about American life and character.

Let us look first, then, at the heroes. You may recall the five main classes distinguished: *winners,* epitomizing beating others and getting what they want; *splendid performers,* who specialize in making a hit with audiences; *heroes of social acceptability,* who perfect pleasing traits and symbolize belonging; *independent spirits,* who symbolize standing alone; and *group servants,* who are models of solidarity, cooperation, and loyalty.

Variety and Freedom in Heroes Today

The hundreds of American types show a striking variety of role models compared with simpler and more traditional societies, and perhaps even with some modern European ones. Were there a comparable survey of, say, English or Yugoslavian heroes, I suspect we would beat them on variety, if not on other merits. One can sit back, choose from all of these models, and expect that with hard work or "the breaks" he will achieve a status that his father never dreamed of. Even a flagpole-sitter has a good chance for income and recognition in his peculiar line. This is an important dimension of the American role structure, for choice of heroes is almost another name for freedom. It means a wide range of opportunity—not just one door open to one kind of talent, but many. Indeed, looking at our celebrities, one would think almost any kind of person can be famous in America.

Negatively, we have to put up with a lot from our favorites. Ethically, they are a motley crowd; even a broad-minded person would find it hard to approve all of them: drunkenness and promiscuity are not always out of place, even gangsters have been popular heroes. Nor is there much order or hierarchy in the values expressed by all these models: a torch singer may outshine a scientist; a glamour girl may be more "successful" than the founder of a hospital. One gets a topsyturvy impression of the American value system; there is no definite point of judgment; there may be possible conflicts within the individual because of inconsistent models. A variety of models implies that there is little consensus about "highest" or absolute ethical standards: your saint is no better than my pin-up girl. Indeed, it is possible that people could be not only confused but demoralized by too many role choices, whereas a few "safe" models, such as defenders, martyrs, and group servants, would build up a uniform, stable character type throughout the society.

Another disadvantage in having the freedom of role choice is the aggravation of frivolity and faddishness—evident in "sharks," "fiends," "fans," and play heroes of American life. If a person rushes about from one fad or hobby to another he is probably uncertain of his values—even of who he is. Americans find themselves in a kind of bargain basement with a bewildering variety to choose from—the models may not all be equally becoming, but nothing prevents us from trying them on. The American personality, then, is about what one would expect from people shopping around for what they want to be—a hodgepodge rather than integrity: restless change in life styles and personality patterns and a rather poor fit with the styles and patterns one has.

Some characteristic adjustment problems of America seem directly connected with freedom in hero types. One is the role conflict of adolescence. Is it not clear that some of the trouble comes from the bewildering array of choices open to the young people of today—presented both through mass communication and peer groups? There is some group, some marginal area, perhaps, where a juvenile can play roles that are denied in the regular structure—where he has a chance to be himself as he wants to be. In these groups or areas he can try on new models and get more status by being "fast," at least "hep," than by being "square."

Another role conflict related to the variety of hero types is sometimes called the "dilemma of modern woman" or the problem of the "lost sex." Superficially, it is due to the entrance of women into the labor force and the conflict between career and home. But I feel that economic considerations alone do not fully explain either woman's exodus from traditional roles or her sense of conflict about it, unless mention is made of a subjective thing called glory, not found in all roles, not even in all highly paid ones, and to be found in some poorly paid ones. Glory is concentrated in hero types, the bulk of which in American culture—possibly eight-ninths—cannot properly be called feminine. (For instance: "pin-up girl" has a specifically feminine gender, "reformer" is shared by men and women, and "strong man" is solely masculine.) A sample of hero-types, then, shows the following distribution:

Specifically feminine	Shared by both sexes	Specifically masculine	Total
25	136	78	239

There is about one specifically feminine[1] for every three masculine hero types. This imbalance seems to me to mean that there is a greater attraction, in terms of glory, in men's roles than women's roles, or in that neutral field where sex is "lost," that is, does not matter. It is still a man's world when it comes to handing out the medals. When Brunhild really wants to shine, very likely she must enter the lists against Siegfried. But if she does win a masculine prize—identifies herself with a masculine hero type—she will compromise her femininity as a lady boss, self-made woman, girl athlete, woman-about-town, she-wolf of Wall Street, great lover.

Suppose you are a woman and find that you are admitted to a men's field all right but are subtly denied equal honor. Might it not make you all the more determined to crash into the glory, if need be as a Babe

[1] Of course in the above sample there are important, specifically feminine heroic roles, such as beauty contest winner, prima donna, glamor girl, best dressed woman, Lady Bountiful, and self-sacrificing nurses. Tradition also provides attractive models of heroic women: Ruth, Rachel, Cordelia, the Patient Griselda, Cinderella, Penelope, Antigone, Helen of Troy, Madame DuBarry, Cleopatra, and Queen Elizabeth. But it is interesting to note how much choice has actually been confined to two types of glory: the faithful, submissive Penelope-mother-sufferer-helper; or the erotic queen (who may use her attraction as a means to power over men but does not strike out for herself).

Zaharias, cigar-smoking businesswoman, gunmoll, or girl delinquent who acts tough, wears blue jeans, and carries a switchblade knife?

This imbalance in masculine and feminine hero types seems bound to lessen, however, under the impact of mass communication, coeducation, economic and technological developments, and military crises which favor equality of the sexes. One feels sure that Cinderella will have her day, although in a series of roles markedly different from the traditional Cinderella. With increasing Congresswomen, women executives, lady athletes, cowgirls, and so on, it seems reasonable to expect further convergence of the sexes—perhaps even to the point of *men imitating women* as the latter supply more models of achievement.—Could not the trademark "masculine" ultimately disappear from types like tough guy, big operator, wolf?—then, perhaps, we shall know the true meaning of sex.

The main point I have been trying to make is that diversity of hero types means *loss of identity* in any society that does not provide, along with free choice of types: (1) effective agencies of guidance, (2) well institutionalized avenues of validating (proving) oneself in whatever type is chosen, (3) some control to prevent undesirable and inappropriate types from being presented to the masses cafeteria style, and (4) effective agencies for personality repair and readjustment. In other words, a society where personality formation is cafeteria style must expect many people to come out of the line with roles unsuited to them, genuinely confused as to who they are and whether they ought to be what they have chosen.

Accent on the Physical

Another impression is gained by considering types like the strong man, top dog, champ, he-man, cowboy, two-gun man, big operator, big-money boy, stunt artist—the admiration of Tarzans and sale of home exercisers —the tendency to view the solution of life's problems as the knockout of a villain by a hero—the Bunyanesque big swat, big punch, big bankroll, big operation—Li'l Abner with bare chest and sleeves rolled high—models of social acceptability such as pin-ups, it-girls, Miss Americas, charmers, smoothies, and fashion-plates. All have an emphasis on the physical and on the surface, to the neglect, perhaps, of things that do not obviously show.

Various interpretations can be made of the accent on the physical in America. It has been said that it is simply the primitive admiration for strength, physical prowess, and courage—that Americans like Tarzan for much the same reason that the Anglo-Saxons liked Beowulf or Norsemen Sigurd. But such an explanation ignores vast differences in social organization and technology; also that Americans do everything they can to avoid physical exercise, unless it is an occasional sport or hobby or a frantic effort to reduce weight, and will drive their cars a block to mail a letter. How can they put such a high value, then, on muscular development? This explanation also ignores the *mystique* of the primitive toward strength as a kind of mana or magical force (the ancient strong man might be a demigod, have a divine mandate, be supernaturally protected and aided—Aeneas, Moses, Samson, Cuchulain, Archilles, Hercules, Karna, Maui). Such a mystique is a poor way to describe the way Americans regard a strong man. The modern attitude toward achievement is marked by matter-of-factness.[2]

Similarly, I do not care for a complicated psychoanalytical explanation of the American accent on the physical (such as an inferiority complex or Geoffrey Gorer's suggestion that our worship of physique is really fear of being sissies). No doubt such explanations apply to some people, but we need an explanation simple enough to be applied to millions and yet which does not impute neurotic overcompensation to a whole people. Accenting the physical is too simple to be neurotic; it is so simple (because of the absence of mystique) that it is not even primitive. It seems to me that such an explanation is provided by the concept of secularization of values[3]—the paring down of values to sensate qualities appreciated promptly through the senses and without mystical or other complicated interpretation. Loss of value consensus in modern times has been so great that people can agree on little but what is obvious and on the surface.[4] Popular favorites must put their goods on the counter, so to speak: looks, dimples, muscles, physical feats, charm, smooth manners, and such. Sur-

[2] For example, when Babe Ruth made his tremendous homerun records, reporters got out with a tape and measured the length of his drives, experts tested his coordination and neuromuscular equipment, there was a prolonged discussion of the "lively ball" and its contribution to his success—not to debunk him but just to prove that he really was such a fellow. Nor does anybody suppose that there was anything mysterious about mercenary successes such as those of Rockefeller, Carnegie, Ford, Edison, and Morgan.

[3] The theory of secularization has been developed by sociologists such as Howard Becker, "Ionia and Athens" (Ph.D. dissertation, University of Chicago), and Robert Redfield, *The Folk Culture of Yucatan* (University of Chicago Press, 1941). The concept of sensate culture is set forth in Pitirim Sorokin's *Social and Cultural Dynamics* (New York: American Book Company, 1937-1941). For purposes of this study, I am considering the terms "secularized," "secular" and "sensate" as practically equivalent in speaking of values. I am not, however, by using the word sensate implying anything about a trend from one cultural emphasis to another.

[4] As shown by such works as Walter Lippman's *Preface to Morals* (New York: The Macmillan Co., 1929), and *The Public Philosophy* (Little, Brown & Co., 1955); and Pitirim Sorokin, *The Crises of Our Age* (E. P. Dutton & Co., Inc., 1957; first published in 1941).

face qualities have an advantage in mass appeal over those which are inner, spiritual, or require complicated motivations that only comparatively few are likely to share. The secularized hero[5] is the only one really suited on a large scale to a secularized culture. The sensate outlook helps explain the rapid turnover of movie stars and other favorites whose appeal depends upon a surface and vanishes with a wrinkle in the face or a crick in the knee. A sensate people move on when a surface is exhausted or when a more attractive one looms. They are like tourists—sightseeing rapidly, coming and going without deep involvement. To the secularized outlook may also be attributed the decline of the saint as a dominant type[6] and corresponding rise of the do-gooder, whose works are as visible as those of a saint without dispute over spiritual considerations. The secularized outlook also helps us to understand why the cult of celebrities is apparently pushing sanctified traditional figures like Washington into the background in favor of athletes, entertainers, and politicians of the moment—more of which we shall speak later.

Such is the meaning, as I see it, of the cult of the physical that flowers on the bathing beaches, in athletic contests, cheesecake art, and advertising; that emphasizes the tough guy, contempt for softies, the knock-out punch, big bankrolls, horsepower, firepower, manpower and brainpower.

Offsetting the picture somewhat is a perceptible drawing-away from some of the crasser models of success, physique, and sex-appeal, for example, demands for more censorship, "spiritual" best-sellers, popular evangelists like Billy Graham, Fulton J. Sheen, and Norman Vincent Peale. If they are managing to win attention from athletes, erotic queens, and "personalities," I say more power to them. But it should be noted how much evangelical appeals use secular themes—success, wealth, comfort, cures, happiness—and devices of theatricalism. I surely would not cite as examples of a spiritual trend those Hollywood Biblical opuses featuring muscular gladiators, scantily clad slave girls, and a ten million dollar

[5] It is interesting to contrast modern types with folk heroes and see that many of them seem to be watered-down—secularized—versions of figures who in myth would be miraculous supermen. For example:

Modern Type	Mythical Folk Hero
Strong man, champ	Conquering Hero (Achilles)
Smart operator	Clever hero (Maui, Coyote)
Splendid performers	Miraculous feats of Cuchulain, etc
Independent spirit (success)	Cinderella theme
Defender (G-man, etc.)	Dragon-slayer
Do-gooder	Mythical benefactor
Inventor, genius	Culture hero

[6] See John M. Mecklin, *The Passing of the Saint* (Chicago: University of Chicago Press, 1941); also Pitirim Sorokin, *Altruistic Love* (Boston: Beacon Press, 1950).

budget as no small item of the sales pitch. More encouraging is widespread, apparently genuine, admiration for figures like Gandhi and Schweitzer, though (as in all cases where ideals may be compensatory) it is hard to tell whether the image of a Schweitzer helps us to do as he did —or stay the way we are. I shall be convinced of a genuine trend when more people start founding hospitals in underdeveloped countries and Schweitzers outnumber Gables in starring parts.

The Age of Playboys

Another impression of American culture is gained from types like:

fan, fanatic, faddist, jitterbug, shutterbug, zoot-suiter, dance fiend, jazz fiend, camera fiend, rah-rah boy, Joe College, mezzanine hound, rock hound, bopster, bridge shark, life of the party, cut-up, personality kid, high stepper, playboy, party girl, dude, dandy, fashion-plate, lounge lizard, crooner, lady's man, lady killer, grandstander, headline hunter, beach bum, tennis bum, golf widow, golf hustler, joiner, joy rider, hotrodder, dragracer, speed demon, plunger, highroller, daredevil, stunt artist, wastrel, and loafer.

America at play, they seem to say.

Such types reflect an age of leisure, a shorter work week, rising luxury and productiveness (one survey estimates that within a century America will be producing as much in a seven hour day as she now does in a forty hour week), increasing life expectancy, and looming automation with its nightmare of idleness. In such a setting, the hard work ethic can hardly be expected to survive long as an important hero-making force. The serious reason for work, and for admiration of the hero of work, has always been survival. But what sense does that make when the bulk of the population are working for luxuries and a man at the subsistence level in good health (in the Western world at least) is a genuine curiosity? There is also the question of the status-value of leisure. How long will it take time-clock-punchers to find out that status can be gained not only by expensive things but by fads, games, and play that might come cheaply. Those who argue that competition for money and goods will keep the economic system going forget, perhaps, that with survival no longer an issue competition is merely a game—and that bingo, tennis, and beach sports are games too, and that if work can be fun, play can be even more fun. It may be hard to keep people enthralled with the old idea that one has to work in order to be happy and have self-respect. They may see that you can play hard at games, hobbies, entertainments, fads, rituals, and cults with all the status-rewards that now come from work. At any rate, as far as hero types are concerned, I envisage a shift to a play-oriented culture away from the work ethic so important in the past, and a corresponding change in the character of our models—the crooner, playboy, athlete, great lover, entertainer, socialite, best dressed woman, dandy, games-player or dramatic star perhaps looming as large in the national consciousness as work heroes like Franklin, Carnegie, and Edison once did. Our future Edison may well be devoting his talent to improving the pinball machine. A top production man will have to go some to compete for news interest with what a Texas oil millionaire does in Paris with a kootchie dancer. It is quite possible that "playboy" will lose the derisive rating it now has and become a term of esteem—perhaps like disc jockey or master of ceremonies. And there will be playgirls—and further multiplication of play heroes in as yet undiscovered channels of splendiferous leisure.

Much of this development will probably be among those types we have called "splendid performers," because of the increasing prominence of mass communications and spectator sports in the scene of American leisure.

Widespread increase in the spirit of play seems bound to affect other values than work. Carnival has a place in the lives of people who live with discipline, but what if we have carnival most of the time? Can we become a nation of television addicts, and sport and fad followers, and musical comedy fans without, at least, some loss of seriousness, maturity, commitment, and the tragic spirit? I think that emphasis on play favors a hedonistic ethic in which things are evaluated according to whether they are "fun"; there is enthusiasm for the game, but morale is volatile; it is easy to "give up" and not so important to carry the Message to Garcia.

The "Whole Man"—Is He a Hero Today?

With opportunities for self-choice and self-cultivation in the new leisure, shall we find the whole man whom the humanists admire emerging as the hero of modern life?

There have been, and still are, incredibly versatile people (Goethe, Cellini, Leonardo, Bacon, Franklin, Schweitzer, Churchill)—"whole men" fitting Carlyle's specification: "I have no notion of a truly great man that could not be *all* sorts of men." But opposite—almost a caricature—are favorites of today whose appeal consists of one thing (often trivial): pinups and profiles; movie and television stars; crooners and spellbinders; playboys, headliners, and other splendid performers. The athlete comes onto the field for the big sock, the politician gives his great speech, the evangelist thrills twenty thousand people in a stadium—what are these but specialists in a certain kind of impression? What do they have aside from the ability to give the crowd this moment? The specialist appears to be the man of the hour. Considering that both "expert" and "specialist" have univocally heroic ratings, and looking at the current array of American heroes (both as types and as personalities), there seems little reason to say that men of broad ability—"whole men"—are entering the top places of popular choice. On the contrary, what the public seems to be getting—and enthusiastically receiving—most of the time are half-men, quarter-men, or only the surfaces of men.

The hero of surfaces might be a name for leaders and celebrities who are basically showmen who play to the crowd, specialize in impression, and never muff their parts. They are like men wearing sandwich-boards; however familiar to the public, little can be seen of them except their surfaces. They fit peculiarly well into a society where mass communication, audience acceptability and role playing skill—not being a "whole man"—are the new obligations of greatness.

Audience-Direction and the Hero of Surfaces

"So you'd like to break into big-time television. And you think you have talent. You want to be discovered. You want to be a star. And who can blame you! It's exciting. It's glamorous."

ED SULLIVAN[7]

Let us consider the orientation of our society toward heroes of surfaces. Types like the:

star, soloist, virtuoso, artist, entertainer, drum majorette, pompon girl, master of ceremonies, crooner, torchsinger, premiere danseuse, prima donna, disc jockey, maestro, comedian, show girl, showman, fashion model, stunt artist, daredevil, grandstander, water skier, polo-player, big leaguer, headliner, favorite, lion, man of the people, pin-up girl, democrat, celebrity, spell binder, charmer, it-girl, glamor girl, beauty queen, personality kid, and smoothie,

suggest a life style of which the goal is being the center of attention and pleasing audiences. These types show that our lives are oriented, to a large and growing extent, toward shows of one kind or another—we are audience-directed. Mass communication makes it easier for the audience to be involved in a show and harder for a performer to have a private life of his own. Within this setting is the audience-directed person, who does not reject publicity with any old-fashioned insistence on privacy, but lives for

[7] "Break into TV?" San Diego *Union*, Sept. 23, 1956, p. E-7.

a moment of glory before an audience when he has the chance to shine or stand out. The audience-directed person is given names like "stage-struck," "grandstander," "showman," "ham," and "show-off." To him life is a glorious goldfish bowl. If he cannot be a star, then he assigns his highest value to being part of the supporting cast or following of a star (some roles of which are indicated by names like fan, fanatic, autograph hunter, stage-door Johnny, studio audience, or "my public" as stars call their devoted followers). Many devotees have an inner life so directed by mass communication that they carry radios when walking down the street (I suggest they be called communications-zombies).

An audience-directed performer makes the theatre his life in the broad sense, *lives* "for his public," "his art." Ethics are not for their own sake but for the audience; thus a leading disc jockey states his philosophy of integrity:

> I never knock. But at the same time I'm sincere. I have integrity. Nine out of ten records I play, I don't think are good records. But they are commercial records. I play the things they want to hear. Unless I do, I don't have an audience, and therefore I have denied my station, my second integrity, and audience. And the station loses the account of my advertiser, my third integrity. But they're all wrapped up into one integrity—to build the biggest audience there is.[8]

A professional, of course, is more likely to make such a philosophy explicit than a society woman, athlete, or other amateur splendid performer; and is more likely to be audience-directed to the point where *all* other values depend on it. As explained by the television comedian Milton Berle: "I'm the kind of guy who needs an audience." To which his wife added: "Milton will do anything, absolutely anything, to make . . . people laugh."

Audience-direction is often a hidden assumption that flavors the activity of many non-professional performers—teachers, writers, intellectuals, habitual raconteurs, lifes of the party, athletes, and stunt artists.[9] Such people "come into their own" only before a group.

Audience-direction such as I am describing is probably a specific kind

[8] Howard Miller, *Time*, April 29, 1957, p. 50.
[9] Jacqueline Cochrane, the famous woman air-race and stunt-flier, was once asked why she had "spent so much time and energy" on flying and "taken so many risks." She seemed puzzled but said it was something that would have to be rationalized because the needs it met had such deep roots. A revealing observation might be her peculiar vanity—an awareness of audiences—often irritating to other fliers: "I always tried when getting out of my plane, no matter how hard the trip, to look as nearly as possible as if I had just stepped out of a band-box. Even some of the women pilots did not appreciate this flair of mine." Jacqueline Cochrane, *The Stars at Noon* (Boston: Little, Brown & Co., Inc., 1954), pp. 46, 66.

of what Riesman has called the "other-directed" character.[10] Yet there is this important difference: Other-directedness usually means living with a sensitivity to the cues provided by others and responding so as to conform and blend, anxiety being felt at failure to be like others. But the audience-directed person aims to "wow" the crowd, and so may make a point of being as conspicuous as possible, perhaps by being a colorful "character," cut-up, or stunt artist. (There is always the question of how much of "individuality" is really being oneself and how much is trying to make an impression.)

"Getting out in front," it seems to me, is becoming more important in our lives. To meet an audience—how much is it already the ambition of America?—of toastmaster's clubs; of people studying merchandising, leadership, teaching, public relations, and how to improve personalities; of young people working at arts, sports, or spectacular hobbies; of innumerable contestants straining to break records. With opportunities and attractions of getting before an audience increasing, how can our society help but become more audience-directed.

This is hardly more than the price we should expect to pay for living in a world where theatre in the broad sense is so emphasized. There seems no harm in a little playacting and showing off. But we might do well to look at some of the shortcomings of the audience-directed character as he becomes more important in our lives. One shortcoming is that though he thinks of himself as a group servant, he is likely actually to be a showoff and epitomize rank egotism, however skillfully rationalized. Consequently, he illustrates egotism to those who use him as a model (they learn from him not how to be good but how to make a good impression—a difference as vast as that between Jesus and Machiavelli). Another shortcoming of audience-direction in general is that, however pleasing smoothies and showmen can be, as Riesman has pointed out: there is little effective pressure toward morality in an other-directed society. Rather, it is immediate, local, and temporary conformity that pays off—not adherence to principle. The accent is on acceptability of surface. And, as another thinker[11] has pointed out, hidden below acceptable traits may be different traits equally needed for success but not so acceptable (such as craftiness or exploitativeness) and not called by their right names.

So one wonders about the considerable hypocrisy and corruption possible in these heroes of surfaces. All this in people whose charm cannot

[10] David Riesman with Nathan Glazer and Reuel Denney, *The Lonely Crowd* (New Haven: Yale University Press, 1950).

[11] Gustav Ichheiser, "Misunderstandings in Human Relations, a Study in False Social Perception," *American Journal of Sociology*, Sept. 1949, Part II, 32.

be denied; they are easy to live with, easy to love, easy to applaud, easy on the eyes.

The *effective* sanctions of an audience-directed society are not against inherent personal faults but failure to make a good impression. Where the show is everything, standards for criticism tend to be: they are "flops" as showmen, or they lack smoothness or pleasingness as persons. Types like "ham," "corny," "wallflower," "greenhorn," "square," and "odd-ball" fall in this perspective. One of the main villains of an audience-directed society is the "troublemaker," the antithesis of goodfellow, smoothie, and splendid performer because he fails to make a good impression, disrupts the act, and offends the audience. Although our society frowns on trouble-makers, this is no assurance of a high standard of conduct. The smoothies may be worse intrinsically than troublemakers (an honest troublemaker, in my opinion, is sometimes worth two smoothies), but their defects do not show and they usually have the consent of the crowd. Only the surface and the style, not the person or thing itself is criticized. As the popular song goes, "It ain't what you do, it's the way that you do it"; do it in style and you can do about anything. The unforgivable failure is to lose the audience by clumsy performance or lack of interest in the part.[12] Those who meet the audience situation best become expert role-players, brilliant entertainers, and smart publicists. They make themselves supremely acceptable by having glamor, charm, verve, chic, or "it." They know how to play to the crowd and can steal the show from less agile performers. Even the "plain man" may be an agile performer.

An inner-directed person may protest against the excessive role playing of modern society,[13] as did Anne Lindbergh in *Gift from the Sea*: "The most exhausting thing in life is being insincere. That is why so much of social life is exhausting." But for a smoothie, charmer, goodfellow, or splendid performer role playing is not necessarily a source of inner stress (at least, if so, it is also a major route to success). Successful audience-directed living requires a bewildering variety of roles, or a tiring monotony of the same one, for it is subject to the rule of trying to "please everybody." An old-fashioned person lives according to a few styles with

---

[12] True, to *steal a show* unscrupulously is also a fault (gloryhog, show-off), but venial when done smoothly—even a kind of heroism.

[13] Types like the climber, joiner, crasher, favorite, celebrity, showman and stunt-artist show the frantic effort to ingratiate oneself, if necessary to crash into group recognition by any means, whether stripping for cheesecake photography or going over Niagara in a barrel. C. W. Mills describes self-alienation as one of the prices of role-playing in business, *Whitecollar*, pp. 184-188. Also see William H. Whyte's incisive analysis of the neuroses of the organization man, especially at the top executive level. *The Organization Man*, Chap. XII.

which he has had experience; but the audience-directed hero of today may play with ease parts ranging from men-about-town to pillar of the church. He is at home anywhere, has "stage presence," and always manages to land on his feet.

Whether people, however amused and amusing, can find real satisfaction in an audience-directed orientation is another question. The effort to keep up front, put on a show, capture the crowd, has in it a frustration that might be likened (however tritely) to grasping for bubbles—as the "hits" or "kicks" of satisfying an audience may be called. This is the emptiness expressed in Ecclesiastes. However skilled a performer, he never knows when the day will come that he loses his audience (whether because they are frivolous or he is slipping). Showmen know it well; so do hostesses; some teachers find such a disappointment late in life: they have always been "popular" and devoted themselves unsparingly to pleasing their audiences, but now they no longer "draw"; the students think they are old fogeys and pack the classrooms of younger teachers. There are also frustrations for the audience, first for the audience member who wants to get out in front but hasn't made it; he watches, green with envy; then for audience members who just sit there for show after show, debauched by entertainment, jaded by "pitches" of one kind or another. They see so many shows that they forget which is which—receiving experiences which do not (except by luck) fit their precise needs. They are in the same plight as the Christmas shopper who doesn't know what he is looking for, and can't find it anyway because it is lost in piles of goods on the counters. They don't get what they really want, but they pay the price anyway, applauding with politeness and growing ennui, while the performers "break their backs" to "wow" the blasé audience. Such seems to me to be the circular frustration built into the audience-directed life, whether for the performer, who fears the day when he will slip, or the spectators, who applaud and yearn, but also sigh with boredom.

Is not audience-direction a sign of more than just the opportunities of mass communication and increased leisure, a sign also of a craving for prominence as an antidote for mass anonymity? The splendid performer may be a former "nobody" who triumphs over audience after audience while other nobodies (fans) share in his glory. If this is so, then fame for celebrities goes hand in hand with the mass' loss of identity, and audience-direction is, in part, a symptom of the underlying ills of modern society, an unwitting effort of people to restore something to their lives—an effort which, as we have suggested, is probably not being rewarded

Cult of the Good Joe: Squares, Sissies, and Eggheads

Many types seem to support the idea that the American character is intensely democratic, especially goodfellows and certain fool and villain types that have a leveling function (stuffed shirt, snob, authoritarian). The good Joe is friendly and easygoing; he fits in and likes people; he never sets himself above others but goes along with the majority; he is a good sport—but also a he-man who won't let anyone push him around where basic rights are concerned. Most of the time he is so modest that he seems almost self-effacing: even if he is president of the company you can call him by his first name; he is embarrassed to be waited on by domestic servants (or, if not, he is nudged by the impulse to say, "Let me get it for you; you got it for me the last time."); with Europeans he sometimes seems to have a kind of inferiority complex—foreigners tell him he is an "ugly American," "go home Yankee," and he may say conscientiously, "You are probably right," or "Everyone's opinion is worth listening to."

If any types have a right to be called the central theme of the American ethos, it is probably, in my opinion, this cluster: dislike of bullies, snobs, authoritarians, and stuffed shirts; sympathy for the underdog; and liking for the good Joe or regular fellow who, for all his rough-and-ready air wouldn't try to dominate anybody, not even his wife. Let us call this cluster the good Joe complex. Innumerable popular favorites and elected candidates show how important it is to the American people; the last four Presidents seem to have embodied aspects of the good Joe more successfully than their opponents. It may well be the key to success at the polls—to be a better Joe than the other fellow. It is without doubt an enormous source of generosity and justice in the American character, doing much to offset—even throw into confusion—those who believe in the stereotype of Yankee acquisitiveness.

I place good Joe at the center of the complex because it seems to me that he provides the positive ideal which is a reason for the others. The key to mockery of squares and oddballs may be a liking for and wish to be like a good Joe; similarly contempt for eggheads: a fair amount of "anti-intellectualism" in America may mean not dislike of intellect per se, not even an overpowering practicality, but simply the wish to be a good Joe. Likewise, reaction against prudes, bluenoses, sticklers, and such, may not spell "revolt" against puritanism so much as a dislike of people who are too stiff and fussy to be regular fellows. A dude may offend our sense of democracy and may also be a sissy, but most important his fancy manners hint to us that he is not a good Joe—were he to display the redeeming traits of the good Joe, we could forgive him many conceits (as cases like F. D. R. and Diamond Jim Brady show).

Placing good Joe so high among the American values implies that the strong man (champ, cowboy, bronc-buster, strong and silent man, and so on) no longer occupies center stage among American hero types. Are there not signs of a change in the American heroic image—more of the good Joe and less of the tough guy—weakening of the father's role—equality of the sexes (implying less of the strong man in men—or more of it in women)—obligations of the salesman and organization man to be a good talker—even a little gabby—at Toastmaster's clubs, winning friends and customers? As Joe talks more and gets along with people better, he must stop asserting himself, must act in a softer fashion than the old strong man ideal would allow—and more and more, words like sissy will lose their sting.

Failure to understand the good Joe complex I believe is a major source of the misunderstanding of Americans by non-Americans. Joe is a native type, as distinctive of America as jazz and rock-and-roll; there is probably no precisely corresponding type complex in any other country. The Germans surely do not have it; English "fair play" is not good Joeism. Is Khrushchev's burly clowning the Russian equivalent? Do they also favor the underdog and dislike the bully and authoritarian? It seems to me that outsiders who do not have an equivalent concept stereotype Americans as greedy imperialists (they don't appreciate Joe's generosity and live-and-let-live spirit)—or mistake Joe's equalitarianism, tolerance, and wish to be a good sport for weakness, lack of dignity, unsureness of self, or even vulgarity. Americans make mistakes, to be sure; they commit crimes; but a people cannot be properly judged for either their achievements or failures unless the world understands what they are trying to be.

Democracy carries a question mark in the hands of good Joe, for, although he is an equalitarian in opposition to bullies, authoritarians, stuffed shirts, dudes, and snobs, and wouldn't impose on anybody, you can't make a very good case that he favors a liberal democracy of the kind envisaged by J. S. Mill. Joe is tolerant enough; but he doesn't debate well; he is too good natured to push the point home; he doesn't value himself for independence of opinion (a legislature of good Joes would probably not need congressional immunity for speech), nor does he appreciate the eccentricity so prized by Mill. The democracy which good-fellows favor emphasizes belongingness and conformity, the negative side of which holds squares and eggheads in contempt. Surely good Joe democracy is not a laissez-faire individualism, for Joe is too well adjusted to be an independent spirit, too friendly to be uncooperative. He might even be a symbol under which a disguised trend toward collectivism could gather force, as William H. Whyte has suggested. Let us look, however, a little more at the part played by goodfellows in the corporateness of American life before reaching an opinion, for the prevalence of good Joeism could indicate more than it seems to.

Corporateness and Pseudo-Integration

We have just seen three facets of American society—admiration for specialists, audience-direction, and the good Joe complex—which seem to show greater integration of American life—whether a vast drama of mass communication or interdependence in which people work together more closely and smoothly. The growing corporateness has been evident at least since 1932, when John Dewey heralded the passing of the old individualism and called for a new individualism consistent with the fact that "associations tightly or loosely organized more and more define the opportunities, the choices, and the actions of individuals." It seems plain that America is becoming a land of overlapping or shoulder to shoulder structures in which there is no frontier, and even the forests and wild life are managed by a staff of rangers. In this crowded world where leisure and "getting away from it all" are deceptively symbolized by the fishing pole and the trailer, leisure seems only to plunge us into more corporateness, whether audience participation, bureaucratized play, or countless clubs, hobby, country, health, athletics, books, drama, and so on.

But granting pervasive corporateness, what is the nature of social integration where specialists, smooth role-players, and good Joes are major models? It is doubtful that we are being forced into a closer fit simply by technological development and population growth. The actual integration of corporate life may be quite different from what appears on the surface —weak when it seems strong, loose and individuated when it seems close knit, transient when it seems durable, poorly adjusted when it seems well adjusted—because of, for one thing, *role playing*. I suspect that whenever demands are put on people today, the first thing they do is play a role; after that they figure out what to do or how to change themselves, if necessary (but it is often not necessary). Role playing is one of the cheapest ways of adjusting to almost any situation, from a mother-in-law who irks you to the prospect of a concentration camp. Moderns are more versatile role-players than the tradition bound men of yesterday; they can give you almost anything you want, within reason. Splendid performers and many heroes of social acceptability are models of skillful role-playing. Skilled role-players, amateur or professional, are able to give a pretty good facsimile of whatever is required; they can provide (in organizations at least), team spirit, camaraderie, sympathy, love, devotion to duty, or knowledge of the job. Discounting types (stuffed shirt, phoney, etc.) do not counteract role playing but simply weed out its crasser forms and favor the skillful. However, since such role playing is not a genuine commitment, it cannot be a strong and durable social bond, however much it looks like one. Let us, therefore, call any relationship where role playing implies a greater degree of solidarity than actually exists *pseudo-integration*.[14] I would say that our versatile role-players—embodied in types like the goodfellow, gladhander, smoothie and smart operator—show that a kind of solidarity is beginning to prevail in American life, a solidarity that is neither close cooperation and togetherness nor individualism, but a facade of fellowship that often disguises anomie and soothes some of its pains.

To describe this condition, let me distinguish several views of what is happening to American solidarity. One is of a rather simple swing from individualism to collectivism; it can be seen in Orwell's *1984,* Hayek's *Road to Serfdom,* or Whyte's *Organization Man.* The main problem in such a trend is to keep one's autonomy. On the other side, the anomie school, following Durkheim and Mayo, paints an almost opposite picture of modern society: decaying human relations, loss of consensus and the capacity to work together. The solution suggested by Durkheim and Mayo is to build morale. How are these pictures to be reconciled?—we can hardly have decaying solidarity and growing collectivism at the same time. Nor is it safe to say that either is wrong. A somewhat more complicated view accepts the fact of anomie and explains totalitarianism as a kind of compensation for it. This view is expressed

[14] Pseudo-solidarity or pseudo-*Gemeinschaft* will do perhaps as well. What I mean is something pretty close to what Tonnies referred to as the inherent hypocrisy of *Gesellschaft,* except that role-playing ability in modern mobile society has increased beyond what Tonnies could be expected to have visualized—for example, faking on personality-tests as recommended by Whyte, or political staging. I mean something more all embracing than pseudo-*Gemeinschaft* as defined by Merton: "a device for improving one's economic and political position . . . subtle methods of salesmanship in which there is feigning of personal concern with the client in order to manipulate him better." Robert K. Merton, *Social Theory and Social Structure* (Glencoe, Illinois: Free Press of Glencoe, Inc., 1949), pp. 103, 220. The meaning is broader, and bears comparison with Wilhelm Ropke's: "The place of a genuine integration created by genuine communities, which requires the ties of proximity, natural roots and the warmth of direct human relationships, has been taken by a pseudo-integration . . ." created by the market, central organization, secondary controls, mass amusements, and mass education. *The Social Crisis of Our Time* (Chicago: University of Chicago Press, 1950), p. 10. Role playing versatility is the essence of this pseudo-integration as I see it: the freedom that enables an actor to *leave* as well as to take part in the play.

by Erich Fromm (*Escape from Freedom* and *The Sane Society*) and by Eric Hoffer, *The True Believer*. Discontented people escape from responsibility for themselves (freedom) by plunging into totalitarian movements. The important thing, as Fromm points out, is to relieve the unhappiness of the alienated people in modern society by a constructive form of solidarity—democratic communitarianism—before we get something much worse. Solidarity is, then, an escape from, or a cure for, lack of solidarity; but, unlike the anomie school, solidarity is viewed as a threat to the individual.

I would like to make a picture not quite as alarming as looming totalitarianism, but dismal enough for those who hope to repair anomie and build morale. It seems to me that modern society is building a *facsimile of solidarity* by adjustment techniques and expert role playing. This facsimile is quite different from—probably not even an approach to—totalitarian, sectarian, or *Gemeinschaft* integration. Pseudo-solidarity is comforting to those who like to believe that fellowship is replacing loneliness—just as it is alarming to those who fear totalitarianism. It comforts people by purporting to fill an actual lack in society. It is neither plain anomie nor the dreadful organization of Whyte and Orwell, but a pseudo-integration that has the earmarks of solidarity but lacks its most essential component—loyalty.

Even when joining and belonging seem at an all time high,[15] we must consider the possibility that much of this "organization" is pseudo and has inner weaknesses. Take, for example:

a corporation employee who loyally turns out for company parties as a "command performance" but whose feeling is "Buick today, Ford tomorrow";

a community church where in spite of large turnouts members change from Methodist to Presbyterian or Baptist to Congregational depending upon how convenient it is for their children or the distance they must walk;

[15] One has to put pictures such as the kaffeeklatsching and "hotbed of participation" described by Whyte alongside the tremendous mobility of Americans and the great amount of non-affiliation in urban areas. Studies show that from a quarter to as much as three-quarters of dwellers in some urban areas are non-affiliated aside from nominal church membership. Affiliations increase with such things as education, Protestantism, nonmanual work, marriage, number of friends, and home ownership. John C. Scott, Jr., "Membership and Participation in Voluntary Associations," *American Sociological Review*, 1957, 22:315-26. Thus one can build an argument that Americans are hyperactive joiners (at least in some classes and occupational groups) or that many in urban areas suffer from anomie and isolation.

a suburban community with all the appearance of rootedness (trees, well-kept lawns, large families, home improvement projects, active neighborliness), but people sell out in a year or two and a new family picks fruit from the trees an old family watered;

a trailer community with remarkable neighborly spirit, but people who have been talking together like old friends one evening say "Bye bye" the next morning and never see each other again.

Such examples show the lack of commitment—indeed the casualness—characteristic of membership in modern society—extending even to friendship and marriage. One does not get an uncomfortable feeling of shallowness, however, because of the profusion of superficial feelings and the ease with which relationships are established—with the same person or someone else—at the drop of a hat, as it were.

Let me here try to say more fully what the weakness consists of. First, the permanence is only an illusion created by an easily assumed role. When we Americans want to draw closer, we do not establish true solidarity, but instead we play a part that (like the lines of a romantic play) looks like the real thing but would be the same were a different actor to enter the play between scenes and continue in the part. Thus, we are able to generate the appearance of fellowship even with strangers—at a party, while camping, on a bus ride, and so on—but this easy camaraderie evaporates quickly; the campfire is deserted, only empty glasses remain in the barroom. Expert role-players are able to work together as committee members, team players, and organization men, in varying combinations without undue time lost getting used to one another, even getting to know one another. Another way of saying this is that, by role playing, Americans are pretty good at creating *esprit de corps* but not morale.[16] They can *look* devoted, interested, and so on, but when it comes to something more demanding than a temporary role display, they may be apathetic about community affairs, church, politics, or labor union participation.

One of the signs of pseudo-integration is tension and neurotic conflict in intimate, important, and freely chosen roles. This could be likened to friction in a machine between parts that look well mated. In the human organization the friction comes not from sand in the bearings but from

[16] Herbert Blumer distinguishes three kinds of morale: sacred, romantic, and practical, the last of which might be described as a rational determination to get the job done; in W. F. Ogburn, ed., *American Society in Wartime* (Chicago: University of Chicago Press, 1943), pp. 207-232. My remark about the difficulty of Americans in creating morale applies more to sacred and romantic than to practical.

ambivalent and alienated feelings[17] about work and the people we live with, for example, chronic hypocrisy or distaste for seeming what one does not feel. A passage from Boris Pasternak's *Doctor Zhivago* by no means applies only to Russian society:

> The great majority of us are required to live a life of constant, systematic duplicity. Your health is bound to be affected if, day after day, you say the opposite of what you feel, if you grovel before what you dislike and rejoice at what brings you nothing but misfortune. Our nervous system isn't just a fiction, it's a part of our physical body, like the teeth in our mouth. It can't be forever violated with impunity. . . .

Another aspect of pseudo-integration is not being sure where one stands. Nothing is entirely reliable, however reliable it looks. On the other hand, awareness of unreliability and facade is no excuse for challenging something. Everyone creeps about, not wanting to rock the boat. Fred Demara, the "great impostor," explains his amazing success in infiltrating organizations that should have had enough integrity to quickly find him out:

> If you act like you belong somewhere, even people who know you don't belong are hesitant to call you on it. People are so insecure. Deep in their souls they don't feel they belong either.

Does not Demara symbolize pseudo-integration in American society? In areas where people are unsure of where they stand because everybody is playing roles, it is no surprise to find: outsiders inside, poor adjustment that looks good, work with a wish to escape, easy breakup of relationships, easy breakdown of the man.

Such things, added to obvious mobility—trailerism, migration, rootlessness, employee turnover, religious switching, family breakup, and the like—show society to be stable like the vortex of a whirlpool is stable. The parts are highly interchangeable; there is little attachment for place, person or organization. A smoothly working organization may be efficient for routine operations, but break down in crisis because there is no real interconnection (loyalty, binding obligation) beyond role playing and utilitarian exchange. What I am saying applies to small groups as well as vast bureaucracies.[18] The smoothness of organizations—from small teams to entire staffs, regiments, and labor forces—results

[17] The sense of discomfort and tension in modern relationships is expressed in a "beat" poem by Lawrence Lipton, "A Funky Blues for All Squares, Creeps, and Cornballs, *The Holy Barbarians* (New York: Julian Messner, 1959), p. 211.

[18] Numerous studies, following Durkheim, Cooley, and Mayo, have shown that small groups are the main social units of a large organization and that larger loyalties are weak or merely abstract. See, for example, Edward A. Shils and Morris Janowitz, "Cohesion and Disintegration in the Wehrmacht in World War II," *Public Opinion Quarterly*, XII (1948), 280-315.

from technical and role playing skill, not morale and character—people of very different (even incompatible) attitudes may have the skill to work together and look all right. From a structural standpoint, however, it is a house of cards.

Truly durable integration is only possible, I suppose, where there are lifelong associations and roots, affections resulting in and from real intimacy, and education stressing commitment to one set of shared values as a core of unbreakable morale. These conditions are plainly missing from American life; nor do I suppose that we could return to them. In the present fluid multigroup society, where organizations compete for men who don't stay put, it seems that the tightest structure we are likely to get is pseudo-integration of a convincing, but not durable, kind. All this does not seem to me to approach very dangerously the kind of totalitarianism one might see in Nazi, Japanese, Chinese, or Soviet youth brought up in conditions different from what we have been considering.

Our real path, it seems to me, is not a swing from old-fashioned freedom toward a totalitarian kind of solidarity but rather a different course: pseudo-integration of good Joes and team workers who may look like they would die for the organization but really wouldn't think of it. The movement of American life is a spiral that does not go back to laissez faire any more than it goes toward real belongingness, but picks up anomie and belongingness and incorporates them into a complex structure, elements of which, it seems to me, are: (1) role obligations of a narrow (learnable, exchangeable) character; (2) fluidity and mobility; (3) looseness of relationship (lack of loyalty, commitment, roots); (4) a *facade* of togetherness to smooth over, and try to suppress, the lack of loyalty and compensate people for their loneliness (a facade including roles such as good Joe, gladhand, smoothie, and rituals of rellowship); (5) compensatory types such as independent spirits that are an expression, possibly a safety-valve, for the wish for independence and the distaste we may feel at the hypocrisy of role playing in pseudo-solidarity; and (6) types like the smart operator, representing the *sub rosa* fluidity, mobility, and reality—the necessity for working within situations of "loyalty" and "friendship" in a quasi-Machiavellian manner if one is going to "make out."

In this tenor a closer look needs to be taken at the sociability of American society—the joining and gladhanding, business fraternalism, kaffeeklatsching, cocktail party ritual, teenage gregariousness, TV happy "families" and "friends," and the overdeveloped favorites (especially goodfellows) who embody these ideals—to see how much is compensatory, and how much is expressing and helping build the pseudo-integration I have been trying to describe. For it seems to me that Americans, for all their joining, good Joeism, audience participation, fan behavior, and rocking-and-rolling, are not getting the solidarity of real fellowship, but a make-believe of ritual and roles which compensate for a lack of these very things. In this facsimile of warmth and intimacy, social distance is not broken down unless momentarily, much is vicarious, and people in the audience may lack the qualities that their favorites possess in such lavish and often fraudulent proportions. Underlying all the fun and friendship are discontent and ambivalence.

Do-gooders and Egoists

Consistent with the picture of pseudo-integration, it seems to me, is the fact that "do-gooder" is more or less a mocking term in American society. Ideally it refers to an altruist, perhaps a Schweitzer, Gandhi, Jesus, but it actually implies that the do-gooder is somehow out of touch with the facts in American society.

In view of the obvious social value of altruism, how does one explain that about one out of three think of the do-gooder as a fool? (Somewhat the same applies to types like crusader, reformer, martyr, idealist, lady bountiful, bleeding heart, eager beaver, dollar-a-year man.) Can there be too much of anything as good as altruism?

It seems to me that this ambivalence needs to be understood in the light of certain conditions of American life—for instance, that the do-gooder is not a simple expression of good will nor do we appreciate him as such. For one thing, he runs counter to the common sense of an acquisitive economic system. We can hardly avoid the impression that for many Americans, the do-gooder is "asking for it," a kind of chump. He is also seen as an idealistic meddler who tries to change things too fast—perhaps even a radical who will precipitate us into some kind of collectivism. Such attitudes perhaps help explain why social work developed slowly as a profession in America. Also, of course, the low pay of its workers, and the tendency to regard recipients of public welfare as spongers and its donors as busybodies and bureaucrats.

With such mixed feelings, one could hardly infer that altruism was the dominant norm of American society, even though it is extolled in some quarters and exemplified by some models (martyrs, benefactors, defenders). It might be safer to say that "doing good" is among those ideals that are admired when they shine once in a while, like the lights of Christmas, but would be regarded as a great expense, if not a nuisance, if displayed at other times and places. The do-gooder has his sphere—in community chest drives, on boards of foundling homes, and the like—

but it is restricted, and if he gets into fields where altruism is not the norm, he is resented. Indeed, do we not often applaud an outstandingly generous action with the reservation, "is it practical?" or "that's not for me," rather than with a commitment for similar action ourselves? If these attitudes toward altruism are prevalent, then is not "doing good" a compensatory ritual, providing a symbol of what we would like (some people) to be but aren't ourselves?

This supposition—that the general ethos is basically egoistic and the do-gooder is more of a compensatory symbol than an expression of the real will of our society—seems to fit the fact that over three times as many hero types stress egoistic attainment (show-offs, stars, soloists, strong men, smart operators, top dogs, and so on) as stress group service, judging by a sample of type names with the following breakdown:

	number of type names	per cent
Egoistic achievement	158	60
(Strong men, top dogs, brains, smart operators, great lovers, splendid performers, independent spirits)		
Group servants	43	16
(Martyrs, defenders, do-gooders)		
Heroes of social acceptability	42	16
(Charmers, goodfellows, conformers, favorites)		
Unclassified	23	8
Total	260	100

Throw heroes of social acceptability in with group servants (though there is doubtful justification for this), and there are still twice as many "egoistic" as "altruistic" types.[19]

There may well be a critical shortage of mature love—genuine feeling for one's fellows—in modern life—below the quota necessary for individual or collective well-being.[20] We seem to have a formalism in which

[19] It may be objected, of course, that this is only a linguistic distribution—not an observation of actual behavior. Yet our presumption is that names reflect social facts—that the more roles there are the more names there will be of that kind, and vice versa.

[20] A number of sociologists and psychologists have said this in one way or another. For instance, Pitirim Sorokin, *The Reconstruction of Humanity* (Boston: Beacon Press, 1948); Alfred Adler, *Social Interest, A Challenge to Mankind* (New York: G. P. Putnam's Sons, 1939); Harry Overstreet, *The Mature Mind* (New York: W. W. Norton & Company, Inc., 1949); Karen Horney, *Neurosis and Human Growth* (New York: W. W. Norton & Company, Inc., 1950), p. 300; Karl Polanyi; Elton Mayo; F. J. Roethlisberger, *Management and Moral* (Cambridge, Mass.: Harvard University Press, 1941.)

people act parts for which they lack the heart and do things behind the scenes that do not warm the heart.[21]

Nor is the goodfellow role any proof of the contrary. We have already pointed to the spurious nature of much of this behavior. There are many levels or ways of "doing good," only a few of which deserve respect as the real thing. When a do-gooder appears on the scene, say a dollar-a-year man or a social charity worker, we are likely to analyze his motives unflatteringly, for our experience tells us that many people in America are *not* sincere do-gooders. Hence, mockery. An outright egoist even seems genuine compared with a phoney do-gooder.

In the poverty of altruism, do-gooder heroes have two main functions: the simple one of holding up the ideal of group service; and the compensatory one of filling a void (anomie) for those whose experience of altruism is insufficient, for example:

1) efforts to repair anomie by service and good will—a good part of social work, "morale" programs, workers' benefits, mental hygiene programs, and so on;

2) a "front" or ceremony of good will, to hide the dearth of real altruism, e.g., TV pot-of-gold programs, stories and movies of good-hearted persons, great lovers who bring romance to everyone, Cinderella stories showing reward to the humble (i.e., that the system is basically benevolent); and

3) do-gooders as mocked figures—meddlers, sentimentalists, Quixotes and so forth—to counterbalance the idealism of the ritual front of good will and to justify egoistic and unethical practices.

If such an analysis is correct, then the do-gooder has in the main two choices as symbol: either to simply uphold altruism, or to act in such a way as to mask the lack, even impede the progress, of good will in America. The latter occurs when he acts as a sentimental sop or when a clownish picture of a Quixote encourages people to act selfishly and reject the way of the gallant knight. Possibly, by diverting mass attention to giveaways, movie-hokum, and pseudo-philanthropy, the do-gooder gives aid to a very different underlying reality in America.[22]

In general, I feel that the social types of America are not as encouraging as the simple view of martyrs, do-gooders, and goodfellows would

[21] Charles H. Cooley, *Social Organization* (New York: Charles Scribner's Sons, 1927), pp. 56, 324-355.
[22] Thurman Arnold has developed a theory of how ritual compensates for a disreputable political and economic reality. *Symbols of Government* (New Haven: Yale University Press, 1935); *Folklore of Capitalism* (New Haven: Yale University Press, 1937).

suggest. They show that altruism is in trouble, outnumbered by egoistic and pseudo-altruistic types, and subject to mockery, but still making a strong effort to cut through shams and do some real good. Those who really wish to do good must run a gauntlet including not only the burden of service itself but competition of conformers and others who are really egoists in disguise (Machiavellian types)—for the pose of goodness is too profitable not to attract a lot of egoists. And they must be misunderstood and persecuted by those who feel their interests threatened. And on their crown of thorns they must wear the names "bleeding heart" and "egghead."

Oligarchic Tendency

Another aspect of American society which social types help in understanding is oligarchic tendency. It seems that a front of good Joeism, fellowship, and doing good often hides the fact of oligarchy and compensates us somewhat for it. An autocrat may have to play the good Joe but he is still boss. Good Joeism does not eliminate subordination, but it does make it more bearable. Goodfellows act as a buffer between beliefs in equality and brotherly love and facts such as: people don't really like you (relationships are cold, impersonal, and secondary) or they are bossing you or trying to manipulate you.

Modern sociological studies of power elites seem to support the contention of theorists like Robert Michels that oligarchic tendency is inevitable in democracies—not that it must triumph but that it is a reality to be dealt with and may even exist in disguised form. The problem of a liberal society is to hold it in check. Parallel studies of social class by W. L. Warner and colleagues show in America a social ladder with as many as six steps, and constriction of opportunity as one approaches the upper-upper level, mobility and equalitarianism notwithstanding.

If we ask what American social types tell about all this, I would say they do reflect considerable oligarchy and stratification. You have, of course, the climber and others that reflect climbing, such as the snob, the crasher, the comer, and the self-made man. Many indicate a favored position in the social structure (fat cat, smart operator, V.I.P., big boy), concentration of power in the hands of a few (top dog, big wheel), or decision in the hands of a few (brains and experts). We have noted an oligarchic ("king-of-the-hill") tendency in the whole array of winners—strong men, champs, bosses, top dogs, wheels, smart operators, and others. Conformers and joiners (embodied in heroes of social acceptability) do not necessarily present a different picture: though equalitarian in theme, the regular fellow and good Joe can contribute much to build up the phalanx that supports the man of power. Smoothies and smart operators can climb by "personality" and their front of the good Joe (or other models of social acceptability). The good Joe role can be played by bosses, even dictators (Huey Long in Louisiana, George Orwell's "Big Brother"). Deviant types such as square, crackpot, renegade, and traitor make it harder to stand apart and criticize, and, I suspect, favor the despot and authoritarian. Nor is the message of the splendid performers different. Do they not increase audience dependency and, while stressing "individuality" as color or stealing the show, focus glory on one and become excessively influential as personalities (the "cult of personality"). Such social types seem compatible with oligarchy. One does not get a very clear picture of democracy in America from joiners, crowd-pleasers, and smoothies really climbing into positions of privilege or influence, and top dogs admired for the weight they can throw around.

In opposition, however, are leveling and deflating types (big head, stuffed shirt, snob, brass hat, authoritarian, tyrant, bully) also independent spirits who stand apart from organization, hierarchy, climbing, and powerseeking. But one must take account of the ability of social types to serve as symbols or buffers preventing the awareness of facts discrepant with the ideal (in this case equalitarianism), and the deceptiveness of skilled role playing, which, if anything, is growing in spite of the screening and pruning work of discounting types. We have observed that an independent spirit could stand as a symbol of a liberty that, for the many, does not in fact exist; that bosses can backslap and softsoap their way into popularity by playing the good Joe and smoothie, without being discounted as authoritarians, phoneys, or stuffed shirts. It is conceivable that a leader using such symbols could lead the mass into a stronger oligarchy. Also favoring oligarchy seem to be the sensate emphasis (making Americans susceptible to anyone who can deliver the goods, without close scrutiny of his ethics) and freedom of role choice (seen now not as democratic opportunity but confusion of identity, a loss of the sense of who one is, which can become an anomic need to seek a self in a stronger collectivity, as suggested by writers like Fromm and Hoffer).

I do not, then, see a clear balance in favor of the democratic hero, in spite of the reassuring good Joe, leveling types, romanticizing of independent spirits, and lip service to traditional figures like Jefferson and Lincoln.

The New American: Good Joe, Smart Operator, and Playboy

What, then, is the dominant model of America? Having gone through hundreds of types representing the diversity of the American character, is it possible to point to a few? I have no statistics to present but may, perhaps, give an impression here—that three models (the good Joe, the smart operator, and the playboy) are most typical of the new American character that is forming. I see a composite of these images: the American who wants to be an easy going Joe with plenty of friends; who "lives it up," doesn't work too hard; and is smart enough to get machines or other people to do what he doesn't want to do. I do not see an emphasis on the Machiavellian lion, Neanderthal strong man, hard working puritan, Daniel Boone, or persevering seeker or climber. Top dogs are all right, but who wants ulcers?—better a smart operator getting some of the cream without responsibility. It makes sense that admiration for the smart operator-playboy leads to derision of the physical strong men (who wants muscles in an age when nobody walks?), of the do-gooder, and of other heroes of service and self-sacrifice. Enough alienation is built into the smart operator-playboy that he stops short of an all out effort or full approval of those who go "all the way" for any social cause, job, or ideal. The wish to take part in a show, however, is a real incentive, for he is audience-directed and likes the limelight (especially when one considers that maximum effort is usually required only when the lights are on). This may not be a very inspiring type of man, but he is pleasant and easy to live with—sensible, too (like the turtle, he knows when to pull his neck in). These three types—the good Joe, smart operator, and playboy—seem to me to sum up, as far as three types could, the aspirations and character of one hundred and seventy million different people—what the new American character is coming to be. I think that such a type of man fits a society where pseudo-integration is the prevalent organization. For in pseudo-integration you do not put yourself out too far; you play it smart, act the good Joe, and use leisure as a relief from the tensions of excessive role playing, perhaps even as a quest for self.

Deterioration of the Hero

A final question concerns the general quality of contemporary models. An integrated society would, no doubt, present one character model for all, or at least a well fitted series so that the people who followed them could live and work well together. A good society—whether highly integrated or not—would have models of high caliber—possibly supermen (whether of saintly, military, commercial, intellectual, or other mold). I am sorry to say that my impression from the entire array of American heroes is that they are neither consistent nor predominantly of high caliber. Rather, we seem to have a mélange with confusing effects on identity: sensate emphasis—taking it easy, living it up, showing off—transfer of effort from work to play—decline of the whole man in favor of the specialist—loss of character implicit in the hero of surfaces—cult of the good Joe at the expense of individuality, creativity, and perhaps even democracy—likelihood that many types are serving to compensate for what we really haven't got. Unpleasant realities, such as egoism, exploitation, chiseling, oligarchy, alienation, and pseudo-integration, seem visible through the types.

In other words, I would concur in the view that the hero has deteriorated. Compared with a reasonable standard, whether traditional or arbitrarily defined, he is not holding up a very inspiring picture. This has been said in various ways since Carlyle lamented the loss of the great man in *On Heroes and Hero Worship*. I see no reason to differ with this or with the tenor of more recent remarks about the decline of the titan, the passing of the saint, the age of the common man, the bum as culture hero, the age of celebrity gods,[23] from my own survey. I hope to add, however,

[23] Some studies which throw interesting light on change—or deterioration—in the hero are: Leo Lowenthal, "The Triumph of Mass Idols" in *Literature, Popular Culture, and Society* (Englewood Cliffs, N.J.: Prentice-Hall, Inc., 1961); Sigmund Diamond, *The Reputation of the American Businessman* (Cambridge, Mass.: Harvard University Press, 1955); Patricke Johns-Heine and Hans H. Gerth, "Values in Mass Periodical Fiction, 1921-1940" *Public Opinion Quarterly*, 1949, 13:105-113; H. J. Friedsam, "Bureaucrats as Heroes," *Social Forces*, 1954, 32:269-274; John M. Mecklin, *The Passing of the Saint* (Chicago: University of Chicago Press, 1941); Leo Gurko, *Heroes, Highbrows and the Popular Mind* (New York: The Bobbs-Merrill Company, Inc., 1953); Raymond Giraud. *The Unheroic Hero* (New Brunswick, N.J.: Rutgers University Press, 1957); William H. Whyte's analysis of the organization man in contemporary fiction shows the hero characteristically accepting (succumbing or adjusting to) the system, *The Organization Man*, Part IV; Malcolm Boyd, *Christ and the Celebrity Gods* (Greenwich, Connecticut: Seabury Press, 1958); P. A. Sorokin, *The Crisis of Our Age*, pp. 66-67, holds that heroes of art and literature have deteriorated into pathological types; Margaret Dalziel, *Popular Fiction 100 Years Ago* (Philadelphia: Dufour Editions, 1959) holds heroes of modern fiction are morally debased; Edmund Fuller in *Man in Modern Fiction* (New York: Random House, 1958) claims that writers such as Tennessee Williams, James Jones, Norman Mailler, Philip Wylie, and Jack Kerouac, in depicting slobs and depraved characters as typical of human conduct are expressing self-hatred toward the human race; Joseph Wood Krutch is notable for having stated the thesis of the decline of the tragic hero in *The Modern Temper* (New York: Harcourt, Brace and World, Inc., 1929); nor should we neglect Jose Ortega y Gasset's comments in *The Revolt of the Masses* (New York: W. W. Norton & Co., Inc., 1932) on the character of mass man and his heroes.

in following pages, a few details on ways in which heroic models have deteriorated, as well as some general theory of what it means when this happens to a society.

It seems to me that in any society the hero normally acts as a jack—to lift people above where they would be without the model. Statistically the model must be better than the average in character or achievement if he is to raise the level of aspiration. Indeed, to inspire people, he should be considerably better than the ordinary (without, of course, so passing the ordinary that he no longer seems human). If, on the other hand, models do not stand well above the general level, or are so inconsistent that they cancel out one another, then it might be said that they do not perform their proper function. Worse, if models were *below* the average level of character and achievement in the population, a dismal situation indeed would be expected—demoralization of much of the population, alienation from models because they are unworthy (or because "good" ones seem unrealistic), lowering of morale—perhaps one might properly speak of decadence.

It seems to me that American models have deteriorated in the following ways:

1) the bulk of the positive models are not much, if any, better than the average man, except in some narrowly specialized, often trivial, feature (looks, entertainment gimmick, manner before the camera, and so on);

2) "character" (understood as higher moral or spiritual qualities— nobility, saintliness, intellectual honesty, integrity, or such) is not outstandingly illustrated by most American models; some are downright bad;

3) likable types like the goodfellow and smoothie are easily simulated by people who do not really have the good will implied by the role, so that there is doubt whether they are actually illustrating goodness or just skills of maintaining front;

4) the models are so diverse and contradictory that they do not favor consensus as to basic values or roles required of all;

5) the functions of many models seem to have shifted from the normal one of holding up an ideal that people are trying to achieve, to compensating people for lack of these qualities and making them feel more comfortable about not trying to be that way or pretending to be that way—therefore, in many cases, licensing something different from what the model implies.

Are we not ambivalent toward our heroes at least in part because they give such a confused and uninspiring message, and because we see through them to realities that invalidate the models?

Part of the ambivalence may be that really, underneath, the average man cherishes genuine noble models of which he is almost ashamed to speak[24] and is mildly outraged at what he sees of the American character in public communication. He assents as a member of an audience but secretly resents popular types. Does not a hero of unimpeachable integrity—a Lindbergh, a Schweitzer—bring a sigh of relief? We have no way here of exploring such secret and tender recesses of American idealism. But the superficiality of public models should not lead us to neglect them.

I do not claim, of course, that a survey such as this can answer all of the questions of fact raised by these speculations—what is really going on, how populations compare with models, what proportions of models are compensatory and what proportions are holding up sincere ideals, how to determine the degree of decadence that presumably goes with inadequate models. The questions do need to be asked, and perhaps satisfactory answers will not be long forthcoming. In the meanwhile, I shall, in remaining chapters, explain some ways in which I see the hero to have deteriorated: (1) anomic types, (2) the cult of celebrities, (3) corruption of the hero, and (4) mockery of heroes. Elsewhere I have dealt with the weakness of tragedy in America.[25]

---

[24] Perhaps at the risk of his pose of sophistication (of being called bluenose, corny, Pollyanna, square, or a moral indignant). Also, there is no reason to believe that all models are verbalized and public.

[25] Americans are not a "tragic people." Their insensitivity to tragedy and its hero is analyzed in terms of an unfavorable cultural ethos (optimism, naturalism, determinism); social types such as the villain and fool which "shortcircuit" tragic perception; and actual shrinkage that has occurred in the tragic hero. "Tragedy and the American Climate of Opinion," *Centennial Review*, Vol. II, No. 4, Fall 1958, pp. 396-413; reprinted in John D. Hurrell, *Two Modern American Tragedies* (New York: Charles Scribner's Sons, 1961).

CHAPTER 5

AMERICAN ANOMIC TYPES

Beatniks, Hipsters, and Squares

A group of beatniks in Venice, California, held a protest meeting in retaliation to one by local property owners and developers seeking ways of throwing them out on grounds that they were depressing real estate values. The scene the beats chose for their meeting was an old bingo parlor, The Gas House. Expressing distaste for persons conformist enough to have real estate interests, they taped, to jazz accompaniment, a poem on the falsity of current business values, called "Funky Blues for All Squares, Creeps and Cornballs." [1]

This illustrates the place of one colorful alienated group within American society, and the language of mutual abuse between inhabitants of the "square world" and those who feel "out." The beats are not alone in their

---

[1] Lawrence Lipton, *op. cit.*

contempt for the "Square John" [2] and the "square world." A vast number make up the alienated legion of American society, whose extent we are only beginning to realize and measure accurately.[3] Beats merely draw attention to themselves more effectively. What alienated persons have in common is the need to add meaning to their lives in a society of which they do not feel part. This they do in ways sometimes covert, sometimes colorful, alarming, or criminal, for example, efforts to find "kicks."

What I shall do here is analyze "beat" values and language as an example of typing, expressing anomie[4] in society and characterizing the integration beats achieve in their search for "kicks." While they seem at an opposite pole from "gray flannel suit" conformity, their rebellion, it seems to me, is not against conformity per se (they have plenty of that), but against what I have previously called pseudo-integration—the false role playing and neurotic togetherness—of American society. While they do reject this unhappy order, they are more integrated with it than one might guess from their protest, because their relationship is dependent and parasitic. But parasitism connotes passivity and no one can accuse beats of being meek and quiet, so let us call it rebellious parasitism—a way of life within a society whose values are rejected but whose structure is used—tapped, exploited—for "kicks."

As most know, beatniks are bearded eccentrics and ne'er-do-wells and their women, who have gathered in places such as Grant Street in San Francisco or Venice West in Los Angeles—the Latin quarter in Paris, Harlem or Greenwich Village in New York—attracting attention by

---

[2] Used by criminals to refer to a convict who is farther "in," that is, allies himself with prison officials and maintains close ties with noncriminal elements outside the prison. Clarence Schrag, "A Preliminary Criminal Typology," *Pacific Sociological Review,* Vol. 4, 1961, pp. 11-20; also, *Social Types in a Prison Community* (M.A. Thesis, University of Washington, 1944.)

[3] See Gwynn Nettler, "A Measure of Alienation," *American Sociological Review,* December 1957, Vol. 22, p. 675; also John P. Clark, "Measuring Alienation Within a Social System," *ibid.,* December 1959, Vol. 24, pp. 849-52. Five different meanings of alienation, as the concept is now used, are distinguished by Melvin Seeman, "On the Meaning of Alienation," *ibid.,* pp. 783-91; they are: powerlessness, meaninglessness, normlessness, isolation, and self-estrangement.

[4] Disagreement about the meaning of anomie today parallels that about alienation. About all that everyone agrees on is that we have it. There is a tendency currently, following Merton, to define anomie in terms of failure to reach life goals. I prefer, however, to stay close to Durkheim's conception, as I understand it: rulelessness and lack of control, due to defective social organization, with consequences such as frustration and restlessness. I believe it is fair to suppose that anomie and alienation are related; for the present I assume that alienation is an attitude—a feeling of not belonging and of rejection of the social order with which one is confronted—often found in anomie; whereas the latter is an objective, structural fact of unrelatedness among members of a group, a lack of integration severe enough to deprive them of needed support and control.

pointedly casual, careless, yet intellectually pretentious living, openly contemptuous of a species called "squares." Superficially, they resemble bohemians of a generation ago; but times, scenes, and language have changed —for example, coffeehouses with quaint names like "The Place" and "The Voodoo Man" (where often no liquor is served [5] and the patronage is youthful). Old beats there are too—and I am not trying to say that alcohol and the bistro have been eliminated—but faces of the young show how much beatnikism has spread—whether as fad or more serious movement—to large parts of the population.

The beat style is well reflected in language, terms of which have entered common speech, magazines, comic books, novels, and newspapers. One can easily guess that *beat* itself means tired (of almost everything), dead, flat, broke, and not making the effort to be good, successful, or conventional; the opposite of square.[6] *Cool* is an important attitude, displaying no enthusiasm, even toward what one likes—underplaying everything. *Crazy* or *gone* refers to a kick that is deliciously strange, interesting, and weird. *Dig* is to thoroughly appreciate a kick, character, or scene. *Kick* is the highpoint and meaning of life—conceived hedonistically as transient (you've got to get it now) and ineffable (like Tao or Zen, man). *Man* is an idiomatic reference to the other (serving often as a pause like "ah") implying that both you and he are "in" the exclusive world (similarly with terms like "gone cat," "beat chick"). *Scene* is a place one views, or tours, for the kicks it affords, as in "making the scene." *Pad* is a place, with minimum furnishings, in which to sleep or carry on recreational activities. *Bit* is a term for a role which a beat thinks is of little worth, such as the "making a living bit" or the "marriage bit." A more strenuously negative word is *bugged,* meaning to be about as angry as a cool beat can be. Many of these terms are shared with other groups.[7]

We must note here how it is possible, almost from language alone, to construct a scheme of life that consists of drifting through a social structure without taking part in it, alienation, interest in the scene for kicks but without responsibility for it, an in-group that shares kicks and uses

[5] An effort to avoid costs of licensing and the Federal cabaret tax, which would apply to a place that furnished both liquor and entertainment. Coffeehouses are often "shoestring" operations that can be run closely in harmony with beat values of minimum stake in the economic structure.

[6] Beat is also held by some, such as Jack Kerouac, to refer to beatitude or beatific. This is open to objections, among which is that most beatniks do not even know what beatitude means. Another connotation is the jazz "beat," of which beatniks are so appreciative that it might be said to be a central part of their cult.

[7] Some were borrowed from the jazz world or underworld and were common in those worlds of the late thirties. For example, gone meant high on something, probably marijuana, and cat and chick simply meant men and women in the know of night life.

language to exclude squares from their society, a life organization that does not provide for normal contingencies such as family life, growing old, funerals—in other words, an incomplete organization, and finally, a *cult-like* orientation in which kicks are the central value.

Let me focus on the kick, because it is extremely important, perhaps even the heart of beat life. Kicks show that beats have a positive orientation: they are devotees of certain kinds of experiences which compensate them for the loss of gray-flannel-suit values and which they cultivate within an in-group. They are *cultists* organized around sharing central values by ritual. Their rituals include bongo parties, espresso and other kinds of drinking, poetry to jazz accompaniment, the emphatic practice of sex, and the cultivation of kicks that might range from playing chess in the midst of a jam session to a narcotics jag. (The life of kicks transcends routines and few can say where it will lead.) The "churches" of the cult are hangouts such as bars, coffeehouses, and large pads—even old warehouses—where beat values can be celebrated to the exclusion and negation of those of the conventional world, a kind of secular Devil's mass. It seems plain, however, that beats are far from totally anomic in the sense of lawless, valueless, and individuated; indeed, conformist and religious fits them fairly well (the beat faddism sweeping the country is yet another example of conformity). They do, however, symptomatize anomie in the larger structure, to which their contribution is practically nil.

What is this relationship? It does not fit neatly into the well known categories of Robert K. Merton: retreatism, rebellion, ritualism, and innovation, as major modes of the adaptation of deviants to an anomic order.[8] It is, to be sure, aggressive and rebellious, especially when phrased as a "War Against the Squares," a "calculated vulgarity" to "bug the squares." [9] But, if rebellion, it is a sad one, probably closer to retreatism. Says Granville Hicks, "The consistent Beatnik . . . does not seek to triumph over the Squares nor even to shock them; he simply wants to get away from them and associate with his own kind. What he does is to set up Beatnik enclaves within our overwhelmingly Square society." [10] The fact that hard-core beats often shun places where tourists and weekend beats hang out probably supports this. But neither is retreatism quite

[8] Robert K. Merton, "Anomie and Social Structure," *op. cit.*; amplified by Robert Dubin, "Deviant Behavior and Social Structure," *American Sociological Review*, April 1959, XXIV: 147-164.

[9] Paul O'Neil, "The Only Rebellion Around," *Life*, November 30, 1959, p. 115.

[10] "The Quest for a Quiet Time," *Saturday Review*, November 28, 1959, p. 20.

appropriate, for many beats—real ones, too—are not leaving the scene but hanging around, not just to make themselves obnoxious (as some squares suppose) but to seize the kicks that the scene affords. A phrase of Dr. Kingsley Widmer seems more appropriate than either rebellion or retreatism, "disengagement," from tedium and anxiety, a "negative kind of freedom" [11] *within* society. The beats innovate; but their freedom is more negative than that of a creative bohemian artist or intellectual. It is in good part a colorful way of *not* doing things such as shaving and wearing shoes—of letting things (that do not matter) go to pot. How, then, are they using their freedom within the social structure? I would describe them as *aesthetic parasites,* whose picking and choosing, search for kicks and escape from obligations, require them to view the social order rather aggressively, much as a tramp might view the opportunities of the next town. I am not trying to make them seem worse than they are: but it seems to me that they have something in common with con-men, criminals and bums—except that what they are seeking from society is not handouts, pocketbooks, or easy money but aesthetic pleasures. To them, the entire structure of conventional society is: (1) a prison or workhouse, whose obligations are to be shunned and whose rules are to be gotten around as best one can; and (2) a scene, whose kicks are to be taken (dug) where found (even squares can be kicks to a beat, who looks at them with amusement as tourists do him). Yet, to repeat, they are not at war with the squares, for beats are trying neither to defeat the social order nor convert it; they are not even trying to make trouble; their fundamental rule is: "Thou shalt not bug (disturb) thy neighbor"; they do not try to tell other people how to live; they disregard racial and credal differences that are often a source of conflict among other people.[12] While not destructive, there is little use trying to see them as an artistic or intellectual avant-garde, for they do not seem to be really going any place creatively[13]—that is, building new values that will renovate or augment the existing culture (as, for example, Left Bank artists of Paris or American jazz men did); they are too far "out" for that. The key to their lack of creativity (granting writers like Jack Kerouac and Allen Ginsberg) is the

[11] "The American Road and the Contemporary Novel," public lecture at San Diego State College, October 14, 1959.

[12] This statement of the beat code was made by Alphonse Matthews, a lawyer representing the beatniks of Venice, California, in a hearing in which their license to operate a coffeehouse was challenged by local residents. *Time,* September 14, 1959, p. 28.

[13] John Ciardi has passed such a judgment on the literary product of the beat movement, "Epitaph for the Dead Beats," *Saturday Review,* February 6, 1960, pp. 11-13, 42.

"beat" attitude itself, that work is a "drag"; therefore, so is any sustained, rigorous creative effort. Kicks are too easy without the discipline and drudgery of art.

The beatniks' alienation, however, is not to be carelessly compared with that of bums, criminals, radicals, cultists, and other deviants, without taking account of their special orientation and where it puts them on the scale of how far "out" people are from conventional "square" values. Beats, because of their parasitic relationship, are not as far "out" as many rebels and retreatists. Let me compare beats with a few examples on a hypothetical continuum. As already implied, beats should be distinguished from artistic bohemians who are "out" for the sake of an art pursued with enough dedication to disrupt normal relationships (but not showing a "beat" attitude nor pursuing "kicks" indiscriminately— art is enough). The beat should also be distinguished from the hepcat (hipster)[14] of the jazz culture (although some writers mix the two), because the jazz culture and its hepcats existed many years before the "beat" movement, and beats are basically parasites on jazz rather than makers, or even discriminating listeners; being "hip" (in the know) to a beat means something different from being in the know to a jazz cat; the two circles intersect but by no means coincide.[15] Both the jazz cult and artistic bohemianism have an element of dedication and discipline foreign to the drifting, sprawling, orgiastic, beat search for "way out" kicks. Norman Mailer describes how the jazz cat's artistic goal of "swinging" has become a life goal for the hipster, merging at some points with that of the beat,

[14] This type has been described by various writers, for example, Harold Finestone, *op. cit.;* Norman Mailer; William R. Smith, "Hepcats to Hipsters," *New Republic,* April 21, 1958, pp. 18-20; and Howard S. Becker, "The Professional Dance Musician and His Audience," *American Journal of Sociology,* September 1951, LVII, 136-144.

[15] Jazz cats would maintain their in-group lines against beats and vice versa. "The (jazz) musician . . . sees himself as a creative artist who should be free from outside control, a person different from and better than those outsiders he calls squares who understand neither his music nor his way of life and yet because of whom he must perform in a manner contrary to his professional ideals." Becker, *op. cit.,* p. 139. Jazz cats have an esoteric culture, in spite of the fact that part of the public participates to some degree in jazz. From my own experience as a musician who for a time earned his living in jazz, I would agree that most beatniks would fall in the category of "squares." The following statement by Lawrence Lipton concedes that a jazz cat might well regard a beat as square: "Jazz musicians themselves are often puzzled and some-times irritated by the response of the holy barbarians to their music . . . The holy barbarians, on their part, often fail to discriminate between the sacred ritual elements in jazz and the show that the 'natives' sometimes put on for the tourists—and the *Yanqui dólar.* The beats are so hungry that they wolf down everything in sight. . . ." *Op. cit.,* p. 207.

but the last sentences (which I have italicized) indicate where "beat" and "hipster" diverge:

> The language of Hip is a language of energy, how it is found, how it is lost . . . To swing is to be able to learn, and by learning take a step toward making it, toward creating . . . Whereas if you goof (the ugliest word in Hip) . . . or if you flip, if you lose your control . . . then it is more difficult to swing the next time, your ear is less alive, your bad and energy-wasting habits are further confirmed, you are farther away from being with it . . . To be cool is to be equipped, and if you are equipped it is more difficult for the next cat who comes along to put you down. And of course one can hardly afford to be put down too often, or one is beat, one has lost one's confidence . . . one is impotent . . . and so closer to the demeaning flip . . . indeed closer to dying, and therefore it is even more difficult to recover enough energy to try to make it again, because *once a cat is beat he has nothing to give,* and no one is interested any longer in making it with him . . . *To be beat is therefore a flip* . . .[16]

I have been saying that beats, having quit, are farther "out" than the cults which make a contribution to the existing order, or even promise a new order.

On this last point, a comparison with a religious sect such as Jehovah's Witnesses will be useful. Though sects, too, are "out" of the square culture, many aim at recruiting or reform, rather than letting the ship sink;[17] all aim to create a social and moral (sacred) order. This cannot be said with convincingness of beats, since transitory, hedonistic, secular kicks (however "holy" they may be called [18]) are the focus, and their life shows little sign of building a social, let alone a moral, order. That a religious sectarian would condemn a beat as immoral and a beat would classify a sectarian as square, tells us that the beat is farther "out" from square values. Thus, trying to place the beats on a continuum, we may say that they are farther "out" than constructive types like the bohemian, jazz hepcat, and many religious sectarians. Yet, because of their parasitic and dependent relationship, they are not as far "out" as complete retreatists; nor are they as antagonistic as active rebels and criminals. Therefore, we should place them somewhere as follows on a hypothetical continuum of alienation:

[16] Norman Mailer, "The White Negro; Superficial Reflections on the Hipster," *Dissent,* 1957, Vol. 4, pp. 277-288; republished in Harry C. Bredemeier and Jackson Toby, eds., *Social Problems in America* (New York: John Wiley & Sons, Inc., 1960), pp. 476-481.
[17] Referring to the belief of most sects that their members are "saved" and the rest of the world is "lost"; most sects, however, make some evangelistic efforts; comparatively few, such as the Mennonites of Paraguay, who established an isolated community in the jungle, are wholly retreatist.
[18] Lipton, *op. cit.*

Maximum "outness" (alienation and iso-lation) ↓	The Outsiders			The "Square World" (Squaresville)		
7	6	5	4	3	2	1
Retreatists	Rebels (criminals)	Parasites (beats)	Radical innovators (artistic bohemians, jazzmen, religious sectarians, etc.)	Alienated members (youth)	Square innovators (business entrepreneurs, inventors, scientists, academicians, etc.)	Very square ("gung ho" members, corny, old fogeys)

I would distinguish several major points on this provisional scale:

1) the position of the *very square,* who not only adhere to conventional values but are "wholesome," strict, or old-fashioned about it (gung ho, do-gooder, prig, prude, cornball, corny, old fogey, diehard, puritan—as they might be called by the more alienated);

2) *progressive square;* those who keep "up with the times" and those who innovate within the square framework without questioning basic values of the order itself (for example, business entrepreneurs, most scientists and technical inventors, "progressive" churches, reformers, faddists); these might also be called conservative innovators;

3) *alienated conformers* (or alienated members): the captive population —including some in gray flannel suits, and many youth—who do not like it, but do not express their alienation visibly or who "settle down" after a brief fling at protest;

4) *radical innovators:* those who make their break with the square world and endure a certain amount of ridicule, even vilification, but whose contribution is ultimately or presently acceptable to the square world:

5) *parasitism:* alienated parties who are dependent on a social order which they reject and exploit without contribution; often the relationship is rather antagonistic but not outright rebellion (the position of beats and a good part of the underworld);

6) *rebellion:* rejection of and attack on conventional values with defiance and destructiveness;

7) *retreatism:* a total break with the social order, its values, means, and responsibilities.

It seems to me that the youth culture ranges from moderately square (about position 2) to rebellion (6). The "philistine" world ranges from very square (position 1) to slick fashionableness (2), which might include keeping up with "beat" and "hep" fashions in a "society" way, for example, giving a beatnik costume party. Criminals, it seems to me, range from parasitism (5) to rebels (6), depending upon the aggressiveness with which they repudiate conventional values (clearly a racketeer who drives a Cadillac and sends his daughter to college is much more square than a bank robber).

I am not trying to make a scale here but rather to clarify and communicate a conceptual framework which makes explicit use of that expressive word "square," which is so much in vogue among youth and various alienated groups. What is the common denominator of various meanings of "square" unless it is alienation from standard American values taught by parents, schools, churches, businesses, and military institutions? We should try to specify the degree of alienation from "square" for each deviant group and life style. Of course we have not dealt with some difficult problems, such as where to put overconformists (some native fascists and extreme reactionaries) who look very square but may actually be alienated and quite damaging to the conventional structure.

How Various Types Might Express Anomie

Aside from beatniks, we may use the diagram on page 132 as a chart of the territory of alienation. To make much sense of Hero (H), Villain (V), and Fool (F) types, you have to sort them into two broad classes: those expressing the viewpoint of the "square" world and those expressing the alienated viewpoints of outsiders. A deviant should be expected to have H, V, and F types that pretty well reverse the standard scheme—*his* heroes may be deviants[19] as the square sees them, and square heroes look ridiculous, even villainous to him. A square takes what might be called the standard approved view of things: crime is bad, honesty is good; work is better than loafing; everyone should get married, go to church, be well mannered, and so on. Such a person takes deviants "straight" (without cynical or ironic twists), for example: lawless people as villains, eccentrics as oddballs, "good" models (defenders, martyrs, saints, moralists, do-gooders) without mockery, conformists generally with approval. Indeed, a

---

[19] A statement of a yong jazz musician illustrates the tendency of alienated groups to make deviant heroes: "You know, the biggest heroes in the music business are the biggest characters. The crazier a guy acts, the greater he is, the more everyone likes him." Becker, *op. cit.*, p. 138.

very square person might accept insincere poses, such as the super-good-fellows of mass communication or the patriotism of Yankee Doodle Dandies, that an alienated person would reject as hogwash. So, we must measure a person's relationship to the square world before we can say what his social typing means; villain types that meant anomie for the square world might be heroes outside it and indicate thriving organization of deviant groups or movements.

For the square, V and F types normally catch and label various kinds of deviant behavior. To list some: openly lawless individuals as outlaws, flouters, and rebels (a square is more likely to see the serious than the rogue-and-prankster end of this spectrum); less obvious rule breakers as frauds, chiselers, con-men, grafters, pretenders, crashers, and wolves; shirkers of obligation as traitors, renegades, shirkers, parasites, boon-dogglers, goldbricks, and loafers; and reckless disregarders of common sense as rash fools. Squares normally apply comic types to people who are anomic (eccentrics, crackpots, beatniks—oddities so bizarre that people have a hard time understanding them—communication, consensus, empathy may be breaking down). To speak generally, it seems that the square point of view puts most of the types classified by Merton as retreatists and rebels—as well as many innovators—in categories of the villain or fool. Even conservative innovators such as faddists are viewed with suspicion and ridicule (since they go to extremes for values that are not "worthwhile" and permanent), nor is it any accident that they show the frustration, restlessness, and erratic behavior that Durkheim said was characteristic of anomie.[20] Squares are sensitive to deviations that threaten the conservative order because basically (if only nostalgically) theirs is a closed—a folk—society, in which the scheme of life is sacred—everyone has a place and everything stays put. So the greater the amount of such typing, the more likely is there to be anomie in the square world.

In such an order, when things are going well, the normal meaning of V and F types is not breakdown but high conformity and conservatism. *Some* deviation is occurring, but it is well penalized and, by and large,

[20] According to Durkheim in *Suicide*, inadequate and unsatisfying social organization makes people ready to grasp at novel, bizarre, and exciting things outside the order they are used to, whereas in an adequately cohesive group a person is satisfied—wants what he ought to, is "in harmony with his condition." When cohesiveness is lost, a person finds himself discontent, drifting, wanting things he can't or shouldn't have—and lacking a stable hierarchy of values by which to choose wisely. Life is so empty that almost anything is acceptable to fill it—Russian roulette, it may be—or parachute jumping just for kicks. Faddists, beatniks, criminals, and the like pursue thrills that are new or outside the social order. Were the kick domesticated, at it were, and brought within the social order—say as a cult, a form of heroism, or a custom—then it would cease to be anomic, however dangerous to the individual.

everything is under control. This, of course, is not the world we live in. Large numbers of V's and F's may mean that everything is getting out of hand, disorganization is exceeding organization, that is, square typing is not working.[21] A similar change in function can be seen in fool types which in one situation mean tight control (manners are nice, slight deviations are laughable), and in another mean lax discipline, "anything goes," everybody is calling somebody fool. In short, a few V and F types probably mean successful control, but I think, many mean, that society cannot keep people from being villains and fools. When conservative typing breaks down, you find that V labels lose their punch and deviations become more frequent and flagrant. As this happens, more deviations become positive models and for more people the prevailing sign of V's and F's may change from minus to plus (as can be seen in types like scamp and playboy). Large numbers of V and F types changing into hero models are like white corpuscles indicating disease in the social body.

To understand better how the symptomatic value of V and F types can change drastically, let us visualize three ideally typical situations, one (I) a folk-like society—no strangers, high consensus (norms are uniform and sacred, all sub-groups are consistent), therefore few deviants. Here V and F types indicate a strong social order, indeed most deviations are ritualized rather than real (for example clowning, folklore villains). At the other extreme (III), we might conceive a "society" so dispersed and loosely knit that all are like strangers, no in-groups demand loyalty, norms are individuated and there is no effective consensus (Hobbes' state of nature, total anomie as conceived by Durkheim). In such a state, however much freedom, there could be no deviants and no H's, V's, or F's (because these rest on normative consensus). This doesn't fit our order any more than a folk society. But an intermediate situation (II) fits better and is one in which one would expect maximum H's, V's, and F's: a pluralistic secondary society with much individuation but also with conflicting sub-groups demanding loyalty. There is mutual name calling among these groups (for example, beats versus squares, sect versus sect), and the V's of one may be the H's of another. In such a situation, no labeling is absolute, group viewpoints discount one another, relativism prevails. Because of this relativism and because they may be supported as H's by other groups V and F types fail to deter behavior. In such a situation there are many V's and F's because inconsistent reference causes people to run afoul of one another, and there are many perspectives from which to

---

[21] Such a loss of function is illustrated by the villain type of the heretic which, during the Middle Ages when the church was strong, was a symbol of its control, but during the Reformation showed the inability of the Catholic Church to put down rebellion.

say "villain" and "fool." Numerous V and F types indicate anomie (conflict, fissures, alienation) in the social structure, though not in the total sense of situation III. Such a picture, I believe, is closest to our situation.

Comedy gives another view of how the meaning of typing can change as one moves from situation I to situation II. The normal function of comedy in a closed (folk, square) society is to enforce propriety (as shown in Hopi clowning); the laugh is against the fellow who misbehaves. But a pluralistic civilization offers more opportunities for comedy because of the diversity of sub-groups and perspectives and the possibilities of contretemps and predicaments. The audience can see more jokes and the humorist has more to work with. But the tendency in comedy toward license—to spill over the bounds of propriety—which is normally controlled in a folk society, begins to get out of hand where there are numerous opportunities for, and inadequate sanctions against, "improper" jest. If the philosophy of "anything for a laugh" comes to prevail, jesting invades serious values, spreads irreverence (perhaps a consensus that "nothing is sacred"), and may even break down authority and status. Comedians become bizarre, even morbid [22] in their desperation for new material. An undercurrent of irreverence in American slang (the "hot seat," "nine old men," "Brooklyn Bums," "Holy Joes," "Jesus-jazzers") may also have significance in this respect. Such a development represents an inversion of normal comic function, in which clowning and mockery, instead of supporting social structure, break it down—or signify its breakdown. At this stage, criminality and moral flouting may seem merely funny—a kind of *espièglerie;* the bad manners of buffoons encourage unmannerliness; discounting (of stuffed shirts, authoritarians), so important to democracy, spreads until everything is leveled; traditional models are called by mocking names such as crusader, do-gooder, or cornball; and sacred institutions are debunked. Such indiscriminate extension of comedy moves toward situation III, where heroes, villains, and fools are no longer possible—since they depend on taking a social structure seriously (paradoxically, too many fools means there are no fools—and no values either). Comedy, having exhausted itself by excessive deviation (till nothing is unexpected), dies with total anomie.

I have been trying to explain the *failure of square typing* along a continuum in which H's, V's, and F's change their meaning. Let us focus now on typing by deviant groups, two kinds of which clearly indicate anomie.

[22] As in "sick" humor. For example, a greeting card that says "Love is where you find it" (a girl is pictured looking in a garbage can), or "Despite your many faults . . . you're still a bum."—Comedians called "sickniks" tell jokes in nightclubs emphasizing horror and mayhem, such as, "I hit one of those things in the street—what do you call it, a kid?"

One is *heroization of deviant behavior* by sub-groups in conflict with square values. The sub-groups' heroes (though outlaws) symbolize defiance and triumph over the out-group. Such typing inverts standard morality: the hero is the one who plays it smart, beats the game; the fool is the one stupid enough to be honest or get caught; the villain is a meddler (square John, authoritarian, reformer, do-gooder, rate-buster, cop, umpire, and so on) who spoils a racket, insists on sticking to (formal) rules. In such a situation, outlaws and gangsters who defy cops become champions—con-men and chiselers become smart operators—jailbirds become martyrs—in short, almost any type disliked or feared in the square world can become a hero to a deviant group in proportion to his success in breaking the rules of the larger society or of one of the enemy sub-groups. Since the sub-groups are at war among themselves as well as with square society, there are additional opportunities for deviant heroism: a beatnik "puts down" a jazz cat, a con-man cheats a strong-arm robber, a homosexual takes advantage of a drug addict, a sectarian patronizes another sectarian as a "lost soul." The "gang wars" of the nineteen-twenties spawned heroes who were simply the gunmen who managed to cut down their rivals or had been "put on the spot" in a particularly dramatic fashion. The police had comparatively little part in this tournament of bullets. Such conflicts of subgroups with one another or against square society can produce all kinds of twisted martyrs and champions that spell anomie for the larger structure at least until a sub-group movement succeeds in transforming it—hardly a typical fate of deviant groups.

The obverse of deviant heroes is the *rejection of square models* (H, V, and F). Deviants often take a comic view of approved heroes: Founding Fathers are corny; so are saints, martyrs, do-gooders, G-men, moralistic conformers, and other spiritual and altruistic models. It is not necessary, of course, to be at war with society in order to reject square models; a certain amount of disenchantment is enough; for example, among nurses "Florence Nightingale" is a name for one who is overly devoted to nursing, has no other interests, and seems to be waiting for another Crimean War. Many workers apply terms like eager beaver, glory hog, "hero," job-killer, or fall guy to practically anyone who is trying to do a good job. But when any group starts to mock its own ideals, obviously something is wrong with morale. A badly alienated society may feel that most of its idols have feet of clay, may even repudiate *heroism itself*—the whole idea of dedicated and self-sacrificial striving. Inability to take a firm stand against villains is part of this picture. Anomic people who do not adhere to approved positive models also do not feel very strongly against negative ones; their philosophy may be "Who am I to point the finger?" or "Let sleeping dogs lie." They are in no position to take a firm stand against crime or evil as defined by square society; they will be quick to let the "bad guys" off—not from softness of heart or Christian charity, but because they are sympathizers of "Robin Hood." Similarly in the comic dimension, many fools, as defined by square culture, will not seem funny to a non-square or an anomic ("crackpot," "fairy," or "beatnik," for example). To summarize: the rejection of square models (H, V, or F) along with deviant heroes, is a major sign of anomie.

Another sign of anomie is "soft spots" in social structure revealed by typing. Does not typing of bellyachers, soreheads, square pegs, clumsy fools, Sad Sacks, easy marks, butterfingers, sloppy Janes, wallflowers, wet blankets, drifters, characters, and so on, often designate people ordinarily regarded as "normal," but many of whom are in fact maladjusted enough to be called anomic?[23] Even conformity may have something wrong with it, for example, those who adhere compulsively or rigidly to traditional ways of doing things even when it doesn't get them anyplace[24] (labeled by types like corny, passé, traditionalist, antiquarian, old fogey, diehard, prig, prude, disciplinarian, authoritarian, and reactionary). Some people seem to be eager conformists—carry out rules to the letter, become sticklers and purists, even heroes of sorts—not because they are really enthusiastic but in order to mask their alienation or to present a front for some kind of game.[25] Such over-conformity—labeled by names like eager beaver, often by sincere praise (hard worker, go-getter, old reliable)—is plainly at the opposite pole from the morale it resembles. Others do not try so hard that they become visible by overconformity; they do not win prizes nor kick up any fuss; they seem to want to blend in, to efface themselves, as though they were afraid of sticking their neck out or of being found out; they give little trouble but neither are they very helpful; their principal fault is apathy covered by compliance; they mask their alienation by eva-

[23] David Riesman, in fact, uses anomic as virtually synonymous with maladjusted. *The Lonely Crowd* (New York: Doubleday & Company, Inc., 1954), p. 278.

[24] Merton calls it ritualism, which I think is unfortunate, since ritual is normally meaningful and highly effective in its own way. Cooley's term formalism seems better for this kind of anomie.

[25] Suggesting one answer to the question about overconformity raised by Merton: "Overconformity is the direct counterpart of underconformity. It is a form of social deviation that involves 'too much' just as underconformity involves 'too little' when judged by group standards. This still leaves open the question of accounting sociologically for certain actions being experienced as 'too much' and therefore as social deviation; why, for example, are certain kinds of high performance regarded by the group as a great achievement, and other kinds as being too much of a good thing?" Robert K. Merton, "Social Conformity, Deviation and Opportunity-Structures," *American Sociological Review*, April 1959, XXIV: 184.

sive conformity with the middle of the group.[26] Sometimes types like yes-man, Milquetoast, conservative, bureaucrat, goldbrick, and clockwatcher, catch these rather elusive people—we do not expect them to be named as often as rebels. Such "soft spots" are caught by social typing in our society. Though they do not stand out as colorful deviations, they are often drastic departures from the ideal of conformity, hard work, and loyalty, and are significant in the diagnosis of anomie. I have referred previously to their relationship to pseudo-integration.

The fifth major kind of anomic typing might be called a defensive re-action to the fact of anomie—to relieve and disguise it, even give a picture of morale and well-being. As stated before, *compensatory types* make up for what people haven't got or symbolize what people think they ought to be but aren't really trying to be. One may suspect that hero models like the great lover, gladhand, smoothie, charmer, personality kid, man of the people, and glorified cult leaders often reflect loneliness and inadequacy of primary groups. In a world where the average person is unknown and unimportant, splendid performers, celebrities, grandstanders, headliners, big shots, top dogs, strong men, brains, and smart operators may compensate many for lack of status and recognition. Lawless heroes could also have such a compensatory function. As Merton suggests, anomics are often prevented from getting what they have been encouraged to want by an inconsistent social structure. The resulting hero, then, should be either a magical figure winning pots of gold, or an unscrupulous one who gets otherwise inaccessible values by breaking rules (I suspect Capone was such for many Americans in the nineteen-twenties). Also, I guess that the exaggerated democracy of certain American types—plain men, regular fellows, friends of the people—compensate for the perception that things aren't always like that. A similar function could be performed by great men of the humble stamp (Lincoln, Gandhi, Socrates, Jesus). Much good-fellowship today is florid and overblown, no more a simple expression of friendliness than a four-hundred-pound hog is a simple expression of growth. Our democracy has a clammy gladhand (one discerning ob-server, Stanley Kauffman, calls it inverted snobbery, that is, pretend-ing to like people in order to prove you don't dislike them). Anomie, being a kind of vacuum, creates a need for super-good-fellows to sym-bolize friendliness, charmers and smoothies to symbolize being accepted,

---

[26] Riesman calls it apathetic overconformity. Lippitt notes something very much like it as one response of boys' groups to autocratic leaders. See also Alexander H. Leighton's observation that the bulk of the Niseis in a Japanese Relocation Center "were inclined to be apathetic and cynical and subscribed to the phrase common in Poston, 'Don't stick your neck out.'" *The Governing of Men* (Princeton University Press, 1946), p. 160.

splendid performers to dramatize recognition for insecure and unknown people, moralists for those who are not really trying to be good, Tarzans for people who don't exercise, and men on horseback for those who lack authority. Though such types "fit" these needs, they do not satisfy them any more than a blanket does the chill of a fever patient. People remain pretty much where they were in terms of a true remedy. In brief, anomic heroes reflect not what people are but what they are not: crooners for those who do not sing—happy, friendly jokesters for those who are not happy and friendly—"it"-girls for people without "it"— six-day bike races for those who do not race—success for failures—great lovers for poor lovers—super-friends for those who have no friends. Of course, the functions of a type are by no means simple. It is likely that many types work in both normal and compensatory ways. A hero like Joe Palooka (big muscles and super-friendliness), could have different meanings according to whether people have such traits themselves and whether they live according to the ideals portrayed.

Conclusion

I have tried to show here how various American H, V, and F types, instead of performing their "normal" function of supporting the general, respectable ("square") structure can be taken as signs of anomie and alienation. Five ways have been distinguished: (1) breakdown of square typing, that is, its failure to control deviation; (2) heroization of deviant behavior; (3) rejection of square models; (4) soft spots in morale revealed by typing certain kinds of pseudo-integration; and (5) compensatory types that make up for what people in fact haven't got or aren't trying to do.

Such things help us to see cracks in the social structure. I am far from suggesting, of course, that they are an infallible diagnostic means. At best they are deceptive symptoms which still require interpretation. One must decide, for example, whether inversion of function has occurred—whether a model who looks pretty good may be compensating for what in fact is not there—whether our society as the patient is cleverly playing a role to fool himself or others. America presents a confusing mixture of symptoms: discontent and misbehavior alongside rituals of health, happiness, and "all's well." Pseudo-integration was described in earlier chapters as a structure that could be built by role playing and compensatory types. I am not sure how to read this syndrome, and surely do not claim that most Americans are alienated or anomic. The question is relative (to which structure is one referring?), and, in any case, a matter for measurement, of which there has been comparatively little yet.[27] However, I do think that effective research will show much alienation and anomie in the American social structure.

It seems safe to say that something is wrong with many of our heroes. Let us pursue this theme in the following chapters on deterioration of the hero.

[27] Specific studies have attempted to measure anomie for certain research purposes, such as Leo Srole, "Social Integration and Certain Corollaries," *American Sociological Review*, 1956, 21:709-716. Gwynne Nettler's work, "A Measure of Alienation," *ibid.*, 1957, 22:671-677, is a beginning. See also Amitai Etzioni, *Complex Organizations* (New York: Holt, Rinehart, & Winston, Inc., 1961) for studies of the degree of commitment of participants in prisons, businesses, religious groups, and other organizations.

CHAPTER 6

Deterioration of the Hero

Deterioration of the hero is visible in several aspects of American life. One is the ordinariness of real people before the public eye, which I call the cult of celebrities. Another is confusion in literature and drama between good guys and bad guys, especially certain mixed characters who might be called corrupted heroes.

The Cult of Celebrities

Modern communication has brought into prominence a new class of celebrities which is setting the tone and standards of American life. This class is characterized by ordinariness. Admiration of celebrities amounts, I would say, to a cult which is displacing traditional reverence for great men, even encroaching on and draining from religion itself;[1] and, because it isn't based on real merit or achievement, has a debasing effect on American values.

What is the cause of the ordinariness? First, modern celebrities do not recognize an obligation to hold up a high standard before the public but instead assert a right to their "private lives" even though they spend a great deal of time trying to get into the public eye. The very fidelity of modern communication invades their private lives and shows them as they are. For the most part, they are showmen of one kind or another, whose achievements are due to specialties and gimmicks rather than real ability and character. Outside their specialty, many are far from exemplary—they are involved in scandals, fights, and divorces, get arrested while drunk, and show that their standards are no better (one could argue they are worse) than the man on the street.

As a result, they fail to act for the public as hero models should. A hero cult should raise the general level of aspiration, make people try to be better than they are. What is one to say of a society where entertainers have fame surpassing Einstein's, where bathing beauties, romantic vocalists, boxers, and disc jockeys are in the front rank? A glance at the magazine racks will show who get the real popular devotion in America—not persons like Jefferson and Lincoln, but celebrities whose faces and bodies get more publicity in a week than great men get in a year. It was Babe Ruth who, years ago, pointed to the irony that when he stood beside doctors, engineers, and statesmen, the crowd cheered him instead.

Plenty of Americans are less fervent in their worship of God than of celebrities. No Caesar ever got more frantic adulation than any of a dozen singers in America do now. Fans wait for hours, even days, for the personal appearance of stars, collect pictures, autographs, handkerchiefs, and recordings with all the devotion due a saint's relics. There is widespread and continuing preoccupation with the bodies, personalities, and private affairs of celebrities, as is shown by gossip columns, "human interest" news, fan magazines, and the like. The real purpose of such information is seen in fan magazines, which are plainly for pin-up and scrapbook purposes (they might as well put dotted lines around the pictures with directions, "Cut here"): to supply images which people can incorporate into their own lives. The "personal appearance" is the supreme communion of the public with its idol. Recognizing this, leading television shows ("What's My Line?," "The Ed Sullivan Show") have worked

---

[1] See Malcolm Boyd, *Christ and the Celebrity Gods* (Greenwich, Conn.: The Seabury Press, 1958).

celebrity cult into their format, a main purpose being to give the public a feast of celebrities. Contributing to such feasts is a far flung network of amateur shows, talent scouts, booking agencies, sports arenas, nightclub circuits, public relations agencies, and studio-build-ups, which might be looked on as recruiting agencies for the celebrity cult.

Now, as to the impact of these people on American life, I would make four charges. First, they fail to hold up higher *intellectual* types to anywhere near the extent that a civilization with our achievements and problems needs. First-rate thinkers, like T. S. Eliot or Arthur Compton, do not get fair representation in American mass communication.

Second, the celebrity cult does not adequately hold up higher *moral* and *ethical* types. A hundred celebrities taken at random, say, from the *Celebrity Register,* would likely be no better than a hundred taken off the city street.

Third, the models are so miscellaneous and disproportions of emphasis so great that no *consistent* effect can be produced. There is no common denominator of excellence; every noble or civilized example is counteracted by one—perhaps a dozen—showing the opposite. The result is a paralyzing relativism, a lack of any generally accepted standard. Surely our celebrities do not support values held up by school and church.

Fourth, values of *entertainment* and *showmanship* are encroaching other areas of American life—religion, education, politics. Young people are comparing themselves with entertainers, measuring their own worth in terms of making a hit, getting a hand. "High society" is being corrupted by "Publi-ciety," as clearly pointed out by Cleveland Amory.[2]

In all this, I see confirmation of Carlyle's lament that the modern era tends to eat away the foundations of the great man. The celebrity cult celebrates the triumph of ordinariness—charm without character, showmanship without ability, bodies without minds, information without wisdom. Hero-worship looks horizontally, even downward, to a "man like myself."

From the standpoint of the social system, this is Plato's ideal merit system upside-down. The high places are crowded with second- and third-raters teaching that real quality is not needed for success. Anyone who commands a microphone or gets himself filmed or written about is, almost by definition, first-rate. To deplore this lack of discrimination is consistent with democracy, which depends on making what merit there is visible so people can see and use it. Carlyle has been criticized for his attitude

[2] *Who Killed Society?* (New York: Harper & Brothers, 1961). See some comparable observations in C. W. Mills, *The Power Elite* (New York: Oxford University Press, 1956), pp. 71-93.

toward the great man, but was he not just asking for a society where merit has the highest place? "We shall either learn to know a Hero . . . when we see him, or else go on to be forever governed by the Unheroic."

Corruption of the Hero

Deterioration of the hero is reflected not only in mediocre celebrities, but also in certain dramatic and fictional characters—bad people in the hero's role—who confuse the judgment of right and wrong and, because we identify with them, are more demoralizing than outright villains would be.

"Who are the good people and who are the bad people?" my six-year-old daughter sometimes asks me while viewing one of those harrowing television plays supposedly designed for children. I answer as glibly as I can, wishing that there really were some difference. A television serial, "Maverick" (awarded an "Emmie" for the best Western of 1959) illustrates the problem of confusion of good guy and bad guy. The twin heroes Bret and Bart bear little resemblance to the standard good guy; according to their creator and producer, Roy Huggins, Maverick is "not a hero but a bum." He is a coward and sissy: if there is to be a shooting, his first thought is to saddle up and get out of town; he handles a six-gun like a girl and is so squeamish that he closes his eyes while branding a calf. He cheats when it is his deal in a poker game. (The heroine, Samantha, is equally remote from the ideal represented by the Girl of the Golden West.[3]) We may note the Broadway musical-movie-novel *Pal Joey* (in the movie starring Frank Sinatra), portraying a little nightclub heel as a smart operator, underneath it all a good Joe.[4] For an example in American humor, take a cartoon in a national magazine showing a man and wife reclining in beach chairs beside their swimming pool; a butler is bringing them drinks from a mansion in the background; the husband says, "If I had to do it all over again, I guess I still would embezzle the $70,000."

Not only in fiction but in real life confusion between good guys and bad guys occurs. Since Edwin H. Sutherland's epochal studies, Americans have gotten rather used to the idea that a whitecollar criminal looks very

[3] The producer admits that in producing these unheroic heroes he intended to turn the conventional Western inside-out: "I wanted to see how many rules we could break and get away with it." *TV Guide*, August 1, 1959, pp. 17-19. Another example of confusion in the character of the hero is the knife-throwing television character "Jim Bowie," who alternates rapidly from kindness to meanness, fair-mindedness to dishonesty.

[4] In case you are in doubt as to whether anyone could admire Joey, I know a man who has named his son after this dubious character.

like an honest businessman. Expense account chiseling, kickbacks, payoffs, tax evasion, even a little fraud or larceny, may be all in a day's work. If the old distinction between honesty and dishonesty has become blurred, no less has the quaint notion that "crime does not pay" (if you want to get a laugh from an audience, just smile when you say this). When the Brinks Express robbers were caught a few years back, a housewife remarked, "I was kind of sad. It seemed a shame, when they had only a few days to go before the statute of limitations would have let them keep all that money." A strange kind of casting is occurring today—good guys do not have to live up to codes, bad guys do not have to be caught and punished (especially if they look enough like good guys); it may be that the distinction is ceasing to be important.[5]

The historical roots of this confusion go back in part to the tradition of the romantic outlaw.[6] Even today annual celebrations are devoted to Jesse James at Northfield, Minnesota (because he happened to ride through and rob a bank there), and to Wild Bill Hickock at Deadwood, South Dakota. Were a proposal made to abolish the outlaw tradition, there would probably be a storm of protest from movie-makers, writers, and the public. Crooks like John Dillinger, the "Yellow Kid" Weil, and Al Capone, get wrapped in glamor, even outlaws from other countries, such as Pancho Villa, who, in spite of train robberies and murders, became as much of a celebrity in America as Buffalo Bill; reporters stayed with his staff to tell of the women he kidnapped or how he ordered a thousand-dollar bathtub from a firm in Chicago.

When a scalawag is made into a charming fellow for literary purposes,

[5] But the distinction is important to moralists like Senator J. W. Fulbright who, after a Congressional inquiry into graft, said there is in America a corruption "beyond the reach of law," extending into the higher circles of government, and requiring extraordinary action by a commission of private citizens to check the "moral deterioration . . . so evident to all" lest it "continue to its logical conclusion . . . the destruction of our free democratic system."

[6] Tales are told of James, that when he robbed a train, he would go through the cars bestowing kisses on the women, young and old, and taking valuables only from the men (which enabled one clear-minded fellow to save his money by slipping it to his wife). A whimsical mixture of amusing, even endearing traits can do wonders in redeeming an obnoxious character. You might find in a robber extreme good looks, a debonair manner, chivalry toward ladies, bravado or baffling cleverness in defying the law, carrying off deeds with a rollicking joke, generosity with stolen money, soft heartedness—even loyalty such as Sam Bass' refusal to peach on his pals as he lay dying. Why kissing ladies or giving the public back some of its money—or not taking all of it—should be an endearing trait in a bandit will, perhaps, never be explained logically; but it is such droll little inconsistencies that help make a Robin Hood out of a blackguard. The basic theme of the Robin Hood rogue is found in many cultures. See my "The Clever Hero," *Journal of American Folklore*, Jan.-March 1954, Vol. 67, pp. 21-34.

he is usually called picaresque. It is said that in him breathes the spirit of Rabelais, of Tyl Eulenspiegel. Literature seems full of characters interesting, in part, *because* of their badness—famous thieves and adventurers like Volpone, Gil Blas, François Villon, and Casanova, also bittersweet characters like Thackeray's Becky Sharp, Wilde's Lord Harry, Stendhal's Julien Sorel, and Mann's confidence-man Felix Krull, or the amiable Devil of Shaw's *Man and Superman,* who is so engaging that he seems a perfect dinner guest and even overshadows Don Juan himself (whom we see as a high minded philosopher). Villain seems too strong a name to call them, but neither is hero entirely satisfactory. Only a combination of opposite qualities could produce their spiciness. This is the heart of our problem. We *remember* colorfully bad people at least as well as those who, like Nathan Hale or Joan of Arc, present a pure aspect of goodness. To reform a rogue is to ruin him from the standpoint of entertainment, for his piquancy comes *partly from the fact that he is morally reprehensible.* Who could hope to improve on Don Juan by patterning him after Sir Galahad? We may have a dilemma between a bad man in whom everyone is interested and a good one about whom no one cares to hear.

This is, as I would call him, the corrupted hero—too good to be a villain, too bad to be a hero, too serious to be a mere clown, too interesting to forget.

Presumably his effect, in news, TV, literature, or real life, is to carry a person who identifies with him *beyond the range of where he would normally go* (impossible with a conventional villain, so unattractive that most people will not identify with him). Mr. X is that special case where sin assumes its most appealing form. He is a vehicle of demoralization when we say, after vicariously experiencing his deed, "If he, why not I too?"

Let us turn to some contemporary types that deserve to be described and evaluated as native American corrupted heroes. I shall here deal with five: (1) the *tough guy,* (2) the *smart operator,* (3) the *wolf,* (4) the *bad-good character,* and (5) the *false goodfellow.* Their range in our society is much wider than illegal behavior; they might be found in a drawing room, on the streets, in the movies, almost anywhere. And they are often not easily visible. That is, obvious hoodlums are thrown in jail where they can be counted, but what about the others?

First, the *tough guy.* Looking back over a year's output of better crime stories, the *Saturday Review of Literature* reported optimistically, "I cannot recall a single instance of an arm being twisted off at the shoulder, or of initials being etched with a stiletto into a squealer's back. Brutality has not, of course, altogether disappeared; an occasional face is pounded to a pulp, but . . . invariably in the interest of law and order."[7]

One reason for not being encouraged by such an appraisal aside from the question of its accuracy,[8] is that brutality *in* the interest of law and order is the very worst place for it to occur. In the part of the hero it gives most cause for concern. For example, Jimmy Porter (of John Osborne's play *Look Back in Anger*) has been called "the most disagreeable hero in modern literature, a bully, a self-centered sadist filled with self-pity but pitiless with others, he is, in a word, a cur." [9] The peak of the trend in popular America, however, is probably Mickey Spillane's detective "Mike Hammer," who has deservedly been deplored as one of the most alarming fictional characters of this generation. Statistics on the Hammer exploits compiled by one critic[10] show that in five cases thirty-four people, all innocent of the crime in question, died as a result of the activities of the hero.

Some brutality has come from the honest effort to write naturalistically. Ernest Hemingway gets perhaps more than his share of credit for a style that antedates his work and is found among people who do not read Hemingway. Leslie Fiedler, in "Dead-End Werther: the Bum as American Culture Hero," says the trend is to be traced from London and

[7] Sergeant Cuff, "The Toughie Submerged," *Saturday Review of Literature,* December 24, 1955, p. 14. Leo Gurko shows some of the same optimism, opining that the tough guy is giving way to more genteel and mature types. *Heroes, Highbrows and the Popular Mind* (Indianapolis: The Bobbs-Merrill Company, Inc., 1953), pp. 192-3.

[8] The rest of popular culture did not give the impression that brutality was lessening. For instance, the movies shown on a single day in the same month in one town included the following titles: *The Violent Years* ("Gun Girls of the Pack Gang taking their Thrills without Shame—'I shot a cop . . . so what!!!' ", *Running Wild, The Lawless Breed, Two Guns and a Badge, Lone Gun, The Gunfighter, Gunpoint, Love Me Madly, The Man with the Golden Arm, Blood Alley,* and *Killer is Loose.*—In the comic strip "Little Orphan Annie," a heroic detective when he reaches the barricaded outlaw kicks him to death; "yes," says an awe-stricken cop, "he kicked'm, just kicked'm and kicked'm, with those number twelves." By the end of 1956, the *Saturday Review* revised its estimate: "A year ago we noted that one of the more encouraging phenomena of 1955's mystery picture was 'the submergence of the toughie yarn.' This conclusion was almost certainly inspired by thoughtless wishing. One mystery writer took us goodnaturedly to task for this rather offhand generalization—said he wasn't able to sell anything else, much as he wanted to forego pistol-whipping, toe-stamping, shin-kicking, and groin-kneeing in favor of sweetness, light, and nice clean corpses. Well, let us generalize again and say that 1956 saw a resurgence of the toughie. . . . We have assigned the verdict 'literate toughie' far more frequently than in any previous year." Sergeant Cuff, "Prime Crimes of '56," *Saturday Review,* December 22, 1956.

[9] Robert Coughlan, "Why Britain's Angry Young Men Boil Over," *Life,* May 26, 1958, p. 138.

[10] Richard W. Johnston, "Death's Fair-Haired Boy," *Life,* June 23, 1952, pp. 79-95.

Dreiser to modern novels and movies like James Jones' *From Here to Eternity*. We are invited by bad language, sordid characters, crudeness, and cheap thrills to join the "Utopia of the Natural"—the heaven of the low-brows. In this heaven, virtue is having faith in "toughness in a world gone soft, the only force that can save America." The ruling passion is to "allow yourself to be butted and slugged by your comrades to test how long you can take it," to "spit out teeth, to be beaten and scarred, to be hurt past endurance . . . to anticipate the promise of death." [11]

The sensate emphasis of American culture also probably favors a hero of force. But, whatever the cause, the tough guy is more successful in American life than good Joeism and the Christian ethos, taken by themselves, would lead one to expect. Unforgettable portraits have emerged from time to time—the "Little Caesar" of Edward G. Robinson, the ruthless fighter portrayed by Kirk Douglas in *The Champion*, and the political tough guy who evokes admiration for his ability to ride roughshod over eggheads and bleeding hearts. In perfected form, he is a magnificent heel who loves them and leaves them, beats them up, looks out for himself, and has only contempt for softies.

To repeat, it is as hero, not villain, that the tough guy is a problem. Though Americans usually see him as a villain, a comparison of ratings shows that the attitude varies considerably and it is not just being on the side of law or justice that decides. About one out of two rate Billy the Kid as a hero (they see the courage and prowess of a champ gunfighter; some sympathize for the cowardly way in which he was assassinated). About one in four see the two-gun man as a hero (whereas about half rate him villain). One in six see the desperado as a hero (five out of seven as a villain). The tough guy himself is rated by one in seven as a hero (one in two as villain). Force gets a better rating with slightly varying labels. "Strong" does not have the same unpleasant meaning as "tough." Two-thirds rate strong man as a hero, seven-tenths iron man, nine-tenths champ, five-sixths he-man, two-thirds strong and silent man, one-half the bronc-busting and pistol-packing cowboy. If we consider head guy and wheel as strong men (important enough to throw their weight around) both are rated as heroes by seven out of ten. Also one out of four rates authoritarian as a hero (bearing in mind that such a type is likely to impose ideas by force). Such ratings suggest that: (1) there is distinct admiration of the man of force in America; (2) much depends on what you call him, however; (3) the boundaries between good and bad violence are not clear; (4) if the framework is legitimate, brutality is likely to get more

---

[11] Leslie A. Fiedler, *An End to Innocence* (Boston: Beacon Press, 1948), pp. 183-190.

approval—a punch in the teeth is more acceptable from a cop than from an outlaw; and (5) in any event we may well worry about the substantial percentage who like the tough guy as he is.

Why does a tough guy appeal? I think fundamentally he is like a champ (you have to hand it to him, he licks the others). So long as this is so, he has the almost universal appeal of the one who can't be beat. Since he usually fights others about as tough as himself, he has a kind of fairness (whereas we should have little trouble rallying against a bully). Another thing that confuses the issue is that sometimes the only one who can beat him is another tough guy—so we find the good guy in the role too, often with little to choose between. Tough guys often display loyalty to some limited ideal such as bravery or the "gang code," which also makes it possible to sympathize with them. Finally, they may symbolize fundamental status needs, such as proving oneself or the common man struggling with bare knuckles to make good.

The impact of the tough guy ideal on American culture is indicated, I think, by such things as hoodlumism, ratpack fights, and the rising rates of violent crimes, though I do not think these prove the effect of such models.

Let us now consider the popularity of the *"smart operator"* (also known as smoothie or fast worker), who might be called the con-man hero of America. He is less offensive than the tough guy, because he exerts himself by adroitness, charm, and guile, and is more likely to be accepted in polite society. His fast work rarely results in a call for a policeman; indeed, he is probably as often on the side of the law (technically speaking) as against it. He is found wherever sharp fellows get together, especially highly competitive fields that place emphasis on wit. About one out of two rate the smart operator or fastworker as a hero; one out of three the smoothie, sharpie, and promoter; one out of five the fast talker; and eight out of ten the diplomat. However, if called a con-man or slicker, then only about one out of ten like him.[12]

Full length portraits can be found in fiction ranging from classics like Stendhal's *The Red and the Black* or Thackeray's *Vanity Fair* to bestsellers like Bud Schulberg's *What Makes Sammy Run?*, John O'Hara's *Pal Joey,* and Cameron Hawley's *Cash McCall*.[13] A visual image was seen

[12] A comic variant of the smart operator is the clown-rogue, whose crafty ways are redeemed by humor and farce. The classic is Falstaff; aspects are seen in well-known American characters such as W. C. Fields, Groucho Marx, Charlie McCarthy, the Kingfish ("Amos and Andy"), Phil Silvers' TV character "Sergeant Bilko," a humorous grifter in uniform, always trying to put one over on somebody.

[13] This novel describes a species of businessman "known by the group name of *operators* . . . they were . . . rigidly individualistic . . . They worked alone, in secrecy

in an Academy Award-winning movie, *Stalag 17*, starring William Holden as an American soldier in a German prisoner-of-war camp: an extremely hard-boiled individualist who, by shrewd trading, captured cigarettes and other prison commodities until he was banker of the barracks. At the climax of the film he escapes and makes his getaway leaving the others behind.

The lesson taught by the smart operator, though subtler than that of the tough guy, is not so very different. The same cynicism, hardness, and egoism are there, expressed in the use of words like "sucker" and "slob" [14] to refer to the public—in Barnum's joke, "This way to the Grand Egress" —in phrases like "on the make" or "a fast nickle is better than a slow dime." What the tough guy gets by force the smart operator gets by smoothness and fast work.

A third American type that often deserves to be called a corrupted hero is found in the field of romance, the *great lover* as a shoddy Prince Charming, a fast worker in affairs of the heart. Because he conquers by charm or a "line," he might be called a slicker of sex. People hurt by him are likely to call him a wolf, but those who admire him may sincerely say great lover.[15] There are two contradictory themes in this type: a Prince

and without confidants, their steely eyes forever alert as they stalked companies that might be turned to their highly profitable purpose." Cameron Hawley, *Cash McCall* (New York: Houghton Mifflin Company, 1955, Pocket Books 1956), p. 155. McCall, however, is not a typical operator in that he is depicted in contrast to the others: he plays fair; and he reforms in the end, realizing that there are social values more important than just making money. See also Frank Gibney, *The Operators* (New York: Harper & Brothers, 1960) for a survey of business and political dishonesty.

[14] The latter word is used by some workers in radio and television to refer to the public. See Al Morgan, *The Great Man* (New York: E. P. Dutton & Co., Inc., 1955), which records some of this idiom. Note also the self-definition as con-men: "What kind of a business do you think you're in? You're a con-man. We all are. We're pushing cigarettes and beer, soap and furniture polish instead of gold bricks or the Brooklyn Bridge, but we're all con-men. So we got an electronic gadget that amplifies our voice, but we're still con-men." *Ibid.*, p. 237.

[15] "Wolf" is predominantly villainous (only 1 in 15 regard him as a hero); but substantial heroic ratings are given Prince Charming and Adonis (2 out of 3), sheik and Romeo (1 of 2), great lover (1 of 3), Don Juan (1 of 4), lady killer and lady's man (1 of 5), Casanova (1 of 6). We must bear in mind that there is an undertone of derision in most of these types. Derision may explain why more do not rate Casanova as hero; but it does not indicate repudiation of the great lover ideal, rather, it is a tribute to it for it rebukes people for not being the real thing. The real thing is what is in question in this chapter.

On the feminine side, types like charmer, Cleopatra, Venus, pin-up girl, beauty queen, it-girl, and glamor girl, are approved; but flirt, coquette, vamp, siren, party girl, and golddigger have villainous connotations. The undertone of derision, however, is missing from all. I suspect this difference is due to the fact that the female role does not lead to pretentious, boastful claims, nor is the sissy image appropriate, both of which may be implied by "lady killer."

Charming symbolizing devoted, chivalrous love; and an erotic champion or master lover, proving skill and charm by repeated conquests, necessarily violating the ideal of fidelity. The same model (John Barrymore, Rex Harrison, Errol Flynn) may, in screen and real roles epitomize both a Sweet Prince and a roué or amorous playboy close to the rogue of whom Don Juan is a prototype. But it is difficult to see how a great lover or erotic queen, unless rigorously faithful on the Doug Fairbanks–Mary Pickford pattern, can avoid favoring the latter theme of sensuality and a "love 'em and leave 'em" attitude. Even gross abuse of romantic ethics does not always disqualify a great lover, as has been shown by numerous examples. In such cases, corrupting hero is the only verdict.

Closely related, though not identical, is a movie type called by Martha Wolfenstein and Nathan Leites the *"good-bad girl."* [16] She either manages to look both sexy and innocent, or she is apparently bad but turns out to be misunderstood and basically good. The phrase "naughty but nice" applies to her, also the words used by *Time* to describe Betty Grable: a "hot-looking number who is really just a good kid waiting for Mr. Right." [17] In comic strips, one sees the fetching, bare-legged Daisy Mae in starry-eyed monogamous devotion to Li'l Abner. By offering sensual indulgence within a frame of prosy morality, the good-bad girl fulfils a wish to enjoy vicariously what is forbidden, to "eat one's cake and have it too." The *"good-bad guy"* is also well known in Hollywood, epitomized by George Raft as the suave gangster, basically decent beneath it all. Though possibly compensatory (helping people to live within a structure which deprives them of things), it seems reasonable that such mixed characters, when they are popular models, favor casuistry and the blurring of moral distinctions.

Last in this review is the ever friendly but *insincere goodfellow*—all charm on the surface but with the same hardness, cynicism, and egoism underneath that we observed in the tough guy and the smart operator. First let me pay a tribute to the American *ideal* of friendliness, embodied in the "'regular fellow" or "good Joe"—in favorites like Arthur Godfrey, Bing Crosby, Tennessee Ernie, Will Rogers, Al Smith, Sophie Tucker, and Lucille Ball (she can be a goodfellow too).

A more pleasant ideal is hard to find. What, then, is wrong with it? The trouble is with the people who play the role. It seems that everyone is trying to pose as a right guy with a heart of gold. As a result, confusion reigns when we find goodfellows acting like wolves and inner hardness

---

[16] Martha Wilfenstein and Nathan Leites, *Movies, a Psychological Study* (Glencoe, Ill.: The Free Press, 1950), pp. 81, 189.

[17] *Time*, August 23, 1948, p. 42.

called by pleasant names. "Genuineness" is doubletalk today; as often as not, a theatrical term for projection of simulated warmth by a skillful performer.

There is a point, then, at which the ideal turns sour. Let us call it Machiavellian goodfellowship when people *use* friendliness rather than simply being that way. Exploitation of friendship for economic or political advantage marks the powerseeker who pulls himself up by a handshake, calling people by first names, and winning over even enemies by personal contact. Barriers melt for him; his magic is multiplied by radio and television. The essence is that the Machiavellian is friendly for a strategic reason—to get something. This distinguishes him from a genuine goodfellow, who wants to be liked simply for its own sake and follows amiable impulses without consideration of strategy. Nowadays a simple goodfellow would be considered by many in the practical world as a kind of fool, and this is yet another proof of the existence of the Machiavellian type (who is a good Joe outside but a fox inside). His friendliness is not an absolute commitment but a convenient role, and his achievement would not be possible were he committed to every person he had expressed devotion to. In short, it is success, not friendship, that makes him a hero. And let me reiterate that, for having so acted, he is not a villian but a popular and much admired man.

Cultivation of a vast, superficial, and useful friendliness has itself become a heroic ideal in American society. Few would ask that this goodfellow actually return to the Epicurean or Emersonian pattern of the true friend. The goodfellow is distinctly proud of having flexible dramatic resources, of being able to wield charm, and of the power it implies—a procedure that Franklin Roosevelt Jr. once jocularly referred to as turning on "the old schmoo."

Such a development represents the simultaneous success and failure of the Dale Carnegie ideal which, advising people to be sincere in cultivating friends, must necessarily produce, among those whose personalities are "improved," a bumper crop of polished hypocrites who have convinced even themselves that they are genuine.

The pose of good guy has become so obligatory in America that a politician takes a chance coming on the platform without it. Baby-kissing is no laughing matter. And just try to get along in business without pretending to like practically everybody you see! So one cannot fully blame the man; our system is demanding, and producing, insincere goodfellows at an appalling rate.[18]

[18] The basic cause of this insincerity was long ago indicated by Ferdinand Tonnies in his celebrated analysis of *Gesellschaft* and its exploitative character; "the lie," he said,

We accept the old schmoo because it is pleasant and because it is always more or less advantageous to organizers, hostesses, churchmen, entertainers, almost anyone. It brings a kind of happiness to those who are lonely and do not mind a little play-acting at being a big family of friends. Habituation also soothes protest—indeed, the old schmoo has become so much a part of our social fabric that (like those breakfast cereals advertised on TV) we may be persuaded that our health depends on it.

You may, indeed, ask, if our society *wants* the insincere goodfellow, and if he is so pleasant, then what is so bad about having him? Isn't it a sign of adjustment to "play the social game," whatever it is?

I would answer that there are drawbacks to having the insincere goodfellow around, ranging from uncomfortable to downright sinister and many of which are not even recognized under their right names. One is the strain of excessively gregarious and friendly role playing, which can evoke symptoms that often look like neurosis. Worse are moral effects: corrosion of the ideal of sincerity, loss of integrity and identity (possibly tragedies such as Willy Loman's), inability to tell truth from falsehood, and the endless scurrility that may underly friendliness. Of course, when a deception is too crude, we are sharp enough in rebuking the false goodfellow ("hypocrite," "two-faced," "fair-weather friend" catch the worst offenders, others get the Bronx cheer as fool types: applepolisher, yes-man, joiner, softsoaper, gladhander, bunk-shooter, "handing out a line"). But the trouble is that such rebukes do not protect sufficiently— they penalize mainly failures—the slow, clumsy, or unlucky—not the ones who get away. For, unlike the desperado, who *must* be known, the Machiavellian goodfellow's deeds go largely unnoticed and he is usually seen on his favorable side. If you want to see the wolf lurking beneath the pose of friendliness, you may have to wait for a trial where some big operator is brought to bay—if only momentarily, before being escorted out by legal counsels. Or occasionally a false goodfellow drops his guard, as in that brutal scene in Thomas Wolfe's *You Can't Go Home Again*, where, in a confidential chat with an employee behind a partition, the cheery, ever-smiling boss turns into a terrifying Simon Legree and then back into the good guy again. But where shall we find

"is characteristic of *Gesellschaft*." However, new trends, such as the anomic need for goodfellows to compensate for lack of fellowship, probably aggravate this. Also, the role demand of democracy for equality makes it expedient, if not necessary, to pretend to like, and be like, everybody else. On the economic side, see C. Wright Mills' discussion of the "personality market," *Whitecollar* (New York: Oxford University Press, 1951), pp. 182-188; also William Whyte's incisive analysis of pseudo-goodfellowship in the top executive role, with its attendant neuroses, *The Organization Man,* pp. 166-172.

many obvious examples of a role whose nature is, like the chameleon's, to blend? And how shall we count such types? Shall we poll goodfellows on how sincere they are?

Consistent with this picture is the fact that our lush good Joeism is associated with a critical lack of real altruism and mutual help.[19] Also certain kinds of high-class and skillful dirty work seem at an all-time high. When we run out of bad guys, why not suspect pseudo-goodfellows? The average American knows in general that a game is being played, has learned to ask, "What's the gimmick?" when he gets a friendly approach from a stranger; but he lacks reliable criteria for knowing when he's being bamboozled, by whom, how, and for what. He cannot reject everyone in a coonskin cap (real good guys sometimes wear them too), so he may be caught in a demoralizing suspension of judgment, a dilemma solved perhaps by taking all "good" guys on the same basis, or rejecting them cynically as do-gooders. But if the essence of ethics is choice, this inability to discriminate is unethical.

I have now mentioned some representative corrupted heroes on the American scene and tried to judge their likely effects. It is possible that the prevailing models of America are not the good guys at all but corrupted types (heels in the good Joe role, wolves as great lovers, tough guys as protectors of security, and so on) teaching lessons that a good guy is not supposed to. To the extent that this were so, a society could have nominally high ideals and at the same time little underlying consensus that such things as violence and trickery are bad. I suggest that one of the reasons for the unpopularity of Americans abroad is that outsiders, seeing qualities beneath the surface, criticize the "ugly American."

At any rate, it is time we looked more closely and took stock of the problem of corrupted heroes. What to do about it is beyond the scope of this limited essay, a problem perhaps as formidable as reforming an entire culture. One thing needed, it seems to me, is a study of how to maintain more effective control over the personality types presented in mass communication—a screening of the *kinds of people presented in the hero's role.* As pointed out, practically any kind of person can be a celebrity or star before the camera or microphone. I do not know how to keep bad men from becoming celebrities and presenting themselves as popular models, especially when they get power, but perhaps one might hope that the communication agencies could exercise tighter criteria of what is newsworthy and of human interest. A positive approach would be to spotlight desirable models more effectively—a public relations for

[19] As pointed out by Pitirim Sorokin, *Reconstruction of Humanity* (Boston: Beacon Press, 1948).

morality, one might say. I see no reason why there should not be a government subsidy for the publicity of high types of character, either in real life or in fiction and drama. When people are *cast* in dramatic parts, we should focus attention on the role of the hero, not the obviously bad guy. People are not much affected by what a bad guy does so long as they do not identify with him; but when the most appealing personalities are selected for parts portraying vice, crime, violence, hypocrisy, and egoism, one should not be surprised if demoralization results. To cast a popular favorite as a criminal might be itself almost a crime against the public.[20] Above all, watch the hero's role, never mind what the villain does.

Censorship, of course, is beset by so many problems that it may well prove as bad as the corruption it proposes to combat. Indeed, it might just restrict the freedom of mass media without reducing the number of corrupted models (even give them better and more exclusive political billing). On the other hand, as practiced now, with self-imposed "codes" (dictated by tactical considerations, without much knowledge of actual effects of media content) censorship—for screening out subtle types we have been talking about—is like a tennis net for catching tsetse flies.

However, by half measures, by some start, perhaps we could move toward changing the general culture and the institutional structure—we could change economic ways, like the hard sell, the soft sell, and the fast buck, that makes types like the smart operator and pseudo-good Joe necessary. Would it be possible to de-emphasize the cultivation—that amounts to a cult—of good Joeism as a key to adjustment, success, and everything else? Would it be possible for people to be more genuine and show what they really feel? Could we stand the momentary expense of this—in jobs, sales, contracts, contacts, box-office ratings, and votes? Perhaps the real question is, could we stand ourselves?

[20] A case in point might be some of Frank Sinatra's roles—the gambler in *Guys and Dolls*, the drug addict in *The Man With The Golden Arm*, the heel in *Pal Joey*.

CHAPTER 7

Mockery of the Hero

A significant thing about the age in which we live is its antiheroism—its tired, apathetic, cool, and beat rejection of lofty goals. Common expressions such as "Don't stick your neck out" show a consensus in some quarters about the way to live, that might be summed up by the phrase, "heroism is for other guys." In modern literature we find an inadequate hero whose shortcomings are, on the whole, comic rather than tragic or pathetic—a little man in a big pair of shoes—a go-getter who doesn't rise, possibly because the organization defeats him—or who does rise but is a heel, and we are sorry to see him succeed—or his victory is hollow, and we see that he is a fool. The common theme is an inadequacy to meet the grand part, which may be freely admitted by the hero, as in T. S. Eliot's "The Love Song of J. Alfred Prufrock":

> No! I am not Prince Hamlet, nor was meant
> to be;

Am an attendant lord, one that will do
To swell a progress, start a scene or two,
Advise the prince; no doubt, an easy tool.
Deferential, glad to be of use,
Politic, cautious, and meticulous;
Full of high sentence, but a bit obtuse;
At times, indeed, almost ridiculous—
Almost, at times, the Fool.

What is the meaning of a hero who fails or rejects the grand part, even accepts the role of fool? Why do people mock heroes? I see mockery of heroes as expressing an attitude toward certain roles, in part, distaste for the bureaucratic role, but also alienation from heroism itself when conceived as nobility, austerity, or striving above the ordinary level. In the latter case, discounting heroes is a defensive tactic by which people preserve themselves from commitment, possibly because they do not believe in the value of the role, or, it may be, because they perceive a danger in it—no small part of which is that overconformity (the spirit of "gung ho," doing good) where society is pseudo-integrated may cause you to plunge first, encouraged by others, only to find that you swim alone. So, what I am analyzing here is not just a literary type or a name in popular speech but the morale of American society as it is reflected in certain types. Mockery of heroes seems to mean a low level of aspiration—either because the hero is too "good" or not good enough.

Too good or not good enough—are these not aspects of the same thing when analyzing models? Let me explain. For a model to function well, it should not seem so high or so low that it discourages emulation. Our society (as pointed out previously) gives a prominent place to mediocre types. Whether the public really likes them is an open question (attitudes are highly ambivalent toward many). Even when one identifies with a model, it is another thing to say that one has been inspired to higher achievement. Two kinds of reaction seem likely in a society with inferior models: people who hanker for the "higher" types will despise the prevailing mediocre ones, and those satisfied with mediocre models will mock and reject the higher ones. So there are two sources of mockery of heroes: disappointed people with high ideals and people satisfied with low ideals.

This is abstract. Let me illustrate the two kinds of mockery as they correspond to the two modes of alienation. First is the classical type of Don Quixote—a man of high ideals or character who makes a fool of himself while playing an approved role. For example, the valiant knight rescues a lad from a beating, only to cause him a worse beating after his protector has left; the victim later reproaches Quixote for having meddled. The mockery here is that a fiasco results from following a noble, supposedly trustworthy, ideal. The high minded hero is converted into a high minded fool (see Chapter 3). The inference is that something is wrong with the hero, his role, or both—perhaps that high mindedness itself is foolish. I analyzed the reaction of an audience to this episode. Twenty-five college students, after reading it, were asked what they learned from it. Most thought that Quixote's role was strikingly similar to what we today call a do-gooder. Feelings divided, however, about the goodness of the hero and his deed: though approving the general idea of helping people, most did not like the way Quixote went about it—his militant, uncompromising manner and his bad judgment—they saw him as an idealistic fool and meddler, though underlying his defeat they often saw something pathetic, tragic, or noble. Folly was the dominant note, however; and the lesson was that there are certain ways of doing good and sticking your nose into other people's business that do not pay off, however well intentioned you are. The ideal of going good, then, was restricted and qualified—I would say discounted in some degree, though not to the extent that one would not do someone a good turn if it could be done prudently.

Another high minded mock hero is Candide, whose catastrophes before finally learning to mind his own garden are well known. I analyzed the meaning of his story to twelve adults after a two-hour "Great Books" discussion. The majority rated Candide as an idealistic person but a fool, with the qualification, however, that he grew wiser and learned to face the facts by the end of the story. Some reported loss of confidence in Candide's optimistic doctrine "everything is for the best," none reported gain in confidence.[1] It seems to me that such a response shows that this story does discount the ideal of optimism to some degree. It is interesting that this message clashes with important themes in the American ethos, such as the belief in progress and the doctrine of harmony of interests (that an economic system where entrepreneurs are left alone will turn out for the best).

A less classical mock hero comes from James Thurber. His treatment of Longfellow's poem, "Excelsior" (droll cartoons showing a distraught hero in a business suit, carrying a flag, rushing up a mountainside past gaping onlookers) neatly converts idealistic pathos into humor. The last scene, in which the hero is frozen in the snow, his stiffened arm still holding erect the banner, while two Thurber pooches sniff him, completes the fiasco of the quest for the high and noble. These examples—Quixote, Candide, and Thurber's mountain climber—show, it seems to me, basic features of

[1] I am indebted to Helen McCall for collecting this information.

the high minded mock hero who throws an idealistic role into question because of his failure in it or its failure for him.

Now let us turn to the other, more common kind of mock hero. This is an unworthy man cast in a hero's role so that, by contrast, his shortcomings are seen more plainly. To define this type, let us take first a literary classic that seems like Quixote, yet I think is quite different—Samuel Butler's picture of the Puritan knight Sir Hudibras. The knightly trappings and bony steed are the same. But Sir Hudibras is a one-eyed bigot, a canting hypocrite, who carries pullets—not bullets—in his sword hilt (a sword, it may be added, rusty from disuse); in other words, not a sincere idealist but a phoney. We see that Butler has placed within the suit of armor an inferior man whose smallness of mind contrasts with the generosity of Quixote, and the last of whose impulses would be to tilt at windmills at the risk of his own life. This placement of the unworthy person in contrast with what a hero should be is the essence of a kind of mockery very widespread in modern literature that shows the *little man in a big pair of shoes*—or, to put it differently, man as he is versus what a hero ought to be. Such a stultifying contrast can be achieved in various ways. A well known humorous poem, "Casey at the Bat," tells of a baseball player rather like Babe Ruth, who steps up to the plate with bases loaded, proudly lets two good pitches go by, then strikes out. Aldous Huxley's *Antic Hay* shows a "great lover" on a career as ladies' man wearing a false beard to increase his attraction—in other words, a little man who isn't up to Casanova or Prince Charming. Thurber's "The Greatest Man in the World" describes a transoceanic flier (whose fame resembles Lindbergh's) who is in fact a boor so impossible as a popular idol that finally officials push him out of a window to make a martyr of him and keep him from the public view. Al Capp's "Li'l Abner" stresses stupidity ("his brain can absorb only one thought at a time") as a flaw in the "strong man with a heart of gold." Many men of modern fiction are faint-hearted and weak, circumscribed by limitations that would not have stopped Sir Galahad— a daydreaming Mitty or Milquetoast, a bureaucrat defeated by organization, a George Apley who passes up his big opportunity and plays it safe (marries the girl his family wants instead of the one he loves). Some heroes "succeed" so dismally that we see their victory is a kind of mockery (*The Great Gatsby, Citizen Kane, What Makes Sammy Run?, Point of No Return, Room at the Top*[2]); many are rogues (Count Bruga, Elmer Gantry,

---

[2] Another example of dismal success is a Twentieth-Century-Fox movie, *Will Success Spoil Rock Hunter?* whose hero's dream is "to rise from his untouchable caste as TV commercial writer to possession of his own jewel-encrusted key to the executive's washroom." (*Time*, August 19, 1957).

MacHeath in Berthold Brecht's *Threepenny Novel*—or, going back to classics, *Jonathan Wild* and *Volpone*), whose way of acting on the way to success is opposite that of the good guy.[3] Finally, there are little men who do not aspire to the "big" role—who break no rules and undertake no quests—but the author ironically (it may seem pathetically) likens them to a hero of the "great" or chivalrous type: J. Alfred Prufrock (Hamlet), Miniver Cheevy (who longed for the days when swords were bright, but "coughed, and called it fate, and kept on drinking"), C. Green (who never did anything worth getting his name in the papers until he committed suicide by jumping out of a building and landing on his head —a deed which merited his comparison with Sir Francis Drake);[4] not to leave out Leopold Bloom (a Ulysses of the twentieth century, who is cuckolded and at one point in his Odyssey gets a biscuit tin thrown at him).

Such an array of climbers, upstarts, Babbitts, men in gray flannel suits, palookas, has-beens, failures, and misfits in one way or another reverses the formula of the Horatio Alger success story. They have a lack of the all-conquering pluck, luck, and merit which they need to rise to the fortune they deserve. Merely showing an inadequate man, of course, is not mock heroism; but when he is clothed in knightly armor it exposes all the more sharply his shortcomings. Were it not for this comparison, he might escape embarrassment, like so many unknown Milquetoasts, Pru-frocks, and Cheevies.

Such treatment seems to say that the men of today are not what they should be. It expresses disenchantment with current models and appeals, I think, to people who are disappointed with the man of today and (whether they admit it or not) yearn for higher, nobler types. The other

[3] At this point—where mockery is achieved by placing a villainous character in the hero's role—the mock hero merges with the corrupted hero discussed in Chapter VI. Of course, definitions of "hero" and "villain" are stretched at such a meeting point. The villain-in-hero is a black comedy mode of the mock hero. Outrageous scurrilities show how far short of the ideal the "hero" really is. Examples are *Jonathan Wild, Volpone, Tartuffe, Elmer Gantry,* Ben Hecht's *Count Bruga,* and Berthold Brecht's *Threepenny Novel.* In Shaw's play, "Androcles and the Lion," we see a cowardly debauchee, Spintho, playing the part of a Christian martyr.

[4] "No. Green—poor little Green—was not a man like Drake. He was just a cinder out of life—for the most part, a thinker of base thoughts, a creature of unsharpened, coarse perceptions. He was meagre in the hips, he did not have much juice or salt in him . . . We who never saw brave Drake can have no difficulty conjuring up an image of the kind of man he was. . . . But neither Drake nor Spaniard could ever have imagined Green. Who could have foreseen him, this cipher of America, exploded now upon a street in Brooklyn? . . . Our friend has landed on his head—'taken a nose dive,' as we say. . . ." Thomas Wolfe, *You Can't Go Home Again* (Garden City, N.Y.: The Sun Dial Press, 1942), pp. 469-71.

satirical form (exemplified by the windmill-smasher) mocks the high minded role and appeals to people who are satisfied with prosaic models and so debunk higher ones, thus sparing themselves the embarrassment of painful comparisons. For convenience one might call these two classes of audience "disappointed idealists" and "realists satisfied with things as they are"—or, if one prefers, the Quixotes and the Sancho Panzas. Realists easily mock the do-gooder and are less likely to see mockery in treatment of man as he is. They follow the statement of Tolstoy in his later years: "Heroes—that's a lie and invention; there are simply people, people, and nothing else." [5]

Thus I see two kinds of hero mockery. But both (in whatever proportion they may be in the audience or in literature) seem to point to the same thing: alienation from models and whatever roles or values are represented by the models. Higher models are shown to be untrustworthy; inadequate little men seem to say that men are no longer equal to heroism—you shouldn't expect it any more. Therefore both impair the effectiveness of models.

Let me now distinguish three levels of alienation achieved by such satirical devices. First, alienation from a particular person. A famous person may be attacked in this way: Samuel Butler aimed "Sir Hudibras" at Cromwell; Fielding's Jonathan Wild, though named after a famous outlaw, was intended as a portrait of Sir Robert Walpole; Aristophanes' mock heroic treatment of Socrates in The Clouds is credited with helping bring about his death; modern novels such as Hecht's Count Bruga and Al Morgan's The Great Man are thinly disguised caricatures of contemporary celebrities; Charles Chaplin devastatingly lampooned Hitler and Mussolini in his film, The Great Dictator. We see plainly enough that such treatment damages personal prestige and alienates the audience from figures so lampooned.

At the second level, the value or role represented by the "hero" is thrown into question—Hudibras as the puritan bigot, Babbitt as the striving American businessman, Quixote as a symbol of chivalry and the do-gooder, Candide as the eternal optimist, Tartuffe as the religious hypocrite. This is more generalized than personal mockery; let us call it type mockery; the first finds fault with an actor—it says "don't be like him"—the second says "don't be like that"—the fault is not just in the man but in the role or ideal. Personal mockery tends to become type mockery because people forget who the target is, often they do not care;

[5] Statement to Maxim Gorky, quoted by Rufus W. Mathewson, Jr., The Positive Hero of Russian Literature (New York: Columbia University Press, 1958), p. 144.

some stories are universal enough to have meaning regardless of what particular person was uppermost in the author's mind.

This distinction between personal mockery and type mockery is important for social structure, because the first punishes a person for failure to live up to a norm but the second punishes a *norm*, so to speak—that is, throws into question an ideal, a role, or even an entire structure.

As an example I would cite the remarkable amount of social criticism to be found in one episode from Al Capp's "Li'l Abner." The hero is shown in a Quixotic role, that is, a person with a heart of gold getting into trouble by helping others. Abner answers an advertisement by a clothing company for the man with the lowest I.Q. in the world. The job is to risk his neck publicizing zootsuits at a salary of eight dollars a week. (The theory is that the public will be so captivated by such a hero that they will rush to wear whatever he wears.) Clad in a preposterous zootsuit with floppy tie and padded shoulders (his armor?) he undertakes missions to help anyone who calls. In one case, he climbs a tree to rescue a kitten for a lady, but at the top finds a wild cat and falls, all bitten and torn, while the crowd cheers. His exploits finally make him so popular that he is nominated for President of the United States by the "Zoot Suit Progressive Party."—Thus, in one episode, Capp strikes at a number of American value themes: (1) the healthy American boy (naïve enough to be taken advantage of); (2) the ideal of the do-gooder ("Eight dollars a week!!—Oh (sob!), thank you,' gennulmen!—But, honestly—it hain't th' big money which attracks me—it's the chance t' do *good!!*"); (3) judgment of popular majorities (captivated by such a hero); (4) a current political viewpoint; (5) a clothing fashion; and (6) by implication the tone of a society that could provide a scene for such activities. A study of the entire career of this "hero" might show that he was versatile enough to lance at almost any important American ideal. How do people regard Li'l Abner? Analysis of opinion shows that he has the character of both hero and fool (more fool than hero but enough of both to be a true mock hero). One hundred and sixteen college students were given a long list of type categories that might conceivably be applied to Abner. The most frequent ones were: simpleton (22 per cent), chump or easily taken advantage of (20 per cent), superman or dragonslayer (16 per cent), heroic or admirable (12 per cent), greenhorn (12 per cent), a butt always getting the worst of it (7 per cent), idealist or romanticist (6 per cent), clumsy fool (5 per cent) (eleven other categories registered less than 2 per cent). Thus, by combining attributes of fool and hero, Li'l Abner serves as a vehicle to bring accepted values into fiasco and disrepute, doing for comic strip readers what Molière and Joyce might for others.

Beyond type mockery there is yet a third level, repudiation of *heroism itself* as a way of life (the ideal of better than average striving, belief that it is desirable or possible to rise above the common level). Some of this results from the entire array of mock heroes; that is, you can have just so many clowns and Sad Sacks in the hero's role before it begins to look as though heroism itself is discredited. A world without heroism—in which aspiration remained at a dead level—is perhaps impossible; but pictures approximating it can be found in fiction. James Thurber's writing, I would say, is pervasively antiheroic (take his treatment of Grant's meeting with Lee at Appomattox or of Whittier's poem "Barbara Frietchie"). James Joyce's *Ulysses,* as critics have pointed out, brings all values (except art itself) within the realm of comedy; there is hardly a heroic ideal that is not mocked, from Penelope's chastity to Nelson's pillar. Huxley's *Brave New World* is a technological "utopia" with no place for heroism. From such examples we see a perspective in which heroism as a way of life is repudiated.

At this level we see what mockery of heroes ultimately leads to if it becomes the predominant artistic mode of a society or the prevalent view of the man on the street. A man who viewed life consistently in such terms would likely be a "mean spirited clod," incapable of rising to heroism as it is usually conceived. True, he might be thrust into situations where he would have to act desperately ("some are born to greatness, some achieve greatness, and some have greatness thrust upon 'em"), but he would not gratuitously break a lance for some noble cause. I see these levels, then, as stages in the deterioration of morale: (1) mockery of a particular person (possibly a leader) by invidious comparison with what a hero should be, (2) mockery of a heroic ideal or role, and (3) mockery of all heroes.

Let us now turn from literature to the language and thought of the man on the street, which reflect, it seems to me, alienation from heroism at all three of these levels. First, there is in America a tendency to make fun of the man out in front. Criticism—amounting sometimes to heckling—of American Presidents and of the Supreme Court (the "nine old men") are cases in point. Even sacrosanct figures are not immune to mockery. For example, I asked fifty college students to nominate American heroes of history, tradition, or today. The names most frequently mentioned were Lincoln, Washington, Einstein, Eisenhower, Franklin D. Roosevelt, Frank Sinatra, and Marilyn Monroe. Then I gave them a list of two hundred and fifty American fool types, and asked them whether any were appropriate to these figures. The results of this were as follows:

Fool Types Assigned to Persons Nominated as Popular Heroes

Hero	Most frequent derisive types assigned	Average number of terms used by a rater
Einstein	braintruster, character, highbrow, egghead, crackpot	1.4
Lincoln	crusader, hayseed, character, do-gooder, roughneck, wisecracker	1.5
Eisenhower	brass hat, crusader, bigwig, superpatriot, straddler, yes-man	2.8
Washington	highbrow, superpatriot, crusader, blue-nose, boy scout, do-gooder	3.6
F. D. R.	do-gooder, bureaucrat, crusader, glory hog, bigwig, braintruster, highbrow, diehard, spellbinder	4.1
Monroe	flapper, floozy, dumb Dora, prima donna, scatterbrain, slob, phoney, glory hog, eager beaver	8.2
Sinatra	crooner, playboy, lover boy, lady's man, creampuff, punk, Romeo, great lover, pantywaist, shrimp, sissy	16.6

Of course, one expects that movie stars and crooners will draw more mockery than great men; but it is significant that no one was above mockery. Every person could see—and was willing to impute—at least one comic trait to every one of the "heroes" nominated by the same group. He was not so reverent ("gung ho") toward even sacred figures such as Lincoln that he could not see them in a comic light. It is reasonable that leaders less sacred than Lincoln would draw considerably more mockery. Most of our idols seem to have "feet of clay."

Let us note, also, that many esteemed statuses in America have a sort of clownish underside. Politicians have suffered badly in cartooning; there are innumerable jokes about lawyers, doctors, dentists, clergymen, and military men; "Babbitt" and "philistine" have become rather painfully attached to the businessman,[6] who has, after all, one of the central roles of American culture. Such mockery seems to indicate that Ameri-

[6] "I get a little weary of the notion that businesspeople are quite the Philistines that many seem to think." Crawford H. Greenswalt, President of E. I. du Pont de Nemours and Company, "The Culture of the Businessman," *Saturday Review of Literature*, January 19, 1957, p. 11.

cans are inclined to discount higher roles and statuses of their own society, even those that happen to be the focal point of striving. Some of this corresponds to what I would call the second level—generalized mockery of heroic roles and ideals.

Many commonly used words have a mock heroic flavor, and probably enter what I would call level three—repudiation of heroism in general. Do-gooder, crusader, boy scout, eager beaver, fanatic, martyr, and saint are applied disparagingly to people who set a standard higher than others are able or willing to reach. In military organizations, even the term "hero" may refer to a fool who volunteers or who takes unnecessary risks. In industry, rate-buster and eager beaver designate workers who exceed their production quota to a point that is embarrassing or costly to the rest. In business, one often hears terms like "boy wonder" and "fairhaired boy" applied derisively to the young man of unusual zeal and promise—the very one celebrated in the Horatio Alger legend.

Pursuing this matter, I polled one hundred college students on how often they used nominally heroic and complimentary words mockingly —that is, made a fool of a man by calling him a hero. The following titles were "often" used derisively (percentages indicated in parentheses): big shot (77), eager beaver (51), hero (42), Einstein (42), martyr (39), daredevil (33), saint (29), do-gooder (22), brass hat (22), and boy scout (21). Many more said they used the same words "occasionally" in a mocking way, as well as the following titles: star (51), 100% American (39), booster (32), dollar-a-year man (25), Lady Bountiful (24), dragonslayer (18). This shows that mock heroism is congenial idiom to the American college student. I suppose it is not greatly different with the man on the street. In such mockery, the language of praise is used to penalize the overconformer and the high achiever—the one who gets out in front. Of course, it can also be used to discount phoneys, show-offs, weaklings, goof-offs, and con-men (therefore supporting the true hero). I do not know at present how often it is used in one way rather than the other. Where there is much derisive use of heroic titles, however, it seems likely to make a person more cautious in achievement by heroic means, more reluctant to get out in front in a heroic manner—more suspicious, generally, of the whole idea of "being a hero."

Certain phrases also seem mock heroic. One is heard among American college students: "gung ho" (in an unflattering sense, too eager, too full of spirit for the cause—not cool—square).[7] This indicates an ambivalence

---

[7] There is also a flattering meaning: hard-working, loyal, enthusiastic, a fellow who is "with it" and "on the ball." My impression is that this is distinctly less common.

toward the heroic role and a withholding of full commitment. Another interesting term came into use during World War II which, it seems to me, expresses disillusionment with the heroic ideal. American soldiers used the word "liberated" to refer to things they had taken (let us admit, stolen) from occupied countries—guns, cameras, works of art, and the like. What this seemed to say was, certain rewards are legitimate for soldiers who have won; the do-gooder pose is fancy talk for a rather unheroic reality underneath, namely, that people who have power take things from people who lack power. A similar disillusionment was expressed by the phrase "making the world safe for democracy" after World War I. Such mock heroic language could well reflect alienation not only from specific tasks of high achievement but heroism generally.

To sum up, what modest evidence I have mentioned above indicates that mockery of heroes is not only a literary mode—an amusement for satirists and tired intellectuals—but has entered popular thought and is an important feature of American society. How far remains open to investigation. It seems plain, however, that the image of the hero is often used to discount heroism.

Is this necessarily a symptom of low morale and failure of role performance, or could it have a *function* for role discrimination and adequate role playing? Do we, in pointing out the shortcomings of the one out in front, discourage achievement or raise the standard—make it tougher for phoneys, and make the next person work even harder to deserve sincere praise?

I believe both are possible: that the mock hero can be a symptom of alienation and also serve society and individuals in certain ways. Three ways are distinguished here.

One is criticism, which I take it that a progressive society needs continually. The "heroes" of Molière, Aristophanes, Lewis, Thurber, and Capp do much to sharpen people's perceptions of what in their society needs change. A mock hero is an effective device for calling attention to such things as the troubles of the man in the gray flannel suit—role stress and frustration that might be remedied. Climbers like Gatsby and Babbitt, showing hollowness or pettiness of "success," may refocus efforts

---

[8] By ritualize, I mean repeating and institutionalizing certain kinds of experience to build up the nonrational consensus that society needs. This standard sociological conception is stated more fully by the author in *Ritual and Cult, a Sociological Interpretation* (Washington, D.C.: Public Affairs Press, 1956). It is coming to be pretty generally recognized that human psychology is a psychology of perspectives; that the way people think, feel, and act is a function of the way they see situations. If this is so, then we need to give considerable attention to two problems. One is classifying the varying

toward more satisfying things. Probably it is necessary for a progressive civilization to ritualize[8] the mockery which subjects leaders to continual lampooning, as did the ancient Athenians in their comedy.

Another way the mock hero can serve society is by defining bureaucratic roles. Among the lessons of the inadequate hero is one something like this: a "little" role is the kind most people are called upon to perform in a society like this; don't feel guilty if you fail to be a hero; efficient performance, not great achievement is called for—if everyone is a man in a gray flannel suit or a Milquetoast, why not you?—don't become too motivated and involved, or you won't be a mobile, exchangeable unit of our bureaucratic system; above all, don't go to radical extremes, break rules, or make trouble. What we want is neither individualists nor fanatics but steady, efficient, little men. Mockery of the hero expresses the spirit of bureaucratic discipline and routinization against charisma. Thus it defines the role requirements of a bureaucratic system to its members. Not only does it dampen Sir Galahad's ardor but makes him fit better into his groove.

The third function can be looked on both as a symptom of morale in the society and a service to the individual. To the individual it is a defensive adjustment which protects him from overcommitment, especially where morale is poor. For example, much mock heroism seems to me to come from the perception of pose and pretense in role playing. We live in a society where people are playing games of one kind or another—winning and being "taken." Now, in a social game, an overconformer or overachiever ("hero") can be: (1) the winner—a hero in the straight sense; (2) a rash fool, daredevil, or reckless loser like Custer, whose example we would not care to imitate; (3) a person who is pretending to conform, achieve, or be "gung ho" for the sake of impressing others (applepolisher, eager beaver, toady, glory hog, yes-man) or carrying on a different game under the cover of his pose; and possibly, (4) a fellow who is holding up the heroic ideal so that *you* will be "taken"—(make a fool of yourself or a wrong move in a game he is trying to win by other means). Fascism and Nazism were full of the glorification of heroism for the sake of making suckers. If we perceive these traps, we may draw back from overachievement, perhaps heroism as a whole, saying "that's

ways people look at things (one classification of dramatic perspectives might be: melodramatic, tragic, comic, matter-of-fact). The other problem is studying the rituals by which society maintains or evokes these perspectives; as, for example, the Greeks maintained their tragic view of life by myths and dramas of this kind. See Kenneth Burke, *A Grammar of Motives* (Englewood Cliffs. N.J.: Prentice-Hall, Inc., 1945), for a dramatistic mode of analysis.

not for me," with a caution not unlike Sancho Panza's—expressed in phrases like "I'll sit this one out," or "let's you and he fight." [9] Disengagement from commitment might be looked on as a kind of adaptation to conditions in which the individual dares not give whole-hearted belief and support to institutions and ideals because, if he does, he may be sold out. He may shun heroism as a fox does a trap, seeing in it perhaps the device of an organization that gives medals—or three-pen desk sets—for the sake of morale (on the assumption that pride moves men more than material rewards); he may, like some professional soldiers,[10] feel that *not* being a hero is his best chance for survival.

In a world where heroism is suspect though not altogether disqualified, the sensible course would be to beware of fine ideals ("glittering generalities"), to hold a little admiration in reserve for those (rare?) occasions when the true hero appears (with a fervent hope, perhaps, that one can recognize him). The middle course—between outright rejection of heroism and being "taken" by all the spurious idealism that a propagandistic age can generate—is where I think America now is. As individuals, we need a certain amount of discounting of heroes—as well as defensive strategies like goldbricking, featherbedding, and withholding full support —perhaps to survive, at any rate to escape exploitation by others only too ready to take advantage of excess idealism. This seems hardly more than the prudence of *Gesellschaft*.[11] Possibly it is worse—a symptom of severe alienation and anomie.

I will say that the mock hero is an ideal symbol for the alienated person, expressing the kind of world and the kind of heroes that he sees (squares, cornballs, gung ho do-gooders, phoneys, climbers, chiselers, people with low morale posing as conformers). Feeling himself apart from such heroes and such a society, he welcomes the mockery of Joyce, of Thurber, which shows his world to be what it is and gives a healthy, comic, specific antidote for what ails him. The whole literature of alienation[12] will probably appeal to him—the little men who live without attachment to

[9] Or Sam Goldwyn's phrase, "Include me out."

[10] Voluntarily taking risks is an attitude characteristic of starry-eyed recruits, not professional soldiers. See Robert Merton and Alice Kitt, "Contributions to the Theory of Reference-Group Behavior," in Guy E. Swanson, et al., eds. *Readings in Social Psychology* (New York: Holt, Rinehart, & Winston, Inc., 1952), p. 443.

[11] Compare the discussion of role strain, dissensus, and the role "bargain" by William J. Goode, "A Theory of Role Strain," *American Sociological Revue*, 1960, 25: 483-96. By this view, giving less than is demanded is characteristic of role bargains in a society of low consensus.

[12] See Colin Wilson, *The Outsider* (Boston: Houghton Mifflin Company, 1956).

the system, who get ahead without being heroes, or who just live small lives:

> I am no thinker, no mere creature of dreams and imagination. I pay bills, post letters: I buy new bootlaces and put them in my boots. And when I set out to get my hair cut, it is with the iron face of those men of empire and unconquerable will, those Caesars and Napoleons, whose footsteps shake the earth.[13]

Such heroes and people rejecting heroes seem to fit a society where ambitions are truncated (someone has lopped off the top rungs or thrown doubt on whether they are worthwhile); there is a moderate level of striving—less of King Arthur, one might say, and more of Milquetoast and Prufrock.

[13] Logan Pearsall Smith, *More Trivia* (New York: Harcourt, Brace & World, Inc., 1921), p. 97.

EPILOGUE

EPILOGUE

AN EPILOGUE is a place for afterthoughts, perhaps to draw tighter certain threads, or even to mend a fence where hindsight or criticism has revealed the need.

This has been a free interpretation; and biases, perhaps peculiar to me, have entered into it.[1]

[1] One of my presumptions is that we need more value consensus. I think that sheer relativism, or a value hierarchy based on shifting numbers of opinions and including the notion that every opinion is as good as every other, is not an adequate basis for a good society, which must, somehow, solve the problem Plato posed, of putting the best things on top. Also, I accept the view (expressed by writers such as Willard Waller, Karen Horney, and Erich Fromm) that it is possible for a society to be "sick." In other words, the functional approach—the belief that social types comprise an informal structure serving integration and role orientation—does not preclude an illness in society which can be reflected by many of the same types. To me, terms like alienation, anomie, neuroticism, role conflict, lack of consensus, pseudo-integration, Machiavellianism, egoism, sensate emphasis, and corruption of heroes, are terms for a *diagnosis* of what is wrong with society—not just a description of an ongoing, smoothly working—though loosely integrated, pluralistic, and changing system. Again, I have pretty well neglected psychoanalytic interpretations, not because I think there is nothing to them but because I am not a psychoanalyst and therefore am not qualified to enter this tricky realm of what symbols might unconsciously mean.

I suspect some readers may feel that I have overdrawn the deterioration of the hero and underplayed the great positive idealism, which is latent if not always active in the American people. I hasten to repeat that one cannot infer from public models alone what people are doing or capable of doing. Nor must one doubt that some very good models could offset a great many bad ones.

Even if people are disenchanted, there is a deep reservoir of enthusiasm available, especially in the new generation. Being "cool" might be only a pose—a waiting until the right hero or issue comes along. We have seen too often a display of *sang-froid* by people about to go overboard. Mockery of heroes, too, does not always mean that morale is low and people are hopelessly dissatisfied. It is well known, for example, that some of the military units that griped the hardest also fought the best. Mockery of heroes might be directed mainly at reckless and phoney efforts to impress others, and might actually reflect pride in real achievement.

Some trends in heroes, villains, and fools do not fall easily into a simple picture. Readers may be puzzled by apparent contradictions. For example, we have noted in Chapter 2 that, though the number of villains seems to be multiplying in American culture, the attitude against them (the ability to take a stand) is weakening, and they are out of date in the better literature. Both heroes and villains are being "humanized," which in many cases is equivalent to deterioration. It may be asked, then, does this not imply a decline of melodrama and *favor* perception of tragedy, rather than portending its decline as noted in Chapter 4?

I would answer, first, that although the villain is out of date in better literature, popular thought still leans heavily on villains and melodrama (though, it may be admitted, with less conviction of personal responsibility—less willingness, for example, of juries to punish). The prevailing, though weaker, popular tendency to vilify is enough to spoil many possibly tragic perceptions. Second, vilification is not the only thing that interferes with tragedy. Humanization by itself might allow more melodramatic heroes and villains to be seen as tragic. But at the same time, the decline of the belief in free will and responsibility, and the acceptance of determinism have robbed the would-be tragic character of the opportunity to take credit for his action—to freely commit himself to a tragic course rather than being simply victimized by forces over which he has no control. And naturalism has insisted on depicting heroes who by no reasonable stretch of imagination could rise to the level of tragic dignity. Humanizing figures, then, *at a certain level* and *to a point* opens the door of tragedy, but below that point descends to weakness, environmentalism, irresponsibility, pettiness, baseness, or sickness, and quickly closes it.[2] There is a level of "humanness" below tragedy.

Another question presents itself. Does the demand for sharper images of nobility, dealt with in Chapter 6, require a return to a melodramatic world view, appropriate to a folk or sectarian society, or can we, through realism and maturity, reach a sharper distinction between good and evil? Another way of saying this is, are we asking for more stereotyping or a realistic representation of human nature? Two answers can be made. First, it may be that at the popular and juvenile levels it would be better to keep the melodramatic formula rather than foster the trend toward mixed fictional characters that debauch and confuse values. A certain amount of melodrama is good for everybody. The other answer is that realism should be able to do a better job than it is doing of depicting goodness or evil as it occurs in human life. One need not deny the distinction between good and evil to be a realist. Let us search more deeply and conscientiously for the nature of good. This need not commit us to a Platonic view but merely keeps open the hypothesis that good and evil are real and that the searches of science, art, philosophy and religion will find them. I hope that more writers will find a challenge in better than average people for central characters. Let us admit, once and for all, that realism can portray bums, but it can also portray saints. I believe the present trend toward corruption of heroes in fiction is due less to naturalism than to a "trashy" sensational effort to find a gimmick by scrambling the qualities that formerly separated heroes and villains.

One of the larger problems posed by the various American types reviewed in this book is commitment. With so many models, genuine and spurious, before us, which are worth dedication to? How are we to follow that single line known as consistency? How are we to have a national "character" in an integral sense? Which of these types will be the weather-vane of our national moods or the guidepost of our progress in the future? I have made my guess that Americans will follow the dominant role models of good Joe-smart operator-playboy in their affairs at home and in the world. If so—or whatever the correct answer may be—the task at hand is to appraise these "characteristic" roles for strengths and weak-nesses and to plan for more "people like that" in the future.

If we choose to follow types like the smoothie, it seems to me we can expect more pseudo-integration, less commitment, and weaker identity in our society.

On the other hand, if we do not like certain dominant models and react

---

[2] Orrin E. Klapp, "Tragedy and the American Climate of Opinion," *op. cit.*

vigorously enough, I believe much can be done to change our culture. Surely one of the best places on which to focus reform is in hero models. If we can stand back and look at ourselves as a nation, we are in a unique position to do something about it—to say we will, or will not, be that way. If the American character has been deteriorating—and I must regretfully admit that I think it has—the very first thing to arrest the drift is to check the compass, refer to the chart, and set the course. In this book I have tried to do some of the charting necessary.

The Eyewitness Accounts of American History Series

The Classics in History Series

The American Assembly Series